D0789217

Modern Critical Views

JOHN ASHBERY

Modern Critical Views

JOHN ASHBERY

Edited with an introduction by

Harold Bloom

Sterling Professor of the Humanities
Yale University

1985
CHELSEA HOUSE PUBLISHERS
New York

THE COVER:
The cover depicts Ashbery's identification with the painting, "Self-Portrait in a Convex Mirror," which at once inspires and inhibits his own masterpiece of the same title.—H.B.

PROJECT EDITORS: Emily Bestler, James Uebbing
ASSOCIATE EDITOR: Julia Myer
EDITORIAL COORDINATOR: Karyn Gullen Browne
EDITORIAL STAFF: Laura Ludwig, Linda Grossman, Peter Childers
DESIGN: Susan Lusk

Cover illustration by Robin Peterson

Library of Congress Cataloging in Publication Data

John Ashbery.
     (Modern critical views)
     Bibliography: p.
     Includes index.
     1. Ashbery, John—Criticism and interpretation—
Addresses, essays, lectures.   I. Bloom, Harold.
II. Series.
PS3501.S475Z73   1985   811'.54   85–6614
ISBN 0–87754–621–5

Chelsea House Publishers
Harold Steinberg, Chairman and Publisher
Susan Lusk, Vice President
A Division of Chelsea House Educational Communications, Inc.
133 Christopher Street, New York, NY 10014

Contents

Introduction......*Harold Bloom* 1

John Ashbery......*Richard Howard*..................... 17

The Charity of the Hard Moments......*Harold Bloom*...... 49

A Magma of Interiors......*Alfred Corn* 81

Self-Portrait in a Convex Mirror......*David Kalstone*........ 91

The Breaking of Form......*Harold Bloom* 115

The Prophetic Ashbery......*Douglas Crase* 127

Vision in the Form of a Task:
  The Double Dream of Spring......*Charles Berger*........ 145

Understanding Ashbery......*Helen Vendler* 179

The Poetry of John Ashbery......*John Bayley* 195

"Soonest Mended"......*John Hollander* 207

Measuring the Canon:
  "Wet Casements" and "Tapestry"......*Harold Bloom* ... 217

"A Commission That Never Materialized": Narcissism and
  Lucidity in Ashbery's "Self-Portrait in a Convex Mirror"
  Anita Sokolsky 233

Chronology 251

Contributors 253

Bibliography 255

Acknowledgments 257

Index 259

Editor's Note

John Ashbery, incontrovertibly a great poet, remains both difficult and underread, even by his readers. This volume gathers together the published criticism that has attempted most seriously to address Ashbery's difficulty. I have not hesitated to include most of my own critical writing upon Ashbery, both because it is scattered throughout half-a-dozen of my books, and I have received a number of requests to bring it together in one place, and because I seem to be the critic who has been most obsessed by and so most concerned with this poetry.

Except for my "Introduction," this book is chronologically arranged. The "Introduction" is a cento of passages from my books *The Anxiety of Influence* and *A Map of Misreading*, together with some later meditations upon Ashbery that center upon his place in the American Romantic tradition. Richard Howard's celebratory essay then begins the chronological sequence, followed by my own first full-scale attempt to introduce Ashbery to wider circles of readers.

These general essays are complemented by three parallel but very different readings of "Self-Portrait in a Convex Mirror," by the poet Alfred Corn, David Kalstone, and myself. The poet Douglas Crase, himself profoundly influenced by Ashbery, sets Ashbery in our prophetic or Emersonian mode. Charles Berger's comprehensive essay on *The Double Dream of Spring* is followed by Helen H. Vendler's exegesis of some of the later work.

A dissident and British voice enters with John Bayley, whose strictures upon Ashbery are prompted both by Bayley's reactions to Vendler's analysis and to my own, and also by Bayley's ambivalence towards Wallace Stevens, Ashbery's prime precursor. In some sense, Bayley is answered implicitly by John Hollander's forceful reading of "Soonest Mended" and then more aggressively by my readings of "Wet Casements" and "Tapestry," readings that deliberately raise again the issues of the canonical and of Ashbery's central place in the major tradition of American poetry. The final essay, the lucid reconsideration of "Self-Portrait" by Anita Sokolsky, sets polemics aside in order to achieve a new kind of balance and justice in the evaluation of Ashbery.

Introduction

In the exquisite squalors of Tennyson's *The Holy Grail*, as Percival rides out on his ruinous quest, we can experience the hallucination of believing that the Laureate is overly influenced by *The Waste Land*, for Eliot too became a master at reversing the *apophrades*. Or, in our present moment, the achievement of John Ashbery in his powerful poem *Fragment* (in his volume *The Double Dream of Spring*) is to return us to Stevens, somewhat uneasily to discover that at moments Stevens sounds rather too much like Ashbery, an accomplishment I might not have thought possible.

The strangeness added to beauty by the positive *apophrades* is of that kind whose best expositor was Pater. Perhaps all Romantic style, at its heights, depends upon a successful manifestation of the dead in the garments of the living, as though the dead poets were given a suppler freedom than they had found for themselves. Contrast the Stevens of *Le Monocle de Mon Oncle* with the *Fragment* of John Ashbery, the most legitimiate of the sons of Stevens:

> Like a dull scholar, I behold, in love,
> An ancient aspect touching a new mind.
> It comes, it blooms, it bears its fruit and dies.
> This trivial trope reveals a way of truth.
> Our bloom is gone. We are the fruit thereof.
> Two golden gourds distended on our vines,
> Into the autumn weather, splashed with frost,
> Distorted by hale fatness, turned grotesque.
> We hang like warty squashes, streaked and rayed,
> The laughing sky will see the two of us,
> Washed into rinds by rotting winter rains.
> (—*Le Monocle*, VIII)

> Like the blood orange we have a single
> Vocabulary all heart and all skin and can see
> Through the dust of incisions the central perimeter
> Our imaginations orbit. Other words,
> Old ways are but the trappings and appurtenances
> Meant to install change around us like a grotto.
> There is nothing laughable

> In this. To isolate the kernel of
> Our imbalance and at the same time back up carefully
> Its tulip head whole, an imagined good.
>   (—*Fragment*, XIII)

An older view of influence would remark that the second of these stanzas "derives" from the first, but an awareness of the revisionary ratio of *apophrades* unveils Ashbery's relative triumph in his involuntary match with the dead. This particular strain, while it matters, is not central to Stevens, but is the greatness of Ashbery whenever, with terrible difficulty, he can win free to it. When I read *Le Monocle de Mon Oncle* now, in isolation from other poems by Stevens, I am compelled to hear Ashbery's voice, for this mode has been captured by him, inescapably and perhaps forever. When I read *Fragment*, I tend not to be aware of Stevens, for his presence has been rendered benign. In early Ashbery, amid the promise and splendors of his first volume, *Some Trees*, the massive dominance of Stevens could not be evaded, though a *clinamen* away from the master had already been evidenced:

> The young man places a bird-house
> Against the blue sea. He walks away
> And it remains. Now other
>
> Men appear, but they live in boxes.
> The sea protects them like a wall.
> The gods worship a line-drawing
>
> Of a woman, in the shadow of the sea
> Which goes on writing. Are there
> Collisions, communications on the shore
>
> Or did all secrets vanish when
> The woman left? Is the bird mentioned
> In the waves' minutes, or did the land advance?
>   (—*Le Livre est sur la Table*, II)

This is the mode of *The Man with the Blue Guitar*, and urgently attempts to swerve away from a vision whose severity it cannot bear:

> Slowly the ivy on the stones
> Becomes the stones. Women become
>
> The cities, children become the fields
> And men in waves become the sea.
>
> It is the chord that falsifies.
> The sea returns upon the men,

> The fields entrap the children, brick
> Is a weed and all the flies are caught,
>
> Wingless and withered, but living alive.
> The discord merely magnifies.
>
> Deeper within the belly's dark,
> Of time, time grows upon the rock.
> (—*The Man with the Blue Guitar*, XI)

The early Ashbery poem implies that there are "collisions, communications" among us, even in confrontation of the sea, a universe of sense that asserts its power over our minds. But the parent-poem, though it will resolve itself in a similar quasi-comfort, harasses the poet and his readers with the intenser realization that "the discord merely magnifies," when our "collisions, communications" sound out against the greater rhythms of the sea. Where the early Ashbery attempted vainly to soften his poetic father, the mature Ashbery of *Fragment* subverts and even captures the precursor even as he appears to accept him more fully. The ephebe may still not be mentioned in the father's minutes, but his own vision has advanced. Stevens hesitated almost always until his last phase, unable firmly to adhere to or reject the High Romantic insistence that the power of the poet's mind could triumph over the universe of death, or the estranged object-world. It is not every day, he says in his *Adagia*, that the world arranges itself in a poem. His nobly desperate disciple, Ashbery, has dared the dialectic of misprision so as to implore the world daily to arrange itself into a poem:

> But what could I make of this? Glaze
> Of many identical foreclosures wrested from
> The operative hand, like a judgment but still
> The atmosphere of seeing? That two people could
> Collide in this dusk means that the time of
> Shapelessly foraging had come undone: the space was
> Magnificent and dry. On flat evenings
> In the months ahead, she would remember that that
> Anomaly had spoken to her, words like disjointed beaches
> Brown under the advancing signs of the air.

This, the last stanza of *Fragment*, returns Ashbery full circle to his early *Le Livre est sur la Table*. There are "collisions, communications on the shore" but these "collide in this dusk." "Did the land advance?" of the early poem is answered partly negatively, by the brown, disjointed beaches, but partly also by "the advancing signs of the air." Elsewhere in *Fragment*, Ashbery writes: "Thus reasoned the ancestor, and everything/Happened as he had foretold, but in a funny kind of way." The strength of the positive *apophrades* gives this quester the hard wisdom of the proverbial poem he rightly calls *Soonest Mended*, which ends by:

> . . . learning to accept
> The charity of the hard moments as they are doled out,
> For this is action, this not being sure, this careless
> Preparing, sowing the seeds crooked in the furrow,
> Making ready to forget, and always coming back
> To the mooring of starting out, that day so long ago.

Here Ashbery has achieved one of the mysteries of poetic style, but only through the individuation of misprision.

II

Another misprision is a haunting lyric of belatedness, Ashbery's recent *As You Came from the Holy Land*, where the parodistic first-line/title repeats the opening of a bitter ballad of lost love attributed to Ralegh, one of whose stanzas lingers throughout Ashbery's gentler poem:

> I have lovde her all my youth,
> Butt now ould, as you see,
> Love lykes not the fallyng frute
> From the wythered tree.

"Her" is the personal past in Ashbery's elegy for the self:

> of western New York state
> were the graves all right in their bushings
> was there a note of panic in the late August air
> because the old man had peed in his pants again
> was there turning away from the late afternoon glare
> as though it too could be wished away
> was any of this present
> and how could this be
> the magic solution to what you are in now
> whatever has held you motionless
> like this so long through the dark season
> until now the women come out in navy blue
> and the worms come out of the compost to die
> it is the end of any season
>
> you reading there so accurately
> sitting not wanting to be disturbed
> as you came from that holy land
> what other signs of earth's dependency were upon you

what fixed sign at the crossroads
what lethargy in the avenues
where all is said in a whisper
what tone of voice among the hedges
what tone under the apple trees
the numbered land stretches away
and your house is built in tomorrow
but surely not before the examination
of what is right and will befall
not before the census
and the writing down of names

remember you are free to wander away
as from other times other scenes that were taking place
the history of someone who came too late
the time is ripe now and the adage
is hatching as the seasons change and tremble
it is finally as though that thing of monstrous interest
were happening in the sky
but the sun is setting and prevents you from seeing it
out of night the token emerges
its leaves like birds alighting all at once under a tree
taken up and shaken again
put down in weak rage
knowing as the brain does it can never come about
not here not yesterday in the past
only in the gap of today filling itself
as emptiness is distributed
in the idea of what time it is
when that time is already past

Ashbery, probably because of his direct descent from Stevens, tends like Stevens to follow rather precisely the crisis-poem paradigm that I have traced in my map of misreading. This model, Wordsworthian-Whitmanian, never restores as much representational meaning as it continually curtails or withdraws, as I have observed earlier. Ashbery's resource has been to make a music of the poignance of withdrawal. So, in this poem, the "end of any season" that concludes the first stanza is deliberately too partial a synecdoche to compensate for the pervasive absences of the ironies throughout the stanza. Ashbery's turnings-against-the-self are wistful and inconclusive, and he rarely allows a psychic reversal any completeness. His origins, in the holy land of western New York state, are presented here and elsewhere in his work with an incurious rigidity that seems to have no particular design on the poet himself, characteristically addressed as "you." The next stanza emphasizes Ashbery's usual metonymic defense of isolation (as opposed to the Stevensian undoing or the Whitmanian regression), by which signs and impulses become detached from one another, with the catalog or census completing itself in the reductive "writing down of names," in which "down" takes on surprising difference and force. The third stanza, one of Ashbery's most radiant, marks the poem's *daemonization*, the American Counter-Sublime in which Ashbery, like Stevens, is so extraordinarily at home. Ashbery's mingled strength and weakness, indeed his deliberate pathos, is that he knowingly begins where Childe Roland ended, "free to wander away" yet always seeing himself as living "the history of someone who came too late" while sensing that "the time is ripe now." Studying his own habitual expression in his prose *Three Poems*, he had compared himself explicitly to Childe Roland at the Dark Tower. Here also, his Sublime sense that a Stevensian reality is happening in the war of the sky against the mind is necessarily obscured by a sunset akin to Roland's "last red leer."

Ashbery's finest achievement, to date, is his heroic and perpetual self-defeat, which is of a kind appropriate to conclude this book, since such self-defeat pioneers in undoing the mode of transumption that Stevens helped revive. Ashbery's allusiveness is transumptive rather than conspicuous, but he employs it against itself, as though determined to make of his lateness a desperate cheerfulness. In the final stanza of *As You Came from the Holy Land*, the most characteristic of Shelleyan-Stevensian metaphors, the fiction of the leaves, is duly revealed as a failure ("taken up and shaken again / put down in weak rage"); but the metalepsis substituted for it is almost a hyperbole of failure, as presence and the present fall together "in the gap of today filling itself / as emptiness is distributed." The two lines ending the poem would be an outrageous parody of the transumptive mode if their sad dignity were not so intense. Ashbery, too noble and poetically intelligent to subside into a parodist of time's revenges, flickers on "like a great shadow's last embellishment."

III

Ashbery has been misunderstood because of his association with the "New York School" of Kenneth Koch, Frank O'Hara and other comedians of the spirit, but also because of the dissociative phase of his work as represented by much of a peculiar volume, *The Tennis Court Oath*. But the poet of *The Double Dream of Spring* and the prose *Three Poems* is again the Stevensian meditator of the early *Some Trees*. No other American poet has labored quite so intensely to exorcise all the demons of discursiveness, and no contemporary American poet is so impressively at one with himself in expounding a discursive wisdom. Like his master, Stevens, Ashbery is essentially a ruminative poet, turning a few subjects over and over, knowing always that what counts is the mythology of self, blotched out beyond unblotching.

Ashbery's various styles have suggested affinities to composer-theorists like Cage and Cowell, to painters of the school of Kline and Pollock, and to an assortment of French bards like Roussel, Reverdy and even Michaux. But the best of Ashbery, from the early *Some Trees* on through "A Last World" and "The Skaters" to the wonderful culminations of his great book, *The Double Dream of Spring* and the recent *Three Poems*, shows a clear descent from the major American tradition that began in Emerson. Even as his poetic father is Stevens, Ashbery's largest ancestor is Whitman, and it is the Whitmanian strain in Stevens that found Ashbery. I would guess that Ashbery, like Stevens, turned to French poetry as a deliberate evasion of continuities, a desperate quest for freedom from the burden of poetic influence. The beautiful group called "French Poems" in *The Double Dream of Spring* were written in French and then translated into English, Ashbery notes, "with the idea of avoiding customary word-patterns and associations." This looks at first like the characteristic quarrel with discursiveness that is endemic in modern verse, but a deeper familiarity with the "French Poems" will evoke powerful associations with Stevens at his most central, the seer of "Credences of Summer":

> And it does seem that all the force of
> The cosmic temperature lives in the form of
>   contacts
> That no intervention could resolve,
> Even that of a creator returned to the desolate
> Scene of this first experiment: this microcosm.

> . . . and then it's so natural
> That we experience almost no feeling
> Except a certain lightness which matches
> The recent closed ambiance which is, besides
> Full of attentions for us. Thus, lightness and
>   wealth.

> But the existence of all these things and
>   especially
> The amazing fullness of their number must be
> For us a source of unforgettable questions:
> Such as: whence does all this come? and again:
> Shall I some day be a part of all this fullness?

The poet of these stanzas is necessarily a man who must have absorbed "Credences of Summer" when he was young, perhaps even as a Harvard undergraduate. Every strong poet's development is a typology of evasions, a complex misprision of his precursor. Ashbery's true precursor is the composite father, Whitman-Stevens, and the whole body to date of Ashbery's work manifests nearly every possible revisionary ratio in regard to so formidable an American ancestry. Though the disjunctiveness of so much of Ashbery suggests his usual critical placement with the boisterousness of Koch or the random poignances of O'Hara, he seems most himself when most ruefully and intensely Transcendental, the almost involuntary celebrator "of that *invisible light* which spatters the silence/Of our everyday festivities." Ashbery is a kind of invalid of American Orphism, perpetually convalescing from the strenuous worship of that dread Orphic trinity of draining gods: Eros, Dionysus, Ananke, who preside over the Native Strain of our poetry.

I propose to track Ashbery back to his origins in another essay, but here I have space only to investigate some poems of his major phase, as it seems developing in his two most recent books. To enter at this point a judgment of current American poets now entering their imaginative maturity, Ashbery and A. R. Ammons are to me the indispensable figures, two already fully achieved artists who are likely to develop into worthy rivals of Frost, Stevens, Pound, Williams, Eliot, Crane, and Warren. Merwin, James Wright, Merrill, perhaps Snyder in the school of Williams and Pound, perhaps James Dickey of a somewhat older generation (if he yet returns to the strength of earlier work) are candidates also. Yet all prophecy is dangerous here; there are recent poems by Howard, Hollander, Kinnell, Pack, Feinman, Hecht, Strand, Rich, Snodgrass, among others, which are as powerful as all but the very best of Ammons, Ashbery, Wright. Other critics and readers would nominate quite different groupings, as we evidently enter a time of singular wealth in contemporary verse.

Ashbery's poetry is haunted by the image of transparence, but this comes to him, from the start, as "a puzzling light," or carried by beings who are "as dirty handmaidens / To some transparent witch." Against Transcendental influx, Ashbery knows the wisdom of what he calls "learning to accept / The charity of the hard moments as they are doled out," and knows also that: "One can never change the core of things, and light burns you the harder for it." Burned by a visionary flame beyond accommodation (one can contrast Kinnell's too-easy invocations of such fire), Ashbery gently plays with Orphic influx ("Light bounced off the ends / Of the small gray waves to tell / Them in the observatory / About the great drama that was being won."). Between Emerson and Whitman, the seers of this tradition, and Ashbery, Ammons and other legatees, there comes the mediating figure of Stevens:

> My house has changed a little in the sun.
> The fragrance of the magnolias comes close,
> False flick, false form, but falseness close to kin.
>
> It must be visible or invisible,
> Invisible or visible or both;
> A seeing and unseeing in the eye.

These are hardly the accents of transport, yet Stevens does stand precariously, in the renewed light. But even the skepticism is Emerson's own; his greatest single visionary oration is *Experience*, a text upon which Dickinson, Stevens and Ashbery always seem to be writing commentaries:

Thus inevitably does the universe wear our color, and every object fall successively into the subject itself. The subject exists, the subject enlarges; all things sooner or later fall into place. As I am, so I see; use what language we will, we can never say anything but what we are. . . . And we cannot say too little of our constitutional necessity of seeing things under private aspects, or saturated with our humors. And yet is the God the native of these bleak rocks. . . . We must hold hard to this poverty, however scandalous, and by more vigorous self-recoveries, after the sallies of action, possess our axis more firmly. . . .

The Old Transcendentalism in America, like the New, hardly distinguishes itself from a visionary skepticism, and makes no assertions without compensatory qualifications. Still, we tend to remember Emerson for his transparencies, and not the opaquenesses that more frequently haunted him and his immediate disciples. I suspect that this is because of Emerson's *confidence*, no matter where he places his emphases. When Stevens attains to a rare transparence, he generally *sees* very little more than is customary, but he *feels* a greater peace, and this peace reduces to a confidence in the momentary capability of his own imagination. Transcendentalism, in its American formulation, centers upon Emerson's stance of Self-Reliance, which is primarily a denial of the anxiety of influence. Like Nietzsche, who admired him for it, Emerson refuses to allow us to believe we must be latecomers. In a gnomic quatrain introducing his major essay on self-reliance, Emerson manifested a shamanistic intensity still evident in his descendents:

> Cast the bantling on the rocks,
> Suckle him with the she-wolf's teat,
> Wintered with the hawk and fox,
> Power and speed be hands and feet.

This is splendid, but Emerson had no more been such a bantling than any of my contemporaries are, unless one wants the delightful absurdity of seeing Wordsworth or Coleridge as a she-wolf. "Do not seek yourself outside yourself" is yet another motto to *Self-Reliance*, and there is one more, from Beaumont and Fletcher, assuring us that the soul of an honest man:

> Commands all light, all influence, all fate
> Nothing to him falls early or too late.

These are all wonderful idealisms. Whitman, who had been simmering, read *Self-Reliance* and was brought to the boil of the 1855 "Song of Myself." Ashbery, by temperament and choice, always seems to keep simmering, but whether he took impetus from Whitman, Stevens or even the French partisans of poetic Newness, he has worked largely and overtly in this Emersonian spirit. Unfortunately, like Merwin and Merwin's precursor, Pound, Ashbery truly absorbed from the Emerson-Whitman tradition the poet's over-idealizing tendency to lie to himself, against his origins and against experience. American poets since Emerson are all antithetical completions of one another, which means mostly that they develop into grotesque truncations of what they might have been. Where British poets swerve away from their spiritual fathers, ours attempt to rescue their supposedly benighted sires. American bards, like Democritus, deny the swerve, so as to save divination, holding on to the Fate that might make them liberating gods. Epicurus affirmed the swerve, ruining divination, and all poetry since is caught between the two. Emerson, though close to Democritus, wants even divination to be a mode of Self-Reliance. That is, he genuinely shares the Orphic belief that the poet is already divine, and realizes more of this divinity in writing his poems. Lucretian poets like Shelley who find freedom by swerving away from fathers (Wordsworth and Milton, for Shelley) do not believe in divination, and do not worship an Orphic Necessity as the final form of divinity. Orphic poets, particularly American or Emersonian Orphics, worship four gods only: Ananke, Eros, Dionysus and—most of all surely— themselves. They are therefore peculiarly resistant to the idea of poetic influence, for divination—to them—means primarily an apprehension of their own possible sublimity, the gods they are in process of becoming. The gentle Ashbery, despite all his quite genuine and hard-won wisdom, is as much in this tradition as those spheral men, Emerson, Whitman, Thoreau, and that sublime egoist, Stevens, or the American Wordsworth.

The Double Dream of Spring has a limpidly beautiful poem called "Clouds," which begins:

All this time he had only been waiting,
Not even thinking, as many had supposed.
Now sleep wound down to him its promise of
dazzling peace
And he stood up to assume that imagination.

There were others in the forest as close as he
To caring about the silent outcome, but they had
gotten lost
In the shadows of dreams so that the external
look
Of the nearby world had become confused with
the cobwebs inside.

Sleep here has a Whitmanian-Stevensian cast ("The Sleepers," "The Owl in the Sarcophagus") and the gorgeous solipsism so directly celebrated here has its sources in the same ultimately Emersonian tradition. Though "he," the poet or quest-hero, is distinguished from his fellows as not having yielded to such solipsism, the poem ends in a negative apotheosis:

He shoots forward like a malignant star.
The edges of the journey are ragged.
Only the face of night begins to grow distinct
As the fainter stars call to each other and are
lost.

Day re-creates his image like a snapshot:
The family and the guests are there,
The talking over there, only now it will never
end.
And so cities are arranged, and oceans traversed,

And farms tilled with especial care.
This year again the corn has grown ripe and
tall.
It is a perfect rebuttal of the argument. And
Semele
Moves away, puzzled at the brown light above
the fields.

The harvest of natural process, too ripe for enigmas, refutes quest, and confirms the natural realism of all solipsists. This poem, urging us away from the Emersonian or Central Self, concludes by yielding to that Self, and to the re-birth of Dionysus, Semele's son. Like his precursor, Stevens, Ashbery fears and evades the Native Strain of American Orphism and again like Stevens he belongs as much to that strain as Hart Crane or

John Wheelwright does. In the recent prose *Three Poems*, he ruefully accepts his tradition and his inescapable place in it:

> Why, after all, were we not destroyed in the conflagration of the moment our real and imaginary lives coincided, unless it was because we never had a separate existence beyond that of those two static and highly artificial concepts whose fusion was nevertheless the cause of death and destruction not only for ourselves but in the world around us. But perhaps the explanation lies precisely here: what we were witnessing was merely the reverse side of an event of cosmic beatitude for all except us, who were blind to it because it took place inside us. Meanwhile the shape of life has changed definitively for the better for everyone on the outside. They are bathed in the light of this tremendous surprise as in the light of a new sun from which only healing and not corrosive rays emanate; they comment on the miraculous change as people comment on the dazzling beauty of a day in early autumn, forgetting that for the blind man in their midst it is a day like any other, so that its beauty cannot be said to have universal validity but must remain fundamentally in doubt.

> *(The Recital)*

The closest (though dialectically opposed) analogue to this passage is the great concluding rhapsody of Emerson's early apocalypse, *Nature*, when the Orphic Poet returns to prophesy:

> As when the summer comes from the south the snow-banks melt and the face of the earth becomes green before it, so shall the advancing spirit create its ornaments along its path, and carry with it the beauty it visits and the song which enchants it; it shall draw beautiful faces, warm hearts, wise discourse, and heroic acts, around its way, until evil is no more seen. The kingdom of man over nature, which cometh not with observation,—a dominion such as now is beyond his dream of God,—he shall enter without more wonder than the blind man feels who is gradually restored to perfect sight.

Ashbery's apocalyptic transformation of the Self, its elevation to the Over-Soul, is manifest to everyone and everything outside the Self, but not to the blind man of the Self. The Emersonian Self will know the metamorphic redemption of others and things only by knowing first its gradual freedom from blindness as to its own glory. Ashbery's forerunners, the makers of *Song of Myself* and *Notes toward a Supreme Fiction*, were primary Emersonians, involuntary as Stevens was in this identity. Ashbery is that American anomaly, an antithetical Transcendentalist, bearer of an influx of the Newness that he cannot know himself.

IV

I leap ahead, past Frost and Pound, Eliot and Williams, past even Hart Crane, to a contemporary image-of-voice that is another strong tally, however ruefully the strength regards itself. Here is John Ashbery's *The Other Tradition*, the second poem in his 1977 volume, *Houseboat Days:*

They all came, some wore sentiments
Emblazoned on T-shirts, proclaiming the lateness
Of the hour, and indeed the sun slanted its rays
Through branches of Norfolk Island pine as though
Politely clearing its throat, and all ideas settled
In a fuzz of dust under trees when it's drizzling:
The endless games of Scrabble, the boosters,
The celebrated omelette au Cantal, and through it
The roar of time plunging unchecked through the sluices
Of the days, dragging every sexual moment of it
Past the lenses: the end of something.
Only then did you glance up from your book,
Unable to comprehend what had been taking place, or
Say what you had been reading. More chairs
Were brought, and lamps were lit, but it tells
Nothing of how all this proceeded to materialize
Before you and the people waiting outside and in the next
Street, repeating its name over and over, until silence
Moved halfway up the darkened trunks,
And the meeting was called to order.
                                    I still remember
How they found you, after a dream, in your thimble hat,
Studious as a butterfly in a parking lot.
The road home was nicer then. Dispersing, each of the
Troubadours had something to say about how charity
Had run its race and won, leaving you the ex-president
Of the event, and how, though many of these present
Had wished something to come of it, if only a distant
Wisp of smoke, yet none was so deceived as to hanker
After that cool non-being of just a few minutes before,
Now that the idea of a forest had clamped itself
Over the minutiae of the scene. You found this
Charming, but turned your face fully toward night,
Speaking into it like a megaphone, not hearing
Or caring, although these still live and are generous
And all ways contained, allowed to come and go
Indefinitely in and out of the stockade
They have so much trouble remembering, when your forgetting
Rescues them at last, as a star absorbs the night.

I am aware that this charming poem urbanely confronts, absorbs and in some sense seeks to overthrow a critical theory, almost a critical climate, that has accorded it a canonical status. Stevens's Whitman proclaims that nothing is final and that no man shall see the end. Ashbery, a Whitman somehow more studiously casual even than Whitman, regards the prophets of belatedness and cheerfully insists that his forgetting or repression will rescue us at last, even as the Whitmanian or Stevensian evening star absorbs the night. But the price paid for this metaleptic reversal of American belatedness into a fresh earliness is the yielding up of Ashbery's tally or image of voice to a deliberate grotesquerie. Sexuality is made totally subservient to time, which is indeed "the end of something," and poetic tradition becomes an ill-organized social meeting of troubadours, leaving the canonical Ashbery as "ex-president / Of the event." As for the image of voice proper, the Whitmanian confrontation of the night now declines into: "You found this / Charming, but turned your face fully toward night, / Speaking into it like a megaphone, not hearing / Or caring." Such a megaphone is an apt image for Paul de Man's deconstructionist view of poetic tradition, which undoes tradition by suggesting that every poem is as much a random and gratuitous event as any human death is.

Ashbery's implicit interpretation of what he wants to call *The Other Tradition* mediates between this vision of poems as being totally cut off from one another and the antithetical darkness in which poems carry over-determined relationships and progress towards a final entropy. Voice in our poetry now tallies what Ashbery in his *Syringa*, a major Orphic elegy in *Houseboat Days*, calls "a record of pebbles along the way." Let us grant that the American Sublime is always also an American irony, and then turn back to Emerson and hear the voice that is great within us somehow breaking through again. This is Emerson in his journal for August 1859, on the eve of being burned out, with all his true achievement well behind him; but he gives us the true tally of his soul:

> *Beatitudes of Intellect.*—Am I not, one of these days, to write consecutively of the beatitude of intellect? It is too great for feeble souls, and they are over-excited. The wineglass shakes, and the wine is spilled. What then? The joy which will not let me sit in my chair, which brings me bolt upright to my feet, and sends me striding around my room, like a tiger in his cage, and I cannot have composure and concentration enough even set down in English words the thought which thrills me—is not that joy a certificate of the elevation? What if I never write a book or a line? for a moment, the eyes of my eyes were opened, the affirmative experience remains, and consoles through all suffering.

V

Of the many contemporary heirs of Whitman and of Stevens, John Ashbery seems likeliest to achieve something near to their eminence. Yet their uncertainty as to their audience is far surpassed in the shifting stances that Ashbery assumes. His mode can vary from the apparently opaque, so disjunctive as to seem beyond interpretation, to a kind of limpid clairvoyance that again brings the Emersonian contraries together. Contemplating Parmigianino's picture in his major long poem, *Self-Portrait in a Convex Mirror*, Ashbery achieves a vision in which art, rather than nature, becomes the imprisoner of the soul:

> The soul has to stay where it is,
> Even though restless, hearing raindrops at the pane,
> The sighing of autumn leaves thrashed by the wind,
> Longing to be free, outside, but it must stay
> Posing in this place. It must move as little as possible.
> This is what the portrait says.
> But there is in that gaze a combination
> Of tenderness, amusement and regret, so powerful
> In its restraint that one cannot look for long.
> The secret is too plain. The pity of it smarts,
> Makes hot tears spurt: that the soul is not a soul,
> Has no secret, is small, and it fits
> Its hollow perfectly: its room, our moment of attention.

Whitman's Soul, knowing its true hour in wordlessness, is apparently reduced here and now to a moment only of attention. And yet even this tearful realization, supposedly abandoning the soul to a convex mirror, remains a privileged moment, of an Emersonian rather than Paterian kind. Precisely where he seems most wistful and knowingly bewildered by loss, Ashbery remains most dialectical, like his American ancestors.

The simple diction and vulnerable stance barely conceal the presence of the American Transcendental Self, an ontological self that increases even as the empirical self abandons every spiritual assertion. Hence the "amusement" that takes up its stance between "tenderness" and "regret," Whitmanian affections, and hence also the larger hint of a power held in reserve, "so powerful in its restraint that one cannot look for long." An American Orphic, wandering in the Emersonian legacy, can afford to surrender the soul in much the same temper as the ancient Gnostics did. The soul can be given up to the Demiurge, whether of art or nature, because a spark of *pneuma* is more vital than the *psyche*, and fits no hollow whatsoever. Where Whitman and Stevens are at once hermetic and off-hand, so is Ashbery, but his throwaway gestures pay the price of an ever-increasing American sense of belatedness.

RICHARD HOWARD

John Ashbery

This poet has been bravely endorsed by his friends ("the illumination of life turned into language and language turned into life"), brutally dismissed by his enemies ("garbage"), and acknowledged with some bewilderment by his reviewers ("words often appear in unexpectedly brilliant new combinations"). All agree broadly, though, that Ashbery is *avant-garde* whatever else he may be, and it is on that consensus I should like to loiter a little, before proceeding, with the poet's help, to a ponderation of the achievements—or what I can recognize as the achievements—in his chief volumes of verse.

The military figure commonly employed to describe the modern artist in his experimental and initiating capacity is so natural to us—we even use it pejoratively, to condemn what appears a timid reliance on the conventional: a *rear-guard* artist is scarcely an artist at all, these days—that it is something of an effort to disengage the notion of *opposition*, of combat and conquest which is the activity we like to associate with the artist as the antagonist of the bourgeoisie, from the notion of *protection*, of scouting and reconnoitre which implies that the vanguard is in advance precisely in order *to guard*. The point—I shall concentrate here on the artist's custodial relation to his art, rather than his hostility to the public—is not to abandon the main body of your troops altogether, but to maintain certain exchanges, to insure certain complicities which will make your own skirmishes up ahead of some service to the more unwieldy forces in the rear—and perhaps the more unwieldy precisely because the more forceful.

From *Alone with America.* Copyright © 1980 by Richard Howard. Atheneum.

In the saving, the conservative sense of the term, Ashbery is, sufficiently to compel our trust, an advance-guard poet. I hope to show how he has kept in touch with the tradition he outdistances, how he has remained ahead of something whose force and weight at his back he is fruitfully (if at times fearfully) aware of. That there are many occasions when, it seems to me, he has allowed his communication-lines with the regulars to be cut speaks neither for nor against him. It is a question of the terrain covered and of the engagements fought. The poet who wrote his master's essay on the novels of Henry Green and who invoked, presenting an *inédit by* Raymond Roussel in the French magazine *l'Arc*, that bewildering author's *particularités qui ajoutent à sa beauté strictement littéraire*—the poet who is also a playful scholiast of the hyperbaton is evidently well prepared to leave us in whatever lurch he finds ineluctable. We need not question his decision, or what seems to us his determination, so to leave us; let us merely remind him that a vanguard, as Roussel himself would certainly have known, is also a variety of hybrid peach valued not so much for its own fruit as for its grafting powers.

I spoke just now of enlisting Ashbery's help in our examination of his work. It is an assistance we have come to look for from those artists whose project is evidently going to make some demand upon our patience, or upon our capacity to be diverted. Lest we remain, like Napoleon, *inamusable*, many writers have provided a clue in the form of an imaginative schema or construct which heightens the work's inner resonance at the same time that it defines the *poetics* by which the contraption operates. For example, as early in his career as 1893, Gide noted the likelihood of such a device (and indeed its appeal, for him, extended to the method of Edouard's *Journal* within *The Counterfeiters* and to the *Journal of the Counterfeiters* published along with the novel):

> I like discovering in a work of art . . . transposed to the scale of the characters, the very subject of that work. Nothing illuminates it better, nothing establishes more surely the proportions of the whole. Thus in certain paintings by Memling or Quentin Metsys, a tiny dark convex mirror reflects the interior of the room where the scene painted occurs. Similarly, in Velasquez' *Meninas* (though in a different way). Finally, in *Hamlet's* play within the play, as in many other dramas. In *Wilhelm Meister*, the marionette scenes or the parties at the château. In *The Fall of the House of Usher*, the passage being read to Roderick, etc. None of these examples is entirely fair. What would be much more so, what would say what I want . . . is the comparison with that method in heraldry which consists of putting a second blazon in the center of the first, *en abyme*.

In Ashbery's case, the blazon *en abyme* occurs at the start, rather than at the center, though in all this poet's larger pieces, there is an impulse to break out of the legalities of a compositional system and to address the reader directly ("But no doubt you have understood / it all now and I am a fool. It remains / for me to get better, and to understand you . . ."). If Ashbery's poems themselves are a *blazon of making*, which is after all what the word poem means, inside them we generally find that second blazon, the inclination to speak up without being mediated by the poem ("That something desperate was to be attempted was, however, quite plain"); the work criticizes its own text by accommodating in its texture an alternative patois. From the start, as I say, Ashbery has afforded us various admonitory nudges and eye-rollings: in the little play "Turandot," a kind of meiotic eclogue in three scenes and a sestina, the princess begins by calling for

> *Laughs and perfect excisions*
> *In which the matter biteth the manner,*

and when the hungry prince asks for her first question, she retorts

> *There are no questions.*
> *There are many answers . . .*

And if that is not quite enough to prepare us for a sestina, surely the only one in English, in which one of the teleutons is "radium," it suggests nonetheless, in a characteristically abrupt way, the embarrassment of riches we must confront. In 1953, the same year *Turandot and Other Poems* was published in a pamphlet by the Tibor de Nagy Gallery (all the poems were reprinted three years later in *Some Trees* except for a three-stanza piece called "White" and "Turandot" itself), this poet's one-act play *The Heroes* was produced off-Broadway (and later published in a collection which also included plays by Merrill and O'Hara). Ashbery's *dégagé* comedy about the heroes of the Trojan War, set in a Long Island house-party strongly reminiscent of the accommodations Henry Green affords *his* personnel, contains four speeches by Theseus, victor over the labyrinth and the minotaur, and one by Circe, sorceress and visionary, which become crucial to our understanding of his poetry—of what it will not do for us as well as of what it must. If we are bewildered by our first encounter with *Turandot and Other Poems*, if we are baffled not only by the imagery but by the syntax and the tonality of lines like these from "White":

> *Where is the tempest buttered? The giants*
> *In their yachts have privately forgotten*

> *by which hand slipped under the door*
> *Its screaming face. I rode into*
> *The scared dead town, parked the Plymouth—*
> *No one in the central dark bar—*
> *"Perhaps Pat is dead" but it buckled,*
> *Came on, all puce zones alight*
> *And in the death of muck and horror*
> *Knelt one on the quiet trapeze of the sky.*

—if we are defeated by such lines, which Ashbery has not chosen to carry over into the canon of his work and which I can therefore quote here without having to say more about them than that they suggest his disconcerting gift for placing a recognizable, even a tantalizing "scene" (as here, from the movies: lines four through seven) among a cluster of irreconcilable propositions—and *disconcerting* must be our normative word here, for it identifies if it does not stigmatize this poet's powerful centrifugal, dissociative impulse—if such lines, then, bewilder, baffle, defeat and disconcert us, we will find our scandal rehearsed and in some senses relaxed and even redeemed by these speeches from *The Heroes*. Reading Theseus on the labyrinth, we are on the way to reading Ashbery on the art of poetry, a tiny dark convex mirror indeed:

> I took advantage of the fact that it was built like a maze. Whenever you do this, even if the problem is just one in algebra, everything becomes simple immediately. Because then you can sit back and get a picture of yourself doing whatever it is. If you do not grant its own peculiar nature to the problem, you can have no picture of yourself and consequently feel harassed and lonely. Without imagination nothing can be easy.
>
> I'd always supposed the world was full of fakes, but I was foolish enough to believe that it was made interesting by the varying degrees of skill with which they covered up their lack of integrity. It never occurred to me that the greatest fake of all [the minotaur] would make not the slightest effort to convince me of its reality . . . not a pretense! But there it was, a stupid unambitious piece of stage machinery! . . . There was nothing to do but give the thing a well-aimed kick and go home . . .
>
> There are large holes in the roof, so the visitor is free, if he wishes, to climb out on top and survey the ground plan of the whole edifice. In short, he is in the dubious position of a person who believes that dada is still alive . . . Now comes the strangest part of all: you have been in the maze several days and nights, and you are beginning to realize you have changed several times. Not just you, either, but your whole idea of the maze and the maze itself . . . The maze looks just the same as ever—it is more as if it were being looked at by a different person. But I was so happy there, for now at last I was seeing myself as I could only be—not as I might be seen by a person in the street: full of

unfamiliarity and the resulting poetry. Before, I might have seemed beautiful to the passerby. I now seemed ten times more so to myself, for I saw that I meant nothing beyond the equivocal statement of my limbs and the space and time they happened to occupy . . . I realized I now possessed the only weapon by which the minotaur might be vanquished: the indifference of a true aesthete . . .

It is almost a catalogue of the modernist principles Ashbery has recited, a post-symbolist enchiridion: the poem as simultaneous structure, impersonal, autonomous, released from the charge of expression, of assertion; the poem as arbitrary construct, absurd, self-destroying, no longer aspiring to convince or even to hoax; the poem as an agent of transformation, equal in value to the poet himself and therefore capable of changing him; the poem as means of escape from identity, leading into a world of contemplation, indifference, bliss. Theseus' final statement of his situation, a *tirade* to Circe, brings us even closer to Ashbery's later poems:

> Let me tell you of an experience I had while I was on my way here. My train had stopped in the station directly opposite another. Through the glass I was able to watch a couple in the next train, a man and a woman who were having some sort of a conversation. For fifteen minutes I watched them. I had no idea what their relation was. I could form no idea of their conversation. They might have been speaking words of love, or planning a murder, or quarreling about their in-laws. Yet just from watching them talk, even though I could hear nothing, I feel I know those people better than anyone in the world . . .

The proposition of a reality that may be identifiable and even beautiful, though it outstrips understanding, is certainly what we shall need in exposing ourselves to Ashbery's first book, which was published by the Yale Series of Younger Poets in 1956 with a remarkably disaffected foreword by W. H. Auden. In the shade of *Some Trees*, I would cite the last of Ashbery's blazons, from the end of *The Heroes*; it is Circe's answer to Theseus' rather blithe assumption that it is enough to *recognize* reality whether one understands it or not. The old witch forces the triumphant hero to acknowledge how much harder it is going to be than he has been prepared to admit—and we stand admonished along with Theseus and Ashbery, *en abyme* in the face of *the poems*:

> So far this play has been easy. From now on it's going to be more difficult to follow. That's the way life is sometimes. Yea, a fine stifling mist springs up from the author's pure and moody mind. Confusion and hopelessness follow on the precise speech of spring. Just as, when the last line of this play is uttered, your memory will lift a torch to the dry twisted mass. Then it will not seem so much as if all this never

happened, but as if parts continued to go on all the time in your head, rising up without warning whenever you start to do the simplest act.

A glance at the table of contents tells us, first of all, how thoroughly aware Ashbery is of his conventions—more than aware, elated to have them at hand: "Eclogue," "Canzone," "Sonnet," "Pantoum" and three sestinas dramatize this poet's fondness for the art's most intricate forms, and his facility with them. Other pieces are named for works of literature themselves—"Two Scenes," "Popular Songs," "The Instruction Manual," "Album Leaf," "Illustration," "A Long Novel," "A Pastoral" —suggesting that Ashbery has none of the advanced artist's habitual hostility to his own medium, for all his dissociative techniques and fragmenting designs. He has even taken Marvell's famous poem, or at least the title of it, and put himself into the photograph: "The Picture of Little J. A. in a Prospect of Flowers"—

> . . . I cannot escape the picture
> Of my small self in that bank of flowers:
> My head among the blazing phlox
> Seemed a pale and gigantic fungus.
> I had a hard stare, accepting
>
> Everything, taking nothing,
> As though the rolled-up future might stink
> As loud as stood the sick moment
> The shutter clicked. Though I was wrong,
> Still, as the loveliest feelings
>
> Must soon find words, and these, yes,
> Displace them, so I am not wrong
> In calling this comic version of myself
> The true one. For as change is horror,
> Virtue is really stubbornness
>
> And only in the light of lost words
> Can we imagine our rewards.

This is but the third section of a poem that runs through much of the diction of English poetry, and even its exaggerated symbolist postures ("the rolled-up future might stink / as loud as stood the sick moment / the shutter clicked") cannot decoy us from the discovery that this poet is obsessed by the most classical of poetic themes: the immortalization of experience by words. For a poet, even one who would leave Andrew Marvell behind him, "the loveliest feelings / must soon find words, and these, yes, / displace them . . . and only in the light of lost words / can we imagine our rewards." The placing of that "yes" betrays the argument Ashbery has had with himself on this subject, and also betokens the victory he has reached over his own love of incoherence (poems called "Errors" and "Chaos"). Most of the poems in the book aim, as one firing buckshot may be said to aim, at a single target: the elusive order of existence which the poet knows to be there, just beyond his reach.

> From every corner comes a distinctive offering.
> The train comes bearing joy;
> For long we hadn't heard so much news, such noise . . .
> As laughing cadets say, "In the evening
> Everything has a schedule, if you can find out what it is."

The notion that The Poem is already there, *in the world*, and must be collected somehow by the poet, is what keeps these pieces going. "Some Trees" itself puts the matter perfectly (though there is a second and probably a third way of reading that title—not only "Several Trees," but also "These Trees as opposed to Others," and even "Trees Indeed!" the way Churchill used to say "Some Chicken—Some Neck!")—

> These are amazing: each
> Joining a neighbor, as though speech
> Were a still performance.
> Arranging by chance
>
> To meet as far this morning
> From the world as agreeing
> With it, you and I
> Are suddenly what the trees try
>
> To tell us we are:
> That their merely being there
> Means something; that soon
> We may touch, love, explain.

By "logic of strange position" rather than by any emotional adequacy or correspondence, any psychological explanation, any moral recovery, this poet sweeps the world's body into his net. It is in this, surely, that Ashbery is truly advanced, even revolutionary—his notion that the world not only contains but *is* his poem, and that he cannot, in order to write it, draw the world into himself as has traditionally been attempted, but must rather extrude himself into the world, must *flee the center* in order to be on the verge at all points. As he had said, in *The Heroes*, "I saw that I meant nothing beyond the equivocal statement of my limbs and the space and time they happened to occupy," so he says in *Some Trees*, "What are lamps / when night is waiting?" and again,

The mythological poet, his face
Fabulous and fastidious, accepts
Beauty before it arrives . . . He is merely
An ornament, a kind of lewd
Cloud placed on the horizon.

Close to the zoo, acquiescing
To dust, candy, perverts; inserted in
The panting forest, or openly
Walking in the great and sullen square
He has eloped with all music
And does not care. For isn't there,
He says, a final diversion, a greater
Because it can be given, a gift
Too simple even to be despised?

Beyond the evident influence of Stevens ("We can only imagine a world in which a woman / walks and wears her hair and knows / all that she does not know. Yet we know / what her breasts are"), and the occasional note of Perse ("Lovely tribes have just moved to the north. / In the flickering evening the martins grow denser. / Rivers of wings surround us and vast tribulation"), the poems in *Some Trees* that most compel our trust in Ashbery's bond with what has already been made, his covenant with the convention, are two which owe most to Apollinaire: "The Instruction Manual" and "Illustration." These strike the note of "a gift too simple even to be despised"—one from inside: "The Instruction Manual," that deploys all of Ashbery's skill with direct statement, the narrative of an achieved indentity confronting the given world; and one addressing the other: "Illustration," about a woman "who acts out," as Auden puts it, "her private mythology and denies the reality of anything outside herself." It is a comfort, in the presence of poems like "Grand Abacus"—the very title suggests the alien and alienating machinery, all those bright beads clicking back and forth on the wires, but not much being accounted for beyond a certain insanely "clever" calculation:

Perhaps this valley too leads into the head of long-ago days.
What, if not its commercial and etiolated visage, could
    break through the meadow wires?
It placed a chair in the meadow and then went far away.
People come to visit in summer, they do not think about
    the head.
Soldiers come down to see the head. The stick hides from them.
The heavens say, "Here I am, boys and girls!"
The stick tries to hide in the noise. The leaves, happy,
    drift over the dusty meadow.

> *"I'd like to see it," someone said about the head, which*
> *has stopped pretending to be a town . . .*

—it is more than a comfort, it is a condition of our engagement to rehearse a poem as evidently entangled with consistency as "Illustration." The suicide about to leap from her cornice is presented to us as a "novice," though we do not at once know whether her novitiate is to life or death. The commandments of man and god against self-slaughter are reviewed in a pun:

> *. . . Angels*
>
> *Combined their prayers with those*
> *Of the police, begging her to come off it.*

The inducements of society (" 'I do not want a friend,' she said"), of adornment, pleasure and selfishness fail to persuade the woman against her resolution; only the blind man offering flowers approaches success,

> *For that the scene should be a ceremony*
>
> *Was what she wanted. "I desire*
> *Monuments," she said. "I want to move*
>
> *Figuratively, as waves caress*
> *The thoughtless shore. You people I know*
>
> *Will offer me every good thing*
> *I do not want. But please remember*
>
> *I died accepting them." With that, the wind*
> *Unpinned her bulky robes, and naked*
>
> *As a roc's egg, she drifted slowly downward*
> *Out of the angels' tenderness and the minds of men.*

There is an exactitude about this, and a wild imaginative choice of analogy ("to move figuratively, as waves caress the thoughtless shore" or "naked as a roc's egg") that conjugate to make something particularly poignant. The private mythology, thirsty for ritual and "monuments," pitted against the trivial life of the crowd watching, is seen as an *illustration* in the old sense (the sense meaning *lustration* as well) in which all objects and incidents are taken, by poetry, as a sanctification of life. The *body* of any symbol, the Church says, is absurd, and Ashbery's practice concurs. In the second part of this poem, which I take it bears a reciprocal relation to the figure of the suicide, each part being the "illustration" of the other, no such preposterous emblems are devised (like "blue cornflakes in a white bowl" for the sea and its curving beach); rather the poet immediately moralizes the fable: "much that is beautiful must be discarded / so that we may resemble a taller / impression of ourselves." And his final vision of the episode's meaning is Ashbery at his most controlled, his most beautiful:

> Moths climb in the flame,
> Alas, that wish only to be the flame:
>
> They do not lessen our stature.
> We twinkle under the weight
>
> Of indiscretions. But how could we tell
> That of the truth we know, she was
>
> The somber vestment? For that night, rockets sighed
> Elegantly over the city, and there was feasting:
>
> There is so much in that moment!
> So many attitudes toward that flame,
>
> We might have soared from earth, watching her glide
> Aloft in her peplum of bright leaves.
>
> But she, of course, was only an effigy
> Of indifference, a miracle
>
> Not meant for us, as the leaves are not
> Winter's because it is the end.

There is the same rueful adieu to experience in "The Instruction Manual," or at least the same note of frustration sounded, as at the end of "Illustration," but because the utterance is made in the poet's own persona there is a waggishness in the wistfulness—the comedian, as Ashbery would say, as the letter A—but lower-case. It is the Apollinaire attitude toward language if not the Apollonian one—the words set down with only so much care as to make them cope—that is most evident here, in this long exercise in projection:

> I wish I did not have to write the instruction manual
>   on the uses of a new metal.
> I look down into the street and see people, each
>   walking with an inner peace,
> And envy them—they are so far away from me!
> Not one of them has to worry about getting out this
>   manual on schedule.
> And, as my way is, I begin to dream, resting my elbows
>   on the desk and leaning out of the window a little
> Of dim Guadalajara! City of rose-colored flowers!
> City I wanted most to see, and most did not see, in
>   Mexico!

There follows a long, exact travelogue, the phrasing so perfect and the feeling so painfully compressed in the objects selected for *émerveillement* that it almost seems as if Mr. James Fitzpatrick had had a possible genre going for himself after all; but then we reach the end, and realize how difficult this "simple" kind of writing must be to carry off, how disabused Ashbery's whimsy is, and how devastating his criticism of himself:

> *How limited, but how complete, has been*
> *our experience of Guadalajara!*
> *We have seen young love, married love, and the*
> *love of an aged mother for her son.*
> *We have heard the music, tasted the drinks, and*
> *looked at colored houses.*
> *What more is there to do, except stay? And that*
> *we cannot do.*
> *And as a last breeze freshens the top of the weathered*
> *old tower, I turn my gaze*
> *Back to the instruction manual which has made me*
> *dream of Guadalajara.*

None of Ashbery's other poems, even in this first book, exploit with such consecution, with such a progressive impulse, these characteristic modes of his; but their tonalities recur throughout the body of his work, no matter how spattered and pointillist the phrases ("murk plectrum" is probably the best—or worst—example), how discrepant the imagery. "The Instruction Manual" and "Illustration" afford us the framing possibilities: the hand-to-mouth music of a self locating its unavailable hopes wherever it can; and the aberrant mind, possessed of its own beautiful truth, disqualifying the accommodations of a cachectic world. I suspect that by now Ashbery is as sick of having these two poems lit upon by his admirers and even by his detractors as Eliot professed to be of having to recite "Prufrock"—in both cases, the poets would deplore the inroads of an early success upon their later style. But in Ashbery's instance, the later style is so extreme, so centrifugal, that it is well to be reminded of its wonderful and central antecedents before, as he says in his title poem,

> *Our days put on such reticence*
> *These accents seem their own defense.*

By the time *Some Trees* was published, Ashbery had moved to Paris where he was to live for a decade. It would be easy to suggest that his experiments in the loosening, explosion and relocation of the poem were a result, or at least a concomitant, of his isolation in a literary milieu where *anything* he might do would be incomprehensible—why not, therefore, do anything? Too easy, and also, I suspect, unjust to the odd strictness of the thirty poems of *The Tennis Court Oath*, published in 1962, six years after his first book. With work as demanding and as bewildering as this, there is always the tendency to cry havoc and let slip the cogs of boredom ("there is a terrible breath in the way of all this"). The compositional techniques of Roussel and of his own understanding of vanguard art brought Ashbery, in his new collection—an extremely long and various one, by the way—to a pitch of distraction, of literal eccentricity, that leaves any consecutive or linear reading of his poems out of the question. In fact, it is only questions that are left. We must be guided in our response ("there are many answers") by the capital statement on poetics which Ashbery appended to his *curriculum vitae* after *The Tennis Court Oath* was published:

> I feel I could express myself best in music. What I like about music is its ability of being convincing, of carrying an argument through successfully to the finish, though the terms of this argument remain unknown quantities. What remains is the structure, the architecture of the argument, scene or story. I would like to do this in poetry. I would also like to reproduce the power dreams have of persuading you that a certain event has a meaning not logically connected with it, or that there is a hidden relation among disparate objects. But actually this is only a part of what I want to do, and I am not even sure I want to do it. I often change my mind about my poetry. I would prefer not to think I had any special aims in mind . . .

Remembering Theseus' image of the couple seen through the train window, whose words could not be made out, though the hero felt an intimacy "just from watching them talk," we know what to expect from these pieces, each of which generally contains its own monument and epitaph *en abyme*, my favorite being one that occurs in the four-page stream of images called "The New Realism":

> *Police formed a boundary to the works*
> *Where we played*
> A torn page with a passionate oasis.

Let me list (in the original sense of the word—to make a border or marginal accommodation) some of the passionate oases in these extraordinary poems—after all, it *is* extraordinary to set so many lines together with an evident concern for music, diction, "a more than usual order," and still remain subliminal in "message":

> *the year books*
> *authored the heart bees—*

> *beers over beads somewhat*
> *broken off from the rest . . .*

In the title poem, then, after the poet has declared "you come through but / are incomparable," he announces "there was no turning back but the end was in sight." In "America" he points to his Pierrot-preoccupations: "tears, hopeless adoration, passions / the fruit of carpentered night." In "Measles":

> *I write, trying to economize*
> *These lines, tingling. The very earth's*
> *A pension . . .*
> *You limit me to what I say.*
> *The sense of the words is*
> *With a backward motion, pinning me*
> *To the daylight mode of my declaration.*

In "The Lozenges" he declares: "We all have graves to travel from, vigorously exerting / the strongest possible influence on those about us." And in "A Last World":

> *But these were not the best men*
> *But there were moments of the others*
> *Seen through indifference, only bare methods*
> *But we can remember them and so we are saved.*

Evidently there is little rhythmic enterprise in these poems, the images being for all purposes assorted one to a line in the cadences of a suburban speech-pattern ("I jest / was playing the piano of your halitosis"), and one supposes much less of an attraction to the closed, conventional forms than in the earlier book. In the first of the "Two Sonnets," for instance, there are only thirteen lines, and though the sonnet "feeling" is there, I suppose, it is difficult to see the force of it, so impatient is Ashbery with his own submission to the form:

> *The body's products become*
> *Fatal to it. Our spit*
> *Would kill us, but we*
> *Die of our heat.*
> *Though I say the things I wish to say*
> *They are needless, their own flame conceives it.*
> *So I am cheated of perfection.*

Here the poet is constantly tweaking his mind in the direction of his poetics ("though I say the things I wish to say they are needless"), and neglecting to pursue to their formal ends the emblems and figures which "the sonnet" ordinarily suggests, though the opening quoted here has all the *panache* of, say, Merrill Moore. There is still a sestina in this volume—a remarkable one called "Faust" which has more to do with Ashbery's earlier mode than with the cut-up-novel pieces like "Europe" that crowd this collection. What is new in "Faust" is a certain narrative glamor, an extension of phrasing that is to become one of Ashbery's surprising strengths, unclotting the preposterous imagery and committing the mind to a sustained experience:

> If only the phantom would stop reappearing!
> Business, if you wanted to know, was punk at the opera.
> The heroine no longer appeared in Faust.
> The crowds strolled sadly away. The phantom
> Watched them from the roof, not guessing the hungers
> That must be stirred before disappointment can begin.

"Thoughts of a Young Girl" and "To Redouté" are further—brief—respites in a host of disproportions—"these things," as Ashbery says in "The Shower," "these things that are the property of only the few." Mostly, *The Tennis Court Oath* is an exasperating book of improper fractions, lovable for its own love of earth:

> . . . Confound it
> The arboretum is bursting with jasmine and lilac
> And all I can smell here is newsprint . . .

or again,

> Nothing can be harmed! Night and day are begin-
>   ning again!
> So put away the book,
> The flowers you were keeping to give someone:
> Only the white, tremendous foam of the street
>   has any importance,
> The new white flowers that are beginning to shoot
> up about now.

and beyond construing, for all its evident and cunning construction. Valéry remarks somewhere that we call beautiful a work which makes us aware, first, that it might not have existed (since its nonexistence would have meant no vital loss), and secondly, that it could not have been other than it is. In these middle poems of Ashbery's, I miss the tug between the first proposition and the second, for there is too much evidence in favor of the possibilities of nonexistence, not enough credence given to inevitability. That Ashbery himself was aware of the discrepancy accounts, I think, for all the self-carping *en abyme*, and leads, happily, into the firmer, fuller achievements of his next volume, which restores the tone of "The Instruction Manual"—diffident, tender and, for all its irony, rapturous!—and the temper of "Illustration"—penetrating, elegiac and, for all its wiliness, truthful.

In 1963, Ashbery interrupted the measured mystery of his expatriation and, on the stage of the Living Theater in New York, gave a reading of new poems to an audience as curious about what had become of him as it was convinced of his accomplishment in the past. In his absence, *The Compromise, or Queen of the Caribou*, a melodrama, had been performed at the Poets' Theater in Cambridge, and *To the Mill*, a kind of Happening *avant la lettre* had been published in Alfred Leslie's one-shot review *The Hasty Papers*. A glance at the end of *To the Mill* will suggest, I think, the quality of the poet's own performance, upon his first appearance in his native land for many years:

> (*The midwife empties a paper bag of dust over Tom & Katherine, who cough and sneeze.*)
> KATHERINE: My sore throat.
>
> (*The midwife disappears behind a rock. Cecilia exits left on the horse. Ernest exits to the left and reappears carrying a drum. The professor enters from the right, also carrying a drum.*)
>
> ERNEST: My leg.
>
> (*Bill exits to the left. Mary enters from the left and Cecilia, on the horse, from the right.*)

CURTAIN

For there was the poet, striding up and down the set of *The Brig*, behind strands of barbed wire (to protect him from us? us from him?), wreathed in clouds of smoke as he consumed one cigarette after the other and with remarkable skill and security read out the poems that already indicated how far he had come from the atomized shocks of *The Tennis Court Oath* ("The arctic honey blabbed over the report causing darkness"). In that last book, he had asked, of course:

> Isn't Idaho the Wolverine state?
> Anyway Ohio is the flower state
> New York is the key state.
> Bandana is the population state.
> In the hay states of Pennsylvania and Arkansas
> I lay down and slept . . .

thereby ringing a change beyond even Mr. Eliot's on "By the waters of Leman" and inventing a badly-needed "population state." This might have prepared us for "Into the Dusk-Charged Air"—a catalogue of 160 lines, each of which contains the name of a river and a characterizing landscape or location:

> *Few ships navigate*
> *On the Housatonic, but quite a few can be seen*
> *On the Elbe. For centuries*
> *The Afton has flowed.*
>   *If the Rio Negro*
> *Could abandon its song, and the Magdelena*
> *The jungle flowers, the Tagus*
> *Would still flow serenely, and the Ohio*
> *Abrade its slate banks . . .*

But there was no predicting the impulse of continuity, of rapt persistence which the other poems exalted to an altogether new pitch of identity; it was as if the poet had come to tell us "about the great drama that was being won":

> *To turn off the machinery*
> *And quietly move among the rustic landscape.*

That curious selfhood of Ashbery's which by fond abnegation found the poem in the world rather than in any centripetal operation or ordering of the sensibility, gathered and gleaned its ready-mades in what seemed, coming from the stage, a furthered capacity to *relate* in both the associative and the narrative senses of the word. And when, in 1966, Ashbery returned from Paris, his third book confirmed the sense one had at his reading three years before that here was perhaps the first poet in history in whose work anxiety (with all its shaping, climax-reaching concerns) had no place, a poet for whom the poem was poem *all through* and at any point, without emphases or repetitions (a maze, a labyrinth, rather than an obstacle-course). This, I think, is why we are rarely able to respond to this *oeuvre* in the way we do to the traditional modes anchored in what Northrop Frye calls the seasonal myths, for recurrence and the cyclical patterns of ritual simply do not apply to Ashbery's poetry in its characteristic extension here. Nothing in *Rivers and Mountains* "depends on everything's recurring till we answer from within" as Frost put it, "because," as Ashbery answers, *"all the true fragments are here."* In the first poems in the book we find, *en abyme*, some more of those apologies for the poems themselves, but they are no longer militant or even apologetic, they are triumphant in accounting for the *over-all* texture of these anti-psychological poems: "continuance quickens the scrap which falls to us . . . a premise of so much that is to come, extracted, accepted gladly but within its narrow limits no knowledge yet, nothing which can be used." And again, most significantly: *"Each moment of utterance is the true one; likewise none are true."* Existence is reported to be as ineffable as in the poems of *Some*

Trees, but no longer beyond the poet's grasp because he is no longer grasping:

> Here I am then, continuing but ever beginning
> My perennial voyage, into new memories, new hope and
>   flowers
> The way the coasts glide past you. I shall never
>   forget this moment
> Because it consists of purest ecstasy. I am happier
>   now than I ever dared believe
> Anyone could be. And we finger down the dog-eared
>   coasts . . .
> It is all passing! It is past! No, I am here,
> Bellow the coasts, and even the heavens roar their
>   assent
> As we pick up a lemon-colored light horizontally
> Projected into the night, the night that heaven
> Was kind enough to send, and I launch into the
>   happiest dreams,
> Happier once again, because tomorrow is already here.

These *dasein*-dazzled lines are from *The Skaters*, a poem of some thirty pages and, with *Clepsydra*, Ashbery's largest statement, a telluric hymn (as the book's title and title poem indicate: "in the seclusion of a melody heard / as though through trees") to a confessed, a welcomed evanescence that somehow guarantees ecstasy. The poem is not about skaters, but takes the image of their action for its own:

> . . . the intensity of minor acts
>   As skaters elaborate their distances,
> Taking a separate line to its end. Returning to the mass,
>   they join each other
> Blotted in an incredible mess of dark colors, and again
>   reappearing to take the theme
> Some little distance, like fishing boats developing from the
>   land different parabolas,
> Taking the exquisite theme far, into farness, to Land's End,
>   to the ends of the earth!
> But the livery of the year, the changing air
> Bring each to fulfillment . . .

And so Ashbery is off, inventorying "the human brain, with its tray of images" filled by his encounters with the world. Over and over, the object of the poem becomes its subject, its making its meaning; except for the late poems of Wallace Stevens, I know no more convincing meditation on the power the mind has to submit itself to forms, and by them be formed:

> . . . this poem
> Which is in the form of falling snow:
> That is, the individual flakes are not essential to the
>   importance of the whole . . .
> Hence neither the importance of the individual flake,
> Nor the importance of the whole impression of the storm,
>   if it has any, is what it is,
> But the rhythm of the series of repeated jumps, from
>   abstract into positive and back to a slightly less
>   diluted abstract.

The long lines, loose though they are, keep a spring, a resilience, in part as a result of "the evidence of the visual," the surprising way Ashbery has of giving "the answer that is novelty / that guides these swift blades o'er the ice," and in part because we recognize the tone of voice as the innocent, astonished, ravished one we had heard in "The Instruction Manual"—only cleared of the old jerkiness, taking now more than bite-size morsels of the earthly meal and discovering "the declamatory nature of the distance travelled." In "Clepsydra," too, Ashbery offers a splendid pledge as much to his achievement as to his intention. The title means a water clock, of course, a contrivance to measure time by the graduated flow of a liquid through a small aperture ("each moment of utterance is the true one"), and in the terms of the poem itself "an invisible fountain that continually destroys and refreshes the previsions." As in "The Skaters," the poem becomes a meditation on its own being in the world:

> . . . it was
> Like standing at the edge of a harbor early on a summer morning
> With the discreet shadows cast by the water all around
> And a feeling, again, of emptiness, but of richness in the way
> The whole thing is organized, on what a miraculous scale,
> Really what is meant by a human level, with the figures of giants
> Not too much bigger than the men who have come to petition them
> A moment that gave not only itself, but
> Also the means of keeping it, of not turning to dust
> Or gestures somewhere up ahead
> But of becoming complicated like the torrent
> In new dark passages, tears and laughter which
> Are a sign of life, of distant life in this case.
> And yet, as always happens, there would come a moment when
> Acts no longer sufficed and the calm
> Of this true progression hardened into shreds
> Of another kind of calm, returning to the conclusion, its premises
> Undertaken before any formal agreement had been reached, hence
> A writ that was the shadow of the colossal reason behind all this
> Like a second, rigid body behind the one you know is yours.

Such poetry is no longer merely the realm, but the means of self-encounter; its method has been to pluck from the world the constituted terms of its being, but Ashbery has exalted his linguistic recognition-scene into something more than a product, a prey, a proof of being-in-the-world. He has made his discourse identical with his experience "in such a way as to form a channel," or again, as he says, "the delta of living into everything." In this way,

> . . . any direction taken was the right one,
> Leading first to you, and through you to
> Myself that is beyond you and which is the same thing as space
> . . . moving in the shadow of
> Your single and twin existence, waking in intact
> Appreciation of it, while morning is still and before the body
> Is changed by the faces of evening.

"THE DOUBLE DREAM OF SPRING"

Our servants, according to the symbolist anchorage in a society of masters—our servants will do our living for us. Our poets, we say now, with the same confidence, the same condescension—our poets, if only we submit to their poems, will do our criticism for us:

"You cannot take it all in, certain details are already hazy and the mind boggles . . . These things could be a lot clearer without hurting anybody. Tomorrow would alter the sense of what had already been learned . . . the moment of sinking in / is always past, yet always in question, on the surface / of the goggles of memory. . . . I am not so much at home with these memorabilia of vision as on a tour / of my remotest properties. There is so much to be said, and on the surface of it very little gets said . . . It is this blank carcass of whims and tentative afterthoughts / which is being delivered into your hand like a letter . . . Strange, isn't it, that the message makes some sense, if only a relative one in the larger context of message-receiving. A light wilderness of spoken words not / unkind for all their aimlessness . . . that sound like the wind / forgetting in the branches and meaning something / nobody can translate . . . But this new way, the way sentences suddenly spurt up like gas / or sting and jab, is it that we accepted each complication / as it came along, and are therefore happy with the result? / Or was it a condition of seeing / that we vouchsafed aid and comfort to the seasons / as each came begging? As though meaning could be cast aside someday / when it had been outgrown . . . our pyramiding memories, alert as dandelion fuzz, dart from one pretext to the next / seeking in occasions new sources of memories, for memory is a profit / until the day it spreads out all its accumulation, delta-like on the plain / for that day no good can come of remembering, and the anomalies cancel each other out. / But until then foreshortened memories will keep us going, alive, one to the other: a kind of activity that offers its own way of life. Perverse notations on an indisputable state of things / open out new passages of being among the correctness of familiar patterns . . . Thus your only world is an inside one / ironically fashioned out of external phenomena / having no rhyme or reason . . . As one figure supplants another and dies, / there is no remedy for this "packaging" which has supplanted the old sensations . . . Ideas were good only because they had to die, / leaving you alone and skinless, a drawing by Vesalius. For this is action, this not being sure, this careless preparing . . . making ready to forget, and always coming back / to the mooring of starting out . . ."

There are three notes at the end of Ashbery's fourth volume of poems (out of which I have stitched together the foregoing poetics of the "turmoil that is to be our route") which help a lot, as the poet says, "to get over the threshold of so much unmeaning, so much / Being, preparing us for its event, the active memorial." Yes, precisely, that is what Ashbery's poems are, an active memorial to themselves, writhing in dissolute, shimmering lines without emphases or repetitions around the column their own accumulation raises until "the convention gapes / prostrated before a monument disappearing into the dark." And if it is true that in reading poems which are habitually a gloss on their own singularity we need all the help we can get, it is also true that Ashbery wants us to enjoy our helplessness all the way: "these things are offered to your participation . . . Each hastens onward separately / in strange sensations of emptiness, anguish, romantic / outbursts, visions and wraiths. One meeting cancels another . . . becoming a medium in which it is possible to recognize oneself. Each new diversion adds its accurate touch to the ensemble, and so / a portrait is built up out of multiple corrections."

Keeping that constant cancellation in mind, then, consider Ashbery's three notes: 1) that the book's title comes from that of a painting by Giorgio di Chirico; 2) that the method of the poems if pursued "with the idea of avoiding customary word-patterns and associations"; and 3) that the title *Sortes Vergilianae* refers to the ancient practice of fortune-telling "by choosing a passage from Vergil's poetry at random."

Ashbery, executive editor of *Art News* who has written with venturesome finickiness about a great many painters, has suggested by several titles in this new book that the plastic arts are a starting-point, an inspiration: *Definition of Blue, Farm Implements and Rutabagas in a Land-scape, Clouds*, and then the poem with Di Chirico's title, suffused as it is with the rural vernality characteristic of most of Ashbery's recent work. I think, too, that Di Chirico has been chosen as the psychopomp and intercessor of the book because his oneiric dissociations are the kind of thing Ashbery himself aspires to: "I would like to reproduce in poetry the power dreams have of persuading you that a certain event has a meaning not logically connected with it, or that there is a hidden relation among disparate objects," the poet has written about his program. Hence *The Double Dream of Spring*, double because it refers to an art of dreams and a dream of art. "In a dream touch bottom", the poet urges in the title poem—and indeed the bottom is so far down that the only way the poet can reach it is by rising to the surface: "I can tell you all about freedom that has turned into a painting."

Ashbery's second note about avoiding customary word patterns and associations is admonitory: only a man utterly oppressed by patterns and associations will seek at such cost to avoid them. As readers of *A Nest of Ninnies*, Ashbery's novel (written with the poet James Schuyler) remember, this poet's strategy is either to collapse helplessly into the customary, the commonplace, the cliché, or else to escape them by convulsive expeditions into "a desert of chance", warning us of "the incredible violence that is to be our route". If the world contains and even secretes Ashbery's poem ("It was the holiness of the day that fed our notions / and released them . . . a kind of fence-sitting / *raised to the level of an aesthetic ideal*"), then what the poet calls customary patterns and associations must not be allowed to distort, to atrophy or distend what is—merely, but also marvellously—there. A persistent derangement of expectation will permit the poem to collect itself from the world, to appear "slowly as from the center of some diamond / you begin to take in the world as it moves / in toward you." This new book, therefore has fewer poems than ever before which exploit or even explode the conventions of poetry, its hereditary intricacies—only one song, one sestina, while the poem "For John Clare" is in prose, and the "Variations, Calypso + Fugue" is, with derisive preposterousness, "on a Theme of Ella Wheeler Wilcox"! No, most of these poems carry on in a language without the tension of negativity, without irony, without the invoked anxiety of a closed form. The lines run on, or peter out, they do not shore up the poem's energy by any kind of rhythmic or musical constant: the poem is endlessly obliging but under no obligations. The longest poem in the book, insistently called "Fragment", is set up in what appear to be stanzas, but they are merely regular clusters, spaced off for the sake of convenience ("refreshment and ease to the statement"). Language in Ashbery's prodigious work is not wielded to convey the disciplinary, punitive passion which has been the art's contribution and resource in the past; it is intended rather—and manages—to convince by letting things alone: "a rhythm of standing still / keeps us in continual equilibrium . . . for each progress is negation, of movement and in particular of number." Recalling that verse is traditionally called "numbers", we can better understand the spell upon us of Ashbery's innumerable art, what he cherishes as "its articulate flatness, goal, barrier and climate."

Ashbery's third note, explaining the *Sortes Vergilianae*, affords the decisive expression: "choosing at random." The accent is on both processes equally, the operation of chance, the operation of choice. The poem is already there, and what Ashbery calls "the secret of the search" is that its given, its constituted existence in the world makes all choosing certain to succeed and therefore eliminates the necessity of choice. The objective of the poem is not subjective, it is the poem's subject, and the poem's "meaning" is in its making: "this banality which in the last analysis is our / most precious possession, because allowing us to / rise above ourselves."

By dilating the poet's notes I have tried to account for his necessities, and I have not hesitated to invoke the poems as their own exegesis. Indeed, the great innovation of Ashbery's poems is that they do not explain or symbolize or even refer to some experience the poet has had, something outside themselves in the world, something precedent. The poems are not about anything, they are something, they are their own creation, and it would be fair to say that the world is, instead, a comment on them, a criticism of them. For all his modesty and mildness, that is Ashbery's great symbolist assertion—that the world may exist to conclude in a book:

> Sly breath of Eros,
> Anniversary on the woven city lament, that assures our arriving
> In hours, seconds, breath, watching our salary
> In the morning holocaust become one vast furnace, engaging all tears.
> (*Poetry*, 1970)

"THREE POEMS"

In his previous collection, it was apparent—no, let us say it was apprehensible, that Ashbery's poems carried on in a language without the tension of negativity, without the invoked anxiety of a closed form. In short, or at length, the poems were moving toward—and some had already moved right in on—*prose*, an utterance unpoliced if not unpolicied (the policy turning out to be "to keep asking life the same question until the repeated question and the same silence become answer"), innovative or advanced, as everyone keeps saying about this writer, because the lines were not wielded to convey the disciplinary, punitive passion which has always been the art's contribution and conventional resource. Now in *Three Poems*, where discourse has "come to mean what it had been called on for," where "our narration seems to be trying to bury itself in the land-scape," there are no lines at all, nor even clusters of enjambed state-ments: there are prose *texts* (something woven, as a snare or *toil*), "a kind of trilogy meant to be read in sequence," Ashbery says, constituting "a glad mess" of the matte instances he had aspired to in that last book as "articulate flatness, goal, barrier and climate," achieved now "far from the famous task, close to the meaningless but real snippets that are today's doing."

The first text, "The New Spirit", about fifty pages long, is said by the poet to record a spiritual awakening to earthly things; and though very few earthly things are vouchsafed, the endeavor is "to formulate oneself around this hollow, empty sphere . . . as objects placed along the top of a wall," for in Ashbery's spiritual exercises the aim is to be aimless, void, abluted, to get out of the way of intention in order to enable "the emptiness that was the only way you could express a thing." The second text, "The System", about the same length, is said by Ashbery to be "a love story with cosmological overtones," material handled, certainly fingered, by a parody of dialectical homiletics. Love here consists of all the possible objections to it ("it prepares its own downfall while never quite begin-ning"), and only comes to exist when it acknowledges "the inner empti-ness from which alone understanding can spring up." The third text, "The Recital", is a much briefer embroidery on the poet's relations to his victories in love and spiritual awakening which are, of course, coincident with his losses ("I am quite ready to admit that I am alone"). But such résumés are merely pretexts—the texts themselves, "provocative but baffling", weave a continuous meditation upon a series of thematic oppositions—self against others or solitude, presence in place and time against all the elsewheres of absence, art against landscape—so many sermons upon Ashbery's real text: "the major question that revolves around you, your being here."

Each poem or fiction (the words mean the same: a *made thing*, what Ashbery calls "the created vacuum") begins with an aporia, a confession of failure or incompetence, and then builds on that admission in a difficult welter of pronouns. "I", "you" and "he" are not easily discriminated, though easily discredited—it is as if Aeschylus had not yet summoned the second actor from the chorus to argue against that first great voice, or as if the persons of the drama here, "the debris of living", were indeed "proposed but never formulated." However, once it is announced that "the system was breaking down," or that "the problem is that there is no new problem", then the contraption can get started: "the note is struck, the development of its resonances ready to snap into place. For the moment we know nothing more than this." And by degrees, in a prose so unfeatured by nomination (the only allusions are to the Tarot deck, Childe Roland, Don Quixote and Alice—all famous problems themselves), so unfettered to events ("things will do the rest . . . I renounce my rights to ulterior commemoration"), that we are forever in danger of wandering from its project, the poems rise to their odd altitude, what Ashbery calls "an erect passivity," on their own apotropaics, "no live projection beyond the fact of the words in which they were written down."

And indeed Ashbery *wants* us to elude the notion of project—it is only when he has warded off choice and emphasis that the poem has, literally, the chance to assume its life—until then, "one senses only separate instances and not the movement of the fall." Again, "nothing is to be learned, only avoided"; *then* the text which started up in self-erasure and which persisted in an articulation of emptiness, can come to its end in fulfillment, its conclusion in Being, "a place of ideal quiet" on which the world is merely a comment, a diacritical marking. "All the facts are here, and it remains only to use them in the right combination," Ashbery exults, for he knows that the "right combination" must exclude any helping hand from *him*. Such is the "cost that reality, as opposed to naturalness, exacts," he muses, and it is an enormous cost, for it makes the poet's problem our own: "Our apathy can always renew itself."

As long ago as *The Tennis Court Oath*, Ashbery had operated by a prosody of intermittence and collage; here, for the same reason—to make poems which are, rather than which are *about*, the world—he invokes a poetics of continuity and encirclement ("I am to include everything: the furniture of this room, everyday expressions, as well as my rarest thoughts and dreams . . . the odd details resolved but nesting in their quirkiness, free to come and go"), the enterprise now being to get it all in rather than to leave it all out, as in the notorious "cut-up" poems like "Europe" of over a decade ago. That is why *Three Poems* must be in prose, the sole medium capable of cancelling itself out, of using itself up: the texts must be capable of proceeding without John Ashbery. How perfectly he knows this! "There comes a time when what is to be revealed actually conceals itself in casting off the mask of its identity." *Three Poems* marks that time.

"SELF-PORTRAIT IN A CONVEX MIRROR"

"I wrote in prose because my impulse was not to repeat myself," Ashbery told an interviewer about his last book, *Three Poems*. His present one is again reponse to those elements of recuperation, of recurrence and reversion which poetry—even such seamless poetry as Ashbery's, which observes beginnings and ends by a prosody of intermittence and collage rather than any such conventional markings as rhyme or repetition—is taken to incarnate, if not to incorporate. He has returned to returning—hence the self-portrait, hence the mirror, hence the convexity: "crooning the tunes, naming the name."

The subject of the self-portrait is the same new thing: if it is all there, the world, "this angle of impossible resolutions and irresolutions", then how do I get into it, how do I find a place in what is already *given*, and if I am already there, how can there be room for all that, "the many as noticed by the one"? The book is a series of meditations on this dilemma:

> And am I receiving
> This vision? Is it mine, or do I already owe it
> For other visions, unnoticed and unrecorded
> On the great relaxed curve of time . . .

long, radiant visions, cross-cut by the usual (usual for Ashbery: no one else could accustom us to "this painful freshness of each thing being exactly itself") opacities of diction and association which—"mutterings, splatterings"—one may like or loathe, depending . . . There is no choice, however, about the title poem and half a dozen others, which are, as everyone seems to be saying, among the finest things American poetry has to show, and certainly the finest things Ashbery has yet shown. "It's all bits and pieces, spangles, patches, really; nothing / stands alone," the poet has written since the book, and we must weave his observation back into the warp of what he calls "a complicated flirtation routine". When I speak of the wide-spread admiration for Ashbery's work, I do not mean to patronize him or his detractors; we are confronted with an utterance at times consistently firm, cool, inclusive, and resolute (and by "times" I mean pages and pages of verse—not since Wallace Stevens, indeed, has there been a voice in which "changes are merely / features of the whole"), and at times by verbal tantrums as preposterous as anything in the long lineage of self-indulgence; as the poet himself glosses the situation: "I tried each thing, only some were immortal and free." But in this book as in no other, the brooding seems to get out from under the allusive looniness that was always Ashbery's resource when the going got rough or smooth; *the ride*, as he says *continues*, and we are presented with "the major movement as a firm digression, a plain that slowly becomes a mountain." The poet, ruminating upon his relation to the past, especially upon the greatness of the past, and to the future, especially upon the grotesquerie of the future, is quite conscious of his idiopathy—as conscious as any of his critics:

> *I know that I braid too much my own*
> *Snapped-off perceptions of things as they come to me.*
> *They are private and always will be.*
> *Where then are the private turns of event*
> *Destined to boom later like golden chimes*
> *Released over a city from a highest tower?*
> *The quirky things that happen to me, and I tell you,*
> *And you instantly know what I mean?*

They are here, those private turns of events, and as Ashbery remarked to his interviewer, "in this kind of meditative verse the things in a room and the events of everyday life can enter and become almost fossilized in the poems." What keeps them from becoming entirely fossilized, what keeps the concrete from becoming concretion and calculus, lethally lithic, immobile, is the sense of before and after, the movement of time which washes through these pages, these long-winded portages across "this wide, tepidly meandering, civilized Lethe" which else would become "choked to the point of silence."

"*The history of one who came too late*," Ashbery puts it in his wonderful poem "As You Came from the Holy Land" (where Harold Bloom was quick to seize upon it, exhibit A in the endless catalogue of belatedness which for him constitutes poetry's knowledge of itself); yet in the title poem, Ashbery puts it conversely: "*All we know / is that we are a little early*": we are here, or there, and the rendezvous has not been kept:

> *. . . everything is surface. The surface is what's there*
> *And nothing can exist except what's there . . .*

So speaks a man whom the world has failed, who is not yet fulfilled by anything except his own existence, his abashed solipsism. The point is not to decide, to determine whether one is early or late, ahead of time or behind *the times* (the past of Parmigianino's portrait, which alas Viking Press has failed to reproduce just where and when we need it, on the book jacket); the point is to discover there is movement, change, and a linking-up, a being-in-league, however bewildering, with all the rest. Again and again, in his room, or under a tree, or looking at an old photograph (girls lounging around a fighter bomber, 1942!), the poet has occasion to remind himself of the recurrence—it is why he has returned to verse, why he has reversed—of the reversion:

> There is some connexion . . . among this. It connects up,
> Not to anything, but kind of like
> Closing the ranks so as to leave them open.

For me the opacities, what used to register as accidents, are now assimilated into the mastery, so that as John Hollander says, what lingers on after their startlingness is their truth. The poet seems to me (it is what I mean by mastery) to have gained access to a part of his experience which was once merely a part of his imagination: he has made his experience and his imagination identical:

> It is both the surface and the accidents
> Scarring the surface . . .
> These are parts of the same body.

And this incorporation, this embodiment has required of his talents that he leave off prose; that he shed those aberrational nuttinesses which are so alluring that "to get to know them we must avoid them"; that he move in on his visions with all the instruments, the devices, the pharmacopoeia of, say, a Parmigianino; as Ashbery says, and never has he proved more accurate about himself, though the proof of the accuracy must *be* himself:

> The great formal affair was beginning, orchestrated,
> Its colors concentrated in a glance, a ballade
> That takes in the whole world, now, but lightly,
> Still lightly, but with wide authority and tact.
>
> (Poetry, 1976)

"HOUSEBOAT DAYS"

After the garland of prizes bestowed in docile succession upon *Self-Portrait in a Convex Mirror*, it is apparent that we have entered a new phase of Ashbery criticism, one we might call post-favorable. I doubt if it is more helpful (though I can see it is more highfalutin) to say, with John Brinnin, that Ashbery's "dazzling orchestrations of language open up whole areas of consciousness no other American poet has even begun to explore" than it was to say, with John Simon in the bad old days, that Ashbery's poems were "garbage". But it would appear that with this new book we are in the presence of a Figure who need not abide our question, "a living contemporary who should be beyond all critical dispute" (Harold Bloom). Here is the opening of a poem, "Bird's-Eye View of the Tool and Die Co.," which I promise is neither harder nor softer than many others in the book, though it begins with a nice reversal of Proust's first line:

> For a long time I used to get up early.
> 20–30 vision, hemorrhoids intact, he checks into the
> Enclosure of time familiarizing dreams
> For better or worse. The edges rub off,
> The slant gets lost. Whatever the villagers
> Are celebrating with less conviction is
> The less you. Index of own organ-music playing,
> Machinations over the architecture (too
> Light to make much of a dent) against meditated
> Gang-wars, ice cream, loss, palm terrain.

I should say that was beyond critical dispute, or should be, simply because it is largely inaccessible to critical procedure. Fortunately (for my enter-prise) not all of Ashbery's work in his new book resists analysis or even interest so successfully. There is a great deal of poetry which is indeed beautiful and beguiling and benign in its transactions with our understand-ing; quite as characteristic as the teratoma I have just instanced is the *whole poem* "Blue Sonata", of which I quote the close, thereby giving equal time to the amazing clarity of this celebrated opacifer:

> It would be tragic to fit
> Into the space created by our not having arrived yet,
> To utter the speech that belongs there,
> For progress occurs through re-inventing
> These words from a dim recollection of them,
> In violating that space in such a way as
> To leave it intact. Yet we do after all
> Belong here, and have moved a considerable
> Distance; our passing is a facade.
> But our understanding of it is justified.

Most of the poems in *Houseboat Days* which I can make out at all are like this bit, deliberations on the meaning of the present tense, its exactions and falsifications, its promises and rewards. "There are no other questions than these, / half-squashed in mud, emerging out of the moment / we all live, learning to like it"—Ashbery is often painfully clear as to what he would wring from his evasive experience ("what I am probably trying to do is to illustrate opacity and how it can suddenly descend over us . . . it's a kind of mimesis of how experience comes to me"), and the pain is there in the tone, now goofy and insolent, then again tender and self-deprecating, vulnerable but not without its gnomic assertions ("It is the nature of things to be seen only once"), various but not without a consistent grimace ("It's all bits and pieces, spangles, patches, really; nothing / stands alone").

The position from which these proceedings flow and flare is rather the converse of what I read in the *Self-Portrait*. Here there is a cool resolution about the dialectic of self and other; the poet seems more or less content (more or less sad) to be at grips with "this tangle of impossible resolutions and irresolutions", but only *for now*. The trouble, and his subject, is that the moment passes, that *now* becomes *then*, losing everything in the process. Whatever is easy-moving, free and pleasant tends to calcify or to rot, leaving dust and ash on the mind's plate: "The songs decorate our notion of the world / and mark its limits, like a frieze of soap-bubbles."

Whence a prosody, as I have called it, of intermittence and collage; no such conventional markings as rhyme or repetition—rather, *seamless verse*, jammed rather than enjambed, extended rather than intense; it must go on and on to keep the whole contraption from coming round again, to work upon us its deepest effect, which is a kind of snake-charming. Quotation occasionally reveals the allure, but not the sense of endless possibilities, of merciless hopes:

> To praise this, blame that,
> Leads one subtly away from the beginning, where
> We must stay, in motion. To flash light
> Into the house within, its many chambers,
> Its memories and associations, upon its inscribed
> And pictured walls, argues enough that life is various.
> Life is beautiful. He who reads that
> As in the window of some distant, speeding train
> Knows what he wants, and what will befall.

The passage is from the title poem, which refers specifically, I believe, to living in the present, one's domicile upon an inconstant element, one's time at the mercy and the rigor of the stream: "The mind / is so hospitable, taking in everything / like boarders, and you don't see until / it's all over how little there was to learn / once the stench of knowledge has dissipated . . ." The misery in this poem, as in all the rest, is that of being deprived by the past and the future of the present; it is only now that the poet can see and seize the clutter as fertilizing, "not just the major events but the whole incredible / mass of everything happening simultaneously and pairing off, / channelling itself into history": experience is wrenched away—is no longer "his"—by the suspect neatness of memory, as by the sacrificial omissions of art, and so these poems are not to record a life, they are not memorials, any more than they are to decorate a tradition, they are not monuments. "What I am writing to say is, the timing, not / the contents, is what matters"—hence almost anything will turn up inside these "parts of the same body", and almost anyone—any pronoun—will become someone else. With a grim chuckle (he actually spells it out: "but perhaps, well, heh heh, temper the wind to the shorn lamb . . .") Ashbery twitches the text away from personality: "I don't think my poetry is inaccessible . . . I think it's about the privacy of everyone." And perhaps that is why they present such brutal clarifications: the privacy of everyone is a hard thing to acknowledge, especially when it is staring at you from the page, hysterically open to distraction, eager to grab the language of packaging and put it into the *perpetuum mobile* of poetry. The texts include everything, they leave out only the necessary transitions and gear-shifts which we call narrative and which have traditionally governed the decorum of our attention. In such a world, "things overheard in cafes assume an importance previously reserved for letters from the front"—and indeed, the front itself shifts to the back room, the view from the kitchen window, the voices overheard in the next bedroom. Of course no poem can keep pace with "eventuality," with the character and quality of existence as it becomes event—not even Ashbery's poem can satisfy him as to the scope and focus of "the present" —but the zany failures mount up as the only important enterprise, undertaking, overdrive:

> And we made much of this sort of materiality
> That clogged the weight of starlight, made it seem
> Fibrous, yet there was a chance in this
> To see the present as it never had existed . . .

The point or the patch is to be at the center of things, the beginning: better not prepare any received standard version of history or fable, "reread this / and the past slips through your fingers, wishing you were there." Better still, take the lesson of painting, which is always in the present, always on hand or it is nothing. So Ashbery's poems will be meditations on how to write his poems, where to begin in order always to be beginning, without that dying fall of classical recital, instead inscribed upon the evanescence of eternity: "a final flourish / that melts as it stays." Painting and music too will help—take the string quartet:

> The different parts are always meddling with each other,
> Pestering each other, getting in each other's ways
> So as to withdraw skillfully at the end, leaving—what?

A new kind of emptiness, may be bathed in freshness,
Maybe not. May be just a new kind of emptiness.

That is the risk this poetry takes, of course: by jettisoning the traditional baggage of the art and assimilating instead the methods and "morality" of the other arts (though not architecture: Ashbery is against architecture the way his critics have learned to be against interpretation), the poet incurs the possibility of "maybe just a new kind of emptiness." But the risk is worth it to Ashbery, who has never dismissed the religious possibility of emptiness—affectlessness, abjection—as *the* condition of fulfillment. (Has he not written, in *Self-Portrait*, "there is some connexion . . . among this. It connects up, / not to anything, but kind of like / closing the ranks so as to leave them open", where he sounds kind of like a SOHO Simone Weil.) It is worth what I call the risk and what he would call the necessity of emptiness—boredom, confusion, irritation, even torment—to reach what he undoubtedly and diligently *does* reach, a world whose terms are refreshed to the point, to the pinnacle, where experience is without anxiety because it is *delivered*, in both senses of that word: presented and released. A world without anxiety, without repression, without the scandal and the labor of the negative. Or as Ashbery puts it:

> Something
> Ought to be written about how this affects
> You when you write poetry:
> The extreme austerity of an almost empty mind
> Colliding with the lush, Rousseau-like foliage of its desire
>   to communicate
> Something between breaths, if only for the sake
> Of others and their desire to understand you and desert you
> For other centers of communication, so that understanding
> May begin, and in doing so be undone.
>
> (New York Arts Journal, 1977)

HAROLD BLOOM

The Charity of the
Hard Moments

Of the American poets now in mid-career, those born in the decade 1925–1935, John Ashbery and A.R. Ammons seem to me the strongest. This essay, an overview of Ashbery's published work to date, is meant as a companion-piece to the essay on Ammons printed in my book of studies in Romantic tradition, *The Ringers in the Tower* (University of Chicago Press, 1971). Ashbery goes back through Stevens to Whitman, even as Ammons is a more direct descendant of American Romanticism in its major formulation, which remains Emerson's. Otherwise, these two superb poets have nothing in common except their authentic difficulty. Ammons belongs to no school, while Ashbery can be regarded either as the best poet by far of the "New York School" or—as I would argue—so unique a figure that only confusion is engendered by associating him with Koch, O'Hara, Schuyler and their friends and disciples.

I remember purchasing *Some Trees*, Ashbery's first commercially published volume (Yale Press, 1956, Introduction by Auden) in December, 1956, after reading the first poem ("Two Scenes") in a bookstore. The poem beings: "We see us as we truly behave" and concludes with "In the evening/Everything has a schedule, if you can find out what it is." A skeptical honesty, self-reflexive, and an odd faith in a near-inscrutable order remain characteristic of Ashbery's work. Also still characteristic is the abiding influence of Stevens. I remember being fascinated by the swerve away from Stevens' "Credences of Summer" in "Two Scenes":

From *Figures of Capable Imagination.* Copyright © 1976 by Harold Bloom. Seabury Press.

> This is perhaps a day of general honesty
> Without example in the world's history
> Though the fumes are not of a singular
>   authority
> And indeed are dry as poverty.

Where Stevens, in a moment of precarious satisfaction, entertained the possibility of overcoming "poverty," imaginative need, the young Ashbery identified self-knowledge with such need. Auden, hardly an admirer of Stevens, introduced Ashbery as an ephebe of Rimbaud, seer "of sacred images and ritual acts." But, actual disciple of Stevens (in his most Whitmanian aspect) and of Whitman ultimately, Ashbery necessarily began in a poetic world emptied of magical images and acts. The highly Stevensian "The Mythological Poet" opposed "a new / Music, innocent and monstrous / As the ocean's bright display of teeth" to "the toothless murmuring/Of ancient willows," sacred images for outworn seers. In the title-poem, clearly the book's best, Ashbery had found already his largest aesthetic principle, the notion that every day the world consented to be shaped into a poem. "Not every day," Stevens warns in his "Adagia," which Ashbery couldn't have read then, but Stevens' point was that on some days it could happen. The point is Emersonian or Whitmanian, and though Ashbery antithetically completes Stevens in this principle, he is ultimately, like Whitman and Stevens, a descendant of Emerson's *Nature*, though at the start a wry one:

> . . . you and I
> are suddenly what the trees try
>
> To tell us we are:
> That their merely being there
> Means something; that soon
> We may touch, love, explain.
>
> And glad not to have invented
> Such comeliness, we are surrounded . . .

The Not-Me, as Emerson said, is nature and my body together, as well as art and all other men. Such a conviction leads Ashbery, even as it impelled Whitman and Stevens, to a desperate quest that masks as an ease with things. The poem is to be discovered in the Not-Me, out in the world that includes the poet's body. Rhetorically, this tends to mean that every proverbial cliché must be recovered, which becomes almost a rage in Ashbery's *Three Poems*. Where the middle Ashbery, the poet of the outrageously disjunctive volume, *The Tennis Court Oath*, attempted too massive a swerve away from the ruminative continuities of Stevens and

Whitman, recent Ashbery goes to the dialectical extreme of what seems at first like a barrage of bland commonplaces. Emerson, in *Nature*, anticipated Ashbery with his characteristic sense that parts of a world and parts of speech are alike emblematic, so that either, however worn out, could yet be an epiphany, though the world *seemed* so post-magical:

> . . . the memorable words of history and the proverbs of nations consist usually of a natural fact, selected as a picture or parable of a moral truth. Thus: a rolling stone gathers no moss; a bird in the hand is worth two in the bush; a cripple in the right way will beat a racer in the wrong; make hay while the sun shines; 'tis hard to carry a full cup even; vinegar is the son of wine; the last ounce broke the camel's back; long-lived trees make roots first . . .

Emerson insisted each worn proverb could become *transparent*. In his rare startlements into happiness, Ashbery knows this transparency, but generally his hopes are more modest. He is, in temperament, more like Whitman than like Emerson or Stevens. Even the French poet he truly resembles is the curiously Whitmanian Apollinaire, rather than Reverdy:

> Et ce serait sans doute bien plus beau
> Si je pouvaise supposer que toutes ces choses
>   dans lesquelles
>   je suis partout
> Pouvaient m'occuper aussi
> Mais dans ce sens il n'y a rien de fait
> Car si je suis partout a cette heure il n'y a
>   cependant que
>   moi qui suis en moi

Let us, swerving away from Apollinaire, call these Ashbery's two contradictory spiritual temptations, to believe that one's own self, like the poem, can be found in "all the things everywhere," or to believe that "there is still only I who can be in me." The first temptation will be productive of a rhetoric that puts it all in, and so must try to re-vitalize every relevant cliché. The second temptation rhetorically is gratified by ellipsis, thus leaving it all out. I suppose that Ashbery's masterpiece in this mode is the long spiel called "Europe" in *The Tennis Court Oath*, which seems to me a fearful disaster. In Stevens, this first way is the path of Whitmanian expansiveness, which partly failed the not always exuberant burgher of Hartford, while the second is the way of reductiveness, too great a temptation for him, as Stevens came to realize. The road through to poetry for Stevens was a middle path of invention that he called "discovery," the finding rather than the imposition of an order. Though there are at least three rhetorics in Stevens, matching these three modes of self-apprehension, none of the three risks Ashbery's disasters, whether of apparently joining together bland truisms or of almost total disjunctiveness. But I think that is close to the sorrow of influence in Ashbery, which is the necessary anxiety induced in him by the siren song of Stevens' rhetorics. Ashbery (who is not likely to be pleased by this observation) is at his best when he is neither re-vitalizing proverbial wisdom nor barely evading an ellipsis, but when he dares to write most directly in the idiom of Stevens. This point, and Ashbery's dazzling deflection of it, will be my concern when I arrive at *The Double Dream of Spring.*

My own melancholy, confronting Ashbery, is provoked by his second public volume, *The Tennis Court Oath* (Wesleyan University Press, 1962). Coming to this eagerly as an admirer of *Some Trees,* I remember my outrage and disbelief at what I found:

> *for that we turn around*
> *experiencing it is not to go into*
> *the epileptic prank forcing bar*
> *to borrow out onto tide-exposed fells*
> *over her morsel, she chasing you*
> *and the revenge he'd get*
> *establishing the vultural over*
> *rural area cough protection*
> *murdering quintet. . . .*

This is from the piece called "Leaving The Atocha Station," which (I am told) has a certain reputation among the rabblement of poetasters who proclaim themselves anti-academic while preaching in the academies, and who lack consciousness sufficient to feel the genuine (because necessary) heaviness of the poetic past's burden of richness. *The Tennis Court Oath* has only one good poem, "A Last World." Otherwise, its interest is now entirely retrospective; how could Ashbery collapse into such a bog by just six years after *Some Trees,* and how did he climb out of it again to write *Rivers and Mountains,* and then touch a true greatness in *The Double Dream of Spring* and *Three Poems?*

Poets, who congenitally lie about so many matters, *never* tell the truth about poetic influence. To address an audience sprinkled with poets, on the subject of poetic influence, is to risk a *sparagmos* in which the unhappy critic may be mistaken for Orpheus. Poets want to believe, with Nietzsche, that "forgetfulness is a property of all action," and action for them is writing a poem. Alas, no one can write a poem without remembering another poem, even as no one loves without remembering, though dimly or subconsciously, a former beloved, however much that came under a taboo. Every poet is forced to say, as Hart Crane did in an early poem: "I can remember much forgetfulness." To live as a poet, a poet needs the illusive mist about him that shields him from the light that first kindled him. This mist is the nimbus (however false) of what the prophets would have called his own *kabod*, the supposed radiance of his own glory.

In *Some Trees*, Ashbery was a relatively joyous ephebe of Stevens, who evidently proved to be too good a father. Nietzsche suggested that: "If one has not had a good father, it is necessary to invent one." Yes, and for a poet, if one's father was too good, it becomes necessary to reinvent one's father's sorrows, so as to balance his glory. This necessity, which Ashbery met in all his subsequent work, is merely evaded throughout *The Tennis Court Oath*, where a great mass of egregious disjunctiveness is accumulated to very little effect. Apollinaire had counselled *surprise* for the modern poet's art, but what is surprising about a group of poems that will never yield to any reading or sustained re-reading? Poems may be like pictures, or like music, or like what you will, but if they *are* paintings or musical works, they will not be poems. The Ashbery of *The Tennis Court Oath* may have been moved by De Kooning and Kline, Webern and Cage, but he was not moved to the writing of poems. Nor can I accept the notion that this was a necessary phase in the poet's development, for who can hope to find any necessity in this calculated incoherence? Yet the volume matters, and still upsets me because it is Ashbery's, the work of a man who has written poems like "Evening In The Country," "Parergon," the astonishingly poignant and wise "Soonest Mended," and "Fragment," probably the best longer poem by an American poet of my own generation, and unmatched I believe by anything in the generation of Lowell.

Isolated amid the curiosities of *The Tennis Court Oath* is the beautiful "A Last World," which in its limpidity and splendor would fit well into one of Ashbery's later volumes. The poem prophesies the restorative aesthetic turn that Ashbery was to take, and reveals also what has become his central subject and resource, the imagination of a later self questing for accommodation not so much with an earlier glory (as in Wordsworth) but with a possible sublimity that can never be borne, if it should yet arrive. Stevens more than Whitman is again the precursor, and the greatness of Ashbery begins to emerge when the anxiety of influence is wrestled with, and at least held to a stand-off.

"A Last World," like any true poem, has the necessity of reminding us that the meaning of one poem can only be another poem, a poem not itself, and probably not even one by its own author. Ashbery emerges into a total coherence when he compels himself to know that every imagining is a misprision, a taking amiss or twisting askew of the poetic *given*. Mature creation, for a poet, rises directly from an error about poetry rather than an error, however profound, about life. Only a wilful *misinterpretation* of a poetry already known too well, loved too well, understood too well, frees a maturing maker's mind from the compulsion to repeat, and more vitally from the fear of that compulsion. This is not what "A Last World" *thinks* it is about, but the poem so presents itself as to compel us to read it as an allegory of this poet's struggle to win free of his own evasions, and not the aesthetic evasions alone, but of everything that is elliptical in the self.

The Stevensian "he" of "A Last World" becomes a constant presence in the next two volumes, modulating from Ashbery as a self-deceiver to a perpetually late learner who is educated with the reader, so as to become a convincing "we":

> Everything is being blown away;
> A little horse trots up with a letter in its
>   mouth,
>   which is read with eagerness
> As we gallop into the flame.

This, the poem's conclusion, is the ostensible focus of "A Last World"; the present is the flame, things vanish perpetually as we come up to them, and we are—at best—romance questers made pathetic as we read the message so charmingly delivered to us, which is hardly going to save us from joining a general state of absence. The poem seems to end dispassionately in loss, yet its tone is serene, and its atmosphere suffused with a curious radiance. This radiance is a revisionary completion of the difficult serenity of late Stevens, a completion that is also antithetical to Stevens' rockier composure, or as his "Lebensweisheitspielerei" calls it, his sense of "stellar pallor":

> Little by little, the poverty
> Of autumnal space becomes
> A look, a few words spoken.
>
> Each person completely touches us
> With what he is and as he is,
> In the stale grandeur of annihilation.

Stevens, contemplating the departure of the proud and the strong, bleakly celebrated those left as "the unaccomplished,/The final human,/ Natives of a dwindled sphere." Ashbery, counterpointing his vision against that of Stevens' The Rock, celebrates loss as an accomplishment, a treasure, a mint flavoring in Stevens' land of hay, which was too ripe for such enigmas:

> Once a happy old man
> One can never change the core of things, and
>   light burns you the harder for it,
> Glad of the changes already and if there are
>   more it will never be you that minds
> Since it will not be you to be changed, but in
>   the evening in the severe lamplight doubts
>   come
> From many scattered distances, and do not come
>   too near.
> As it falls along the house, your treasure
> Cries to the other men; the darkness will have
>   none of you,
>   and you are folded into it like mint into
>   the sound of haying.

Loss is not gain here, and yet Ashbery takes Stevens' vision back from the last world of *The Rock* to "A Postcard from the Volcano" of 1936, where at least we leave behind us "what still is/The look of things." Absence or denudation is the common perception of the two poets, but Ashbery, though always anxious, is too gentle for bitterness, and rhetorically most himself where least ironic. Stevens' "qualified assertions" (Helen Vendler's apt phrase) become in Ashbery a series of progressively more beautiful examples of what we might call "qualified epiphanies," the qualifications coming partly from Ashbery's zeal in tacitly rejecting a poetry of privileged moments or privileged phrases. But this zeal is misplaced, and almost impossible to sustain, as will be seen in his later development.

Rivers and Mountains (1966) is a partial recovery from *The Tennis Court Oath*, though only one poem in it, "The Skaters," seems to me major Ashbery when compared to what comes after. But then, "The Skaters" is nearly half the volume, and its most luminous passages are of the same poetic ambience as the work beyond. With *Rivers And Mountains*, Ashbery began to win back the dismayed admirers of his earliest work, myself included. The curious poem called "The Recent Past," whatever its intentions, seems to be precisely addressed to just such readers, in very high good humor:

> You were my quintuplets when I decided to
>   leave you
> Opening a picture book the pictures were all of
>   grass
> Slowly the book was on fire, you the reader
> Sitting with specs full of smoke exclaimed

> How it was a rhyme for "brick" or "redder".
> The next chapter told all about a brook.
>
> You were beginning to see the relation when a
>   tidal wave
> Arrived with sinking ships that spelled out
>   "Aladdin".
> I thought about the Arab boy in his cave
> But the thoughts came faster than advice.
> If you knew that snow was still toboggan in
>   space
> The print could rhyme with "fallen star".

As far as intention matters, the "you" here is another Ashbery, to whom almost the entire book is directed, as will be the recent *Three Poems*. "These Lacustrine Cities" sets the book's project:

> Much of your time has been occupied by creative
>   games
> Until now, but we have all-inclusive plans for
>   you . . .

"Clepsydra," the longer poem just preceding "The Skaters," is printed as the first attempt at the project's realization, and is a beautiful failure, outweighing most contemporary poetic successes. The water-clock of the title is ultimately Ashbery himself, akin to the sun-flower of Blake's frighteningly wistful lyric. A history-in-little of Ashbery's poethood, "Clepsydra" is Ashbery's gentle equivalent of Stevens' surpassingly bitter "The Comedian as the Letter C," and is as dazzling an apparent dead end. I judge it a failure not because its exuberance is so negative, in contrast to the Whitmanian "The Skaters," but because its solipsism, like that of the "Comedian," is too perfect. Though splendidly coherent, "Clepsydra" gives the uncanny effect of being a poem that neither wants nor needs readers. It sits on the page as a forbiddingly solid wall of print, about as far from the *look* of Apollinaire as any verse could be. From its superbly opaque opening ("Hasn't the sky?") to its ominous closing ("while morning is still and before the body/Is changed by the faces of evening") the poem works at turning a Shelleyan-Stevensian self-referential quality into an absolute impasse. Perhaps here, more than in "The Skaters" even, or in his masterpiece, "Fragment," Ashbery tries to write the last poem about itself and about poetry, last by rendering the mode redundant:

> Each moment
> Of utterance is the true one; likewise none are
>   true,

> *Only is the bounding from air to air, a*
> *serpentine*
> *Gesture which hides the truth behind a*
> *congruent*
> *Message, the way air hides the sky, is, in fact,*
> *Tearing it limb from limb this very moment: but*
> *The sky has pleaded already and this is about*
> *As graceful a kind of non-absence as either*
> *Has a right to expect: whether it's the form of*
> *Some creator who has momentarily turned away,*
> *Marrying detachment with respect . . .*

"Detachment with respect" is Ashbery's attitude towards transcendental experience, for which he tends to use the image of transparence, as Whitman and Stevens, following Emerson, did also. Stevens, as Helen Vendler notes, tends to *sound* religious when his poems discourse upon themselves, and "Clepsydra" like much of the *Three Poems* similarly has an oddly religious tone. All of Ashbery (I am puzzled as to why Richard Howard thinks Ashbery an "anti-psychological" poet), including "Clepsydra," is profound self-revelation. Ashbery—like Wordsworth, Whitman, Stevens, Hart Crane—writes out of so profound a subjectivity as to make "confessional" verse seem as self-defeating as that mode truly has been, from Coleridge (its inventor) down to Lowell and his disciples. "Clepsydra," so wholly self-enclosed, is an oblique lament rising "amid despair and isolation / of the chance to know you, to sing of me/Which are you." The poem's subject overtly is Ashbery's entrapped subjectivity, objectified in the pathetic emblem of the water-clock, and represented in large by the outrageously even tone that forbids any gathering of climaxes. This refusal to vary his intensities is one of Ashbery's defense mechanisms against his anxiety of poetic influences. I can think of no poet in English, earlier or now at work, who insists upon so subtly unemphatic a pervasive tone. As a revisionary ratio, this tone intends to distance Ashbery from Whitman and from Stevens, and is a kind of *kenosis*, a self-emptying that yields up any evident afflatus:

> *Perhaps you are being kept here*
> *Only so that somewhere else the peculiar light*
> *of someone's*
> *Purpose can blaze unexpectedly in the acute*
> *Angles of the rooms. It is not a question, then,*
> *Of having not lived in vain . . .*

The *kenosis* is too complete in "Clepsydra"; the tone, however miraculously sustained, too wearying for even so intelligent a poet rightly

to earn. With relief, I move on to "The Skaters," Ashbery's most energetic
poem, the largest instance in him of the revisionary movement of
daemonization, or the onset of his personalized Counter-Sublime, as against
the American Sublime of Whitman and Stevens. Yet, "The Skaters" is
almost outrageously Whitmanian, far more legitimately in his mode than
Ginsberg manages to be:

> Old heavens, you used to tweak above us,
> Standing like rain whenever a salvo . . . Old
>   heavens,
> You lying there above the old, but not ruined,
>   fort,
> Can you hear, there, what I am saying?

"The Skaters" is not a parody, however involuntary, of *Song of
Myself*, though sometimes it gives that impression. *Song of Myself* begins
where the British Romantic quest-poem is sensible enough to end: with an
internal romance, of self and soul, attaining its consummation. Whitman,
having married himself, goes forth as an Emersonian liberating god, to
preside over the nuptials of the universe. The daemonic parodies of this
going forth stand between Whitman and Ashbery: *Paterson, the Cantos,
The Bridge, Notes toward A Supreme Fiction, Preludes To Attitude, The Far
Field.* What remains for Ashbery, in "The Skaters," is a kind of Counter-
Sublime that accepts a reduction of Whitmanian ecstasy, while re-affirming
it nevertheless, as in the vision early in the poem, when the poet's whole
soul is stirred into activity, flagellated by the decibels of the "excited call"
of the skaters:

> The answer is that it is novelty
> That guides these swift blades o'er the ice
> Projects into a finer expression (but at the
>   expense
> Of energy) the profile I cannot remember.
> Colors slip away from and chide us. The human
>   mind
> Cannot retain anything except perhaps the
>   dismal two-note theme
> Of some sodden "dump" or lament.

One can contrast the magnificent skating episode in Book I of *The
Prelude*, where colors have not slipped away, and the mind has retained its
power over outer sense. The contrast, though unfair to Ashbery, still
shows that there is a substance in us that prevails, though Ashbery tends
to know it only by knowing also his absence from it. His poem celebrates
"the intensity of minor acts," including his self-conscious mode of making-

by-ellipsis, or as he calls it: "this leaving-out business." Putting off (until *Three Poems*) "the costly stuff of explanation," he movingly offers a minimal apologia:

> Except to say that the carnivorous
> Way of these lines is to devour their own nature,
>   leaving
> Nothing but a bitter impression of absence,
>   which as we know
>   involves presence, but still.
> Nevertheless these are fundamental absences,
>   struggling to
>   get up and be off themselves.

"The Skaters," admitting that: "Mild effects are the result," labors still "to hold the candle up to the album," which is Ashbery's minimalist version of Stevens': "How high that highest candle lights the dark." In the poem's second part, Ashbery sets forth on a Romantic voyage, but like Crispin sees every vision-of-the-voyage fade slowly away. The long third movement, a quasi-autobiographical panorama of this poet's various exiles, needs careful examination, which I cannot give here, for nothing else in Ashbery succeeds nearly so well at the effect of the great improviser, an excellence shared by Whitman and by the Stevens of the blue guitar. With the fourth and final section, partly spoken by the persona of a Chinese scholar-administrator, the poem circles to a serene resolution, precisely prophetic of the Ashbery to come. "The whole brilliant mass comes spattering down," and an extraordinary simplicity takes its place. After so many leavings-out, the natural particulars are seen as being wonderfully sufficient:

> The apples are all getting tinted
> In the cool light of autumn.
>
> The constellations are rising
> In perfect order: Taurus, Leo, Gemini.

Everything promised by "The Skaters," Ashbery has performed, in the very different greatnesses of *The Double Dream of Spring* (1970) and *Three Poems* (1972). The first of these is so rich a book that I will confine myself to only a handful of poems, each so wonderful as to survive close comparison with Whitman and Stevens at almost their strongest: "Soonest Mended," "Evening in the Country," "Sunrise in Suburbia," "Parergon," and the long poem "Fragment." Before ruminating on these representative poems, a general meditation on Ashbery's progress seems necessary to me, as I am going on to make very large claims for his more recent work.

Though the leap in manner between *Rivers and Mountains* and *The Double Dream of Spring* is less prodigious than the gap between *The Tennis Court Oath* and *Rivers and Mountains*, there is a more crucial change in the later transition. Ashbery at last says farewell to ellipsis, a farewell confirmed by *Three Poems*, which relies upon "putting it all in," indeed upon the discursiveness of a still-demanding prose. The abandonment of Ashbery's rhetorical evasiveness is a self-curtailment on his part, a purgation that imparts simplicity through intensity, but at the price of returning him to the rhetorical world of Stevens and of the American tradition that led to Stevens. It is rather as if Browning had gone from his grotesque power backwards to the Shelleyan phase of his work. Perhaps Browning should have, since his last decades were mostly barren. As a strong poet, Ashbery has matured almost as slowly as his master Stevens did, though unlike Stevens he has matured in public. Even as Stevens provoked a critical nonsense, only now vanishing, of somehow being a French poet writing in English, so Ashbery still provokes such nonsense. Both are massive sufferers from the anxiety-of-influence, and both developed only when they directly engaged their American precursors. In Ashbery, the struggle with influence, though more open, is also more difficult, since Ashbery desperately engages also the demon of discursiveness, as Hart Crane differently did (for the last stand of Crane's mode, see the one superb volume of Alvin Feinman, *Preambles And Other Poems*, 1964). This hopeless engagement, endemic in all Western poetries in our century, is a generalized variety of the melancholy of poetic influence. It is not problematic form, nor repressed allusiveness, nor recondite matter, that makes much modern verse difficult. Nor, except rarely, is it conceptual profundity, or sustained mythical invention. Ellipsis, the art of omission, almost always a central device in poetry, has been abused into the dominant element rhetorically of our time. Yet no modern poet has employed it so effectively as Dickinson did, probably because for her it was a deep symptom of everything else that belonged to the male tradition that she was leaving out. I cannot involve myself here in the whole argument that I have set forth in a little book, *The Anxiety of Influence: A Theory of Poetry* (1973; see the discussion of Ashbery in the section called "*Apophrades*: or the Return of the Dead"), but I cite it as presenting evidence for the judgment that influence becomes progressively more of a burden for poets from the Enlightenment to this moment. Poets, defending poetry, are adept at idealizing their relation to one another, and the magical Idealists among critics have followed them in this saving self-deception. Here is Northrop Frye, greatest of the idealizers:

Once the artist thinks in terms of influence rather than of clarity of form, the effort of the imagination becomes an effort of will, and art is perverted into tyranny, the application of the principle of magic or mysterious compulsion to society.

Against this I cite Coleridge's remark that the power of originating *is* the will, our means of escaping from nature or repetition-compulsion, and I add that no one needs to pervert art in this respect, since the Post-Enlightenment poetic imagination is necessarily quite perverse enough in the perpetual battle against influence. Wordsworth *is* a misinterpretation of Milton (as is Blake), Shelley *is* a misinterpretation of Wordsworth, Browning and Yeats *are* misinterpretations of Shelley. Or, in the native strain, Whitman perverts or twists askew Emerson, Stevens is guilty of misprision towards both, and Ashbery attempts a profound and beautiful misinterpretation of all his precursors, *in his own best poetry*. What the elliptical mode truly seeks to omit is the overt continuity with ancestors, and the mysterious compulsion operative here is a displacement of what Freud charmingly called "the family romance."

Ashbery's own family romance hovers uneasily in all-but-repressed memories of childhood; his family-romance-as-poet attains a momentarily happy resolution in *The Double Dream of Spring*, but returns darkly in *Three Poems*. Ashbery is a splendid instance of the redemptive aspect of influence-anxiety, for his best work shows how the relation to the precursor is humanized into the greater themes of all human influence-relations, which after all include lust, envy, sexual jealousy, the horror of families, friendship, and the poet's reciprocal relation to his contemporaries, ultimately to all of his readers.

I begin again, after this anxious digression, with "Soonest Mended," and begin also the litany of praise and advocacy, of what Pater called "appreciation," that the later work of Ashbery inspires in me. The promise of *Some Trees* was a long time realizing itself, but the realization came, and Ashbery is now something close to a great poet. It is inconvenient to quote all of "Soonest Mended," but I will discuss it as though my reader is staring at pages 17 through 19 of *The Double Dream of Spring*. The poem speaks for the artistic life of Ashbery's generation, but more for the general sense of awakening to the haphazardness and danger of one's marginal situation in early middle age:

> *To step free at last, minuscule on the gigantic*
> *   plateau—*
> *This was our ambition: to be small and clear*
> *   and free.*
> *Alas, the summer's energy wanes quickly,*

> A moment and it is gone. And no longer
> May we make the necessary arrangements,
>   simple as they are.
> Our star was brighter perhaps when it had
>   water in it.
> Now there is no question even of that, but only
> Of holding on to the hard earth so as not to get
>   thrown off,
> With an occasional dream, a vision . . .

Dr. Johnson, still the most useful critic in the language, taught us to value highly any original expression of common or universal experience. "Has he any fresh matter to disclose?" is the question Johnson would have us ask of any new poet whose work seems to demand our deep consideration. The Ashbery of his two most recent volumes passes this test triumphantly. "Soonest Mended," from its rightly proverbial title through every line of its evenly distributed rumination, examines freshly that bafflement of the twice-born life that has been a major theme from Rousseau and Wordsworth to Flaubert and Stevens. This is the sense of awakening, past the middle of the journey, to the truth that: "they were the players, and we who had struggled at the game/Were merely spectators . . ." Uniquely, Ashbery's contribution is the wisdom of a wiser passivity:

> . . . learning to accept
> The charity of the hard moments as they are
>   doled out,
> For this is action, this not being sure, this
>   careless
> Preparing, sowing the seeds crooked in the
>   furrow,
> Making ready to forget, and always coming back
> To the mooring of starting out, that day so long
>   ago.

Action, Wordsworth said, was momentary, only a step or blow, but suffering was permanent, obscure, dark and shared the nature of infinity. Ashbery's action is Wordsworth's suffering; the way through to it, Ashbery says, is "a kind of fence-sitting/Raised to the level of an esthetic ideal." If time indeed is an emulsion, as this poem asserts, then wisdom is to find the mercy of eternity in the charity of the hard moments. Shelley, forgiving his precursors, said that they had been washed in the blood of the redeemer and mediator, time. Ashbery domesticates this fierce idealism; "conforming to the rules and living/Around the home" mediate his vision, and redemption is the indefinite extension of the learning process, even if the extension depends upon conscious fantasy. The achievement of "Soonest Mended" is to have told a reductive truth, yet to have raised it out of reductiveness by a persistence masked as the commonal, an urgency made noble by art.

The implicit argument of "Soonest Mended" is adumbrated in "Evening in the Country," a reverie rising out of a kind of Orphic convalescence, as another spent seer consigns order to a vehicle of change. "I am still completely happy," Ashbery characteristically begins, having thrown out his "resolve to win further." Yet, this is not the "false happiness" that Stevens condemned, for it is being rather than consciousness, cat more than rabbit. The shadow of Stevens hovers overtly in this poem, the poet of the never-satisfied mind:

> He wanted that,
> To face the weather and be unable to tell
> How much of it was light and how much
> thought,
> In these Elysia, these origins,
> This single place in which we are and stay,
> Except for the images we make of it,
> And for it, and by which we think the way,
> And, being unhappy, talk of happiness
> And, talking of happiness, know that it means
> That the mind is the end and must be satisfied.

Away from this Ashbery executes what Coleridge (in *Aids to Reflection*) calls a "*lene clinamen*, the gentle bias," for Ashbery's inclination is to yield to a realization that the mind had better be satisfied. Somewhere else, Coleridge speaks of making "a *clinamen* to the ideal," which is more in Stevens' mode, despite Stevens' qualifications. Ashbery, in his maturity, tries to be content not to originate an act or a state, though his achievement is to have done so anyway. "Evening in the Country" persuades that Ashbery has "begun to be in the context you feel," which is the context of the mind's surrender to visionary frustration. I quote at length from the poem's marvelous conclusion:

> Light falls on your shoulders, as is its way,
> And the process of purification continues
> happily,
> Unimpeded, but has the motion started
> That is to quiver your head, send anxious beams
> Into the dusty corners of the rooms
> Eventually shoot out over the landscape

In stars and bursts? For other than this we know
  nothing
And space is a coffin, and the sky will put out
  the light.
I see you eager in your wishing it the way
We may join it, if it passes close enough:
This sets the seal of distinction on the success or
  failure of your attempt.
There is growing in that knowledge
We may perhaps remain here, cautious yet free
On the edge, as it rolls its unblinking chariot
Into the vast open, the incredible violence and
  yielding
Turmoil that is to be our route.

Purification here is a kind of Orphic *askesis*, another revisionary movement away from the fathers. The gods or Orphism, at least of that variety which is the natural religion of the native strain in American poetry, are Dionysus, Eros and Ananke. Ashbery's Dionysiac worship, in his recent work, is mostly directed to absence. Eros, always hovering in Ashbery, is more of a presence in "Fragment." Ananke, the Beautiful Necessity worshipped by the later Emerson and all his poetic children, is the governing deity of "Evening in the Country" as of "Soonest Mended" and the *Three Poems*. Purgation "continues happily," while the poet asks the open question as to whether the motion of a new transcendental influx has started. Ashbery's genuine uncertainty is no longer the choice of poetic subject, as it was in *The Tennis Court Oath*, but concerns his relation to his own subject, which is the new birth or fresh being he has discovered in himself, yet which sets its own timing for manifestation.

Nothing is more difficult for me, as a reader of poetry, than to describe *why* I am moved when a poem attains a certain intensity of quietness, when it seems to wait. Keats, very early in his work, described this as power half-slumbering on its own right arm. I find this quality in only a few contemporary poets—Ashbery, Ammons, Strand, Merwin, James Wright, among others. Recent Ashbery has more of this deep potential, this quietness that is neither quietism nor repression, than any American poet since the last poems of Stevens. Webern is the nearest musical analogue I know, but analogues are hard to find for a poem like "Evening in the Country." For, though the poem is so chastened, it remains an Orphic celebration, as much so as Hart Crane at his most ecstatic.

Ashbery's ambitions as a mature poet, rising out of this still Orphic convalescence, are subtly presented in "Sunrise in Suburbia." Ashbery, never bitter, always charged by the thrill of the sun coming up, nevertheless suggests here an initial burden too complex for the poem to bear away from him. This burden is eloquently summed up in a line from "Parergon": "That the continuity was fierce beyond all dream of enduring." Repetition is the antagonist in "Sunrise in Suburbia," which quests for discontinuity or, as the poem calls it, "nuance":

> And then some morning there is a nuance:
> Suddenly in the city dirt and varied
> Ideas of rubbish, the blue day stands and
> A sudden interest is there:
> Lying on the cot, near the tree-shadow,
> Out of the thirties having news of the true
>   source:
> Face to kiss and the wonderful hair curling
>   down
> Into margins that care and are swept up again
>   like branches
> Into actual closeness
> And the little things that lighten the day
> The kindness of acts long forgotten
> Which gives us history and faith
> And parting at night, next to ocean, like the
>   collapse of dying.

An earlier passage in the poem juxtaposes the "flatness of what remains" to the "modelling of what fled," setting the poem in the large tradition that goes from "Tintern Abbey" to "The Course of a Particular." The difficulty, for Ashbery as for his readers, is how to construct something upon which to rejoice when you are the heir of this tradition, yet reject both privileged moments of vision and any privileged heightenings of rhetoric in the deliberately subdued and even tone of your work. Stevens is difficult enough in this kind of poem, yet for him there are times of unusual excellence, and he momentarily will yield to his version of the high style in presenting them. For Ashbery, the privileged moments, like their images, are on the dump, and he wants to purify them by clearly placing them there. Say of what you see in the dark, Stevens urges, that it is this or that it is that, but do not use the rotted names. Use the rotted names, Ashbery urges, but cleanse them by seeing that you cannot be apart from them, and are partly redeemed by consciously suffering with them. Stevens worked to make the visible a little hard to see; Ashbery faces: "a blank chart of each day moving into the premise of difficult visibility." The sounds of nature on this suburban sunrise have a hard tone: "this deaf rasping of branch against branch." These too are the cries of branches that do not transcend themselves, yet they do concern us:

> They are empty beyond consternation because
> These are the droppings of all our lives
> And they recall no past de luxe quarters
> Only a last cube.
> The thieves were not breaking in, the castle was
>   not being stormed.
> It was the holiness of the day that fed our
>   notions
> And released them, sly breath of Eros,
> Anniversary on the woven city lament, that
>   assures our arriving
> In hours, seconds, breath, watching our salary
> In the morning holocaust become one vast
>   furnace, engaging all tears.

Where "The Course of a Particular" rejects Ruskin's Pathetic Fallacy or the imputation of life to the object world, Ashbery uncannily labors to make the fallacy more pathetic, the object world another failed version of the questing self. Yet each day, his poem nobly insists, is holy and releases an Orphic "sly breath of Eros," to be defeated, and yet "engaging all tears." If a poem like this remains difficult, its difficulty arises legitimately from the valuable complexity of its vision, and not from the partial discontinuity of its rhetoric.

The thematic diffidence of "Sunrise in Suburbia" is transformed in the superb short poem "Parergon," which gives us Ashbery's version of pure Shelleyan quest, "Alastor" rather than its parody in "The Comedian as the Letter C." As in "Evening in the Country," Ashbery begins by affirming, without irony, a kind of domestic happiness in his artist's life of sitting about, reading, being restless. In a dream-vision, he utters the prophecy of the life he has become: "we need the tether / of entering each other's lives, eyes wide apart, crying." Having done so, he becomes "the stranger," the perpetual uncompromising quester on the model of the Poet in Shelley's "Alastor":

> As one who moves forward from a dream
> The stranger left that house on hastening feet
> Leaving behind the woman with the face shaped
>   like an arrowhead,
> And all who gazed upon him wondered at
> The strange activity around him.
> How fast the faces kindled as he passed!
> It was a marvel that no one spoke
> To stem the river of his passing
> Now grown to flood proportions, as on the sunlit
>   mall

> Or in the enclosure of some court
> He took his pleasure, savage
> And mild with the contemplating.
> Yet each knew he saw only aspects,
> That the continuity was fierce beyond all dream
> of enduring,
> And turned his head away, and so
> The lesson eddied far into the night:
> Joyful its beams, and in the blackness blacker
> still,
> Though undying joyousness, caught in that trap.

Even as the remorseless Poet of "Alastor" imperishably caught up the element in Shelley that was to culminate in "Adonais" and "The Triumph of Life," so "Parergon" portrays the doomed-poet aspect of Ashbery, of whom presumably we will hear more in his later life. One of the few ironies in Ashbery is the title, which I assume is being used in the sense it has in painting, something subsidiary to the main subject. Yet the poem is anything but bywork or ornamentation. As beautiful as nearly anything in Ashbery, it is central to his dilemma, his sorrow and his solace.

With reverence and some uneasiness, I pass to "Fragment," the crown of *The Double Dream of Spring* and, for me, Ashbery's finest work. Enigmatically autobiographical, even if it were entirely fantasy, the poem's fifty stately ten-line stanzas, orotundly Stevensian in their rhetoric, comment obliquely upon a story never told, a relationship never quite a courtship, and now a nostalgia. Studying this nostalgia, in his most formal and traditional poem, more so than anything even in *Some Trees*, Ashbery presents his readers, however faithful, with his most difficult rumination. But this is a wholly Stevensian difficulty, neither elliptical nor obscure, but a ravishing simplicity that seems largely lacking in any referential quality. I have discussed the poem with excellent and sympathetic students who continue to ask: "But what is the poem *about?*" The obvious answer, that to some extent it is "about" itself, they rightly reject, since whether we are discussing Shelley, Stevens, or Ashbery, this merely distances the same question to one remove. But though repeated readings open up the referential aspect of "Fragment," the poem will continue to inspire our uneasiness, for it is profoundly evasive.

What the all-but-perfect solipsist *means* cannot be right, not until he becomes perfect in his solipsism, and so stands forth as a phantasmagoric realist (one could cite Mark Strand, a superb poet, as a recent example). "Fragment," I take it, is the elegy for the self of the imperfect solipsist, who wavered before the reality of another self, and then withdrew back into an interior world. The poem being beautifully rounded, the title evidently refers not to an aesthetic incompleteness, but to this work's design, that tells us only part of a story, and to its resigned conclusion, for the protagonist remains alone, an "anomaly" as he calls himself in the penultimate line.

The motto to "Fragment" might be from Ashbery's early "Le Livre est sur la table" where much of the enigma of the poet's mature work is prophesied. Playing against the mode of *The Man with the Blue Guitar*, Ashbery made a Stevensian parable of his own sorrows, stating a tentative poetic and a dark version of romance. The overwhelming last stanza of "Fragment" comes full circle to this:

> *The young man places a bird-house*
> *Against the blue sea. He walks away*
> *And it remains. Now other*
>
> *Men appear, but they live in boxes.*
> *The sea protects them like a wall.*
> *The gods worship a line-drawing*
>
> *Of a woman, in the shadow of the sea*
> *Which goes on writing. Are there*
> *Collisions, communications on the shore*
>
> *Or did all secrets vanish when*
> *The woman left? Is the bird mentioned*
> *In the waves' minutes, or did the land*
>   *advance?*

As the table supports the book, this poem tells us, so deprivation supports "all beauty, resonance, integrity," our poverty being our imaginative need. The young poet, deprived of a world he can only imagine, and which he is constrained to identify with "the woman," learns that the sea, Stevensian emblem for all merely given reality, must triumph. Yet, if he is to have any secrets worth learning in his womanless world, it must come from "collisions, communications on the shore," where his imagination and the given meet. "Collisions, communications" is a fearfully reductive way of describing whatever sustenance Eros grants him to live, and is part of an open question. The final question can be read more as a rhetorical one, since the poems got written, and the later work of Ashbery proves that the land did advance.

We need to read this against the splendid final stanza of "Fragment":

> *But what could I make of this? Glaze*
> *Of many identical foreclosures wrested from*

The operative hand, like a judgment but still
The atmosphere of seeing? That two people
    could
Collide in this dusk means that the time of
Shapelessly foraging had come undone: the
    space was
Magnificent and dry. On flat evenings
In the months ahead, she would remember
    that that
Anomaly had spoken to her, words like
    disjointed beaches
Brown under the advancing signs of the air.

He has learned that there are indeed "collisions, communications on the shore," but this apparently crucial or unique instance saw two people "collide in this dusk." Yet this was not failure; rather, the advent of a new time. The stanza's balance is precarious, and its answer to the crucial earlier question, "Did the land advance?" is double. The brown, disjointed beaches seem a negative reply, and "the advancing signs of the air" a positive one.

In the context of Ashbery's development, "Fragment" is his central poem, coming about a year after "The Skaters" and just preceding "Clepsydra," his last major poem written abroad. "Sunrise in Suburbia" and the powerful shorter poems in *The Double Dream of Spring* came later, after the poet's return to this country in the autumn of 1966. My own intoxication with the poem, when I first read it in *Poetry* magazine, led me on to the two recent volumes, and my sense of the enormous importance of this poet. Though I lack space here for any extended account of "Fragment" before I go on to *Three Poems*, I want to give an encapsulated sense of some of its meanings, and the start of the appreciation it deserves, as perhaps the first successful poem of its kind in English since Swinburne's "The Triumph of Time."

The poem opens, as it will close, with the unnamed woman of "a moment's commandment," whom Ashbery sometimes addresses, and sometimes describes in the third person. After a vision of April's decline, "of older/Permissiveness which dies in the/Falling back toward recondite ends,/The sympathy of yellow flowers," the poet commences upon one of these recondite ends, an elegy for "the suppressed lovers," whose ambiguous time together seems to have been only a matter of weeks.

Much of the difficulty, and the poignance, of "Fragment" is generated by Ashbery's quasi-metaphysical dilemma. Committed, like the later Stevens, to the belief that poetry and *materia poetica* are the same thing, and struggling always against the aesthetic of the epiphany or privileged moment, with its consequent devaluation of other experience, Ashbery nevertheless makes his poem to memorialize an intense experience, brief in deviation. This accounts probably for the vacillation and evasiveness of "Fragment," which tries to render an experience that belongs to the dialectic of gain and loss, yet insists the experience was neither. There are passages of regret, and of joy, scattered through the poem, but they do little to alter the calm, almost marmoreal beauty of the general tone of rapt meditation. Even the apparent reference to the death of a paternal figure, in the forty-seventh stanza, hardly changes Ashbery's almost Spenserian pace. The thirtieth stanza sums up Ashbery's inclination against the Stevensian tendency to move from a present intensity to a "That's it" of celebration, "to catch from that / Irrational moment its unreasoning." The strength of Ashbery's denial of "that Irrational moment" comes from its undersong of repressed desire:

> But why should the present seem so particularly
>   urgent?
> A time of spotted lakes and the whippoorwill
> Sounding over everything? To release the
>   importance
> Of what will always remain invisible?
> In spite of near and distant events, gladly
> Built? To speak the plaits of argument,
> Loosened? Vast shadows are pushed down
>   toward
> The hour. It is ideation, incrimination
> Proceeding from necessity to find it at
> A time of day, beside the creek, uncounted stars
>   and buttons.

Of story, "Fragment" gives almost nothing, yet it finds oblique means of showing us: "the way love in short periods/Puts everything out of focus, coming and going." Variations upon this theme constitute almost the whole of the poem's substance, and also its extraordinary strength, as Ashbery's insights in this area of perception seem endless. In its vision of love, "Fragment" hymns only the bleak truth of the triumph of absence:

> Thus your only world is an inside one
> Ironically fashioned out of external phenomena
> Having no rhyme or reason, and yet neither
> An existence independent of foreboding and sly
>   grief.
> Nothing anybody says can make a difference;
>   inversely
> You are a victim of their lack of consequence

> *Buffeted by invisible winds, or yet a flame*
> * yourself*
> *Without meaning, yet drawing satisfaction*
> *From the crevices of that wind, living*
> *In that flame's idealized shape and duration.*

This eloquent despair, Shelleyan in its paradoxical affirmation of love yet acknowledgement of love's delusiveness, ends precisely in Shelley's image of the coming and going of the Intellectual Beauty, "like darkness to a dying flame." Uniquely Ashberyian is the emphasis on *satisfaction*, despite the transitoriness of "living" in so purely "idealized" a shape and duration. "Fragment" alternately explores the saving crevices and the shape of love's flame. Progression in this almost static poem is so subtle as to be almost indiscernible until the reader looks back at the opening from the closing stanzas, realizing then that:

> *This time*
> *You get over the threshold of so much*
> * unmeaning, so much*
> *Being, prepared for its event, the active*
> * memorial.*

The reader's gain is an intensified sense of "time lost and won," never more strongly felt than in the poem's erotic culmination, stanzas 13–20, where Ashbery seeks "to isolate the kernel of/Our imbalance." In stanza 16, Ashbery finds no satisfaction in satisfaction anyway, in the only stanza of the poem that breaks the baroque stateliness and artful rhetorical repetitiveness of its form:

> *The volcanic entrance to an antechamber*
> *Was not what either of us meant.*
> *More outside than before, but what is worse,*
> * outside.*
> *Within the periphery, we are confronted*
> *With one another, and our meeting escapes*
> * through the dark*
> *Like a well.*
> *Our habits ask us for instructions.*
> *The news is to return by stages*
> *Of uncertainty, too early or too late. It is the*
> * invisible*
> *Shapes, the bed's confusion and prattling. The*
> * late quiet,*
> *   This is how it feels.*

"The volcanic entrance to an antechamber," as a dismissal of the inadequacy of phallic heterosexuality to the love meant, is a kind of elegant younger brother to Hart Crane's bitter characterization of this means of love as: "A burnt match skating in a urinal." Ashbery wisely does not pause to argue preferences, but accomplishes his poem's most surprising yet inevitable transition by directly following: "This is how it feels" with a return to childhood visions: "The pictures were really pictures/Of loving and small things." As the interchange of interior worlds continues, Ashbery attains a point of survey in stanza 36 where he can assert: "You see, it is / Not wrong to have nothing." Four years later, writing "Soonest Mended," this joined an echo of Lear's speech to Cordelia to become: "both of us were right, though nothing/Has somehow come to nothing." Expectation without desire is henceforth Ashbery's difficult, more-than-Keatsian attitude, not a distinterestedness nor any longer a renunciation, but a kind of visionary sublimation. This self-curtailing poetic *askesis* is performed as I think the dialectic of poetic influence compels it to be performed by a strong poet, as Ashbery has now become. That is, it is a revisionary movement in regard to the prime precursor, Stevens, who blends with what seems to be the dying figure of Ashbery's own father in the dense and exciting sequence of stanzas 38 through 49. These stanzas are Ashbery's version of Stevens' "Farewell to Florida" and recall its Spenserian image of the high ship of the poet's career being urged upon its more dangerous and mature course. Though Ashbery will back away from this ominous freedom in his final stanza (which I quoted earlier), the quest aspect of his career attains a wonderful culmination in stanza 49:

> One swallow does not make a summer, but are
> What's called an opposite: a whole of raveling
>   discontent,
> The sum of all that will ever be deciphered
> On this side of that vast drop of water.
> They let you sleep without pain, having all that
> Not in the lesson, not in the special way of
>   telling
> But back to one side of life, not especially
> Immune to it, in the secret of what goes on:
> The words sung in the next room are
>   unavoidable
> But their passionate intelligence will be studied
>   in you.

Here, as in so many passages having a similar quality, Ashbery reaches his own recognizable greatness, and gives us his variety of the American Sublime. The "parental concern" of Stevens' "midnight interpretation" (stanza 38) produced the grand myth of the Canon Aspirin in

Notes toward a Supreme Fiction, where Stevens at last, detaching himself from the Canon, could affirm: "I have not but I am and as I am, I am." Ashbery, in his moment most akin to Stevens' sublime self-revelation, affirms not the Emersonian-Whitmanian Transcendental Self, as Stevens most certainly (and heroically) does, but rather "the secret of what goes on." This is not, like Stevens' massive declaration, something that dwells in the orator's "special way of telling," but inheres painfully in Ashbery's vulnerability. As a self-declared "anomaly," Ashbery abides in the most self-revelatory and noble lines he has yet written:

> The words sung in the next room are
> unavoidable
> But their passionate intelligence will be studied
> in you.

That the pathos of "Fragment," a poem of the unlived life, of life refusing revenge upon its evaders, could lead to so lucid a realization, is a vital part of Ashbery's triumph over his earlier opacities. In the recent *Three Poems*, written in a prose apparently without precursors, this triumph expands, though again large demands are made upon the reader. But this I think is part of Ashbery's true value; only he and Ammons among poets since Stevens compel me to re-read so often, and then reward such labor.

Though "The New Spirit," first of the *Three Poems*, was begun in November 1969, most of it was written January to April, 1970. In a kind of cyclic repetition, the second prose poem "The System" was composed from January to March 1971, with the much shorter "The Recital" added as a coda in April. This double movement from winter vision to spring's re-imaginings is crucial in *Three Poems*, which is Ashbery's prose equivalent of *Notes toward a Supreme Fiction*, and which has the same relation as *Notes* to *Song of Myself*. Where Stevens reduces to the First Idea, which is "an imagined thing," and then equates the poet's act of the mind with the re-imagining of the First Idea, Ashbery reduces to a First Idea of himself, and then re-imagines himself. I am aware that these are difficult formulae, to be explored elsewhere, and turn to a commentary upon *Three Poems*, though necessarily a brief and tentative one.

I described "Evening in the Country" as a "convalescent's" displacement of American Orphism, the natural religion of our poetry. *Three Poems* might be called the masterpiece of an invalid of the Native Strain, even a kind of invalid's version of *Song of Myself*, as though Whitman had written that poem in 1865, rather than 1855. Ashbery's work could be called *Ruminations of Myself* or *Notes toward a Saving but Subordinate Fiction*. Whitman's poem frequently is address of I, Walt Whitman, to you or my soul. Ashbery's *Three Poems* are addressed by *I*, John Ashbery writing, to *You*, Ashbery as he is in process of becoming. *I*, as in Whitman, Pater, Yeats is personality or self or the *antithetical*; *You*, as in the same visionaries, is character or soul or the *primary*. Ashbery's swerve away from tradition here is that his *You* is the re-imagining, while his *I* is a reduction.

"The New Spirit," the first poem's title, refers to a rebirth that takes place after the middle-of-the-journey crisis, here in one's late thirties or early forties:

> *It is never too late to mend. When one*
> *is in one's late thirties, ordinary things—like a*
> *pebble or a glass of water—take on an*
>   *expressive*
> *sheen. One wants to know more about them,*
>   *and one*
> *is in turn lived by them . . .*

This "new time of being born" Ashbery calls also "the new casualness," and he writes of it in a prose that goes back to his old rhetorical dialectic of alternating ellipsis and the restored cliché. Indeed, "The New Spirit" opens by overtly giving "examples of leaving out," but Ashbery then mostly chooses to stand himself in place of these examples. Why does he choose prose, after "The Skaters" had shown how well he could absorb prose into verse at length? It may be a mistake, as one advantage, in my experience, of "The New Spirit" over "The System" and "The Recital," is that it crosses over to verse half-a-dozen times, while they are wholly in prose. I suppose that the desire to tell a truth that "could still put everything in" made Ashbery wary of verse now, for fear that he should not be as comprehensive as possible. Speaking again as the poet of "Fragment" he defines his predicament: "In you I fall apart, and outwardly am a single fragment, a puzzle to itself." To redress his situation, the New Spirit has come upon him to renovate a poet who confesses he has lost all initiative:

It has been replaced by a strange kind of happiness within the limitations. The way is narrow but it is not hard, it seems almost to propel or push one along. One gets the narrowness into one's seeing, which also seems an inducement to moving forward into what one has already caught a glimpse of and which quickly becomes vision, in the visionary sense, except that in place of the panorama that used to be our customary setting and which we never made much use of, a limited but infinitely free space has established itself, useful as everyday life but transfigured so that its signs of wear no longer appear as a reproach but as indications of how beautiful a thing must have been to have been so much prized, and its noble aspect which must have been irksome before has now become interesting, you are fascinated and keep on studying it. . . .

This, despite its diffidence, declares what Emerson called Newness or Influx, following Sampson Reed and other Swedenborgians. Sometimes the *Three Poems*, particularly "The System," sound like a heightened version of the senior Henry James. But mostly Ashbery, particularly in "The New Spirit," adds his own kind of newness to his American tradition. At first reading of "The New Spirit," I felt considerable bafflement, not at the subject-matter, immediately clear to any exegete aged forty-two, but at the procedure, for it was difficult to see how Ashbery got from point to point, or even to determine if there were points. But repeated reading uncovers a beautiful and simple design: first, self-acceptance of the minimal anomalies we have become, "the color of the filter of the opinions and ideas everyone has ever entertained about us. And in this form we must prepare, now, to try to live." Second, the wintry reduction of that conferred self is necessary: "And you lacerate yourself so as to say, These wounds are me." Next, a movement to the *you* and to re-imagining of the *I*, with a realization that the *you* has been transformed already, through the soul's experience as a builder of the art of love. With this realization, the consciousness of the New Spirit comes upon the *I*, and self and soul begin to draw closer in a fine lyric beginning: "Little by little/You are the mascot of that time." An event of love, perhaps the one elegized in "Fragment," intervenes, illuminates, and then recedes, but in its afterglow the New Spirit gives a deeper significance to the object-world. After this seeing into the life of things, the growth of the mind quickens. But the transparency attained through the new sense of wholeness "was the same as emptiness," and the sense of individual culmination serves only to alienate the poet further from the whole of mankind, which "lay stupefied in dreams of toil and drudgery." It is at this point of realization that the long and beautiful final paragraph comes, ending "The New Spirit" with a deliberate reminiscence of the end of "The Skaters." Two visions come to Ashbery, to make him understand that there is still freedom, still the wildness of time that may allow the highest form of love to come. One is "the completed Tower of Babel," of all busyness, a terror that could be shut out just by turning away from it. The other is of the constellations that the tower threatened, but only seemed to threaten. They beckon now to "a new journey" certain to be benign, to answer "the major question that revolves around you, your being here." The journey is a choice of forms for answering, which means both Ashbery's quest for poetic form, and his continued acceptance of an "impassive grammar of cosmic unravelings of all kinds, to be proposed but never formulated."

I think that is an accurate account of the design of "The New Spirit," but I am aware such an account gives little sense of how Ashbery has added strangeness to beauty in thus finding himself there more truly and more strange. The transcendental re-awakening of anyone, even of an excellent poet, hardly seems *materia poetica* anymore, and perhaps only Ashbery would attempt to make a poem of it at this time, since his aesthetic follows Stevens by discovering the poem already formed in the world. His true and large achievement in "The New Spirit" is to have taken the theme of "Le Monocle de Mon Oncle," already developed in "Fragment," and to have extended this theme to larger problems of the aging and widening consciousness. Men at forty, Stevens says, can go on painting lakes only if they can apprehend "the universal hue." They must cease to be dark rabbis, and yield up their lordly studies of the nature of man. "The New Spirit" is Ashbery's exorcism of the dark rabbi in his own nature. Its achievement is the rare one of having found a radiant way of describing a process that goes on in many of us, the crisis of vision in an imaginative person's middle age, without resorting to psychosexual or social reductiveness.

"The System" is Ashbery's venture into quest-romance, his pursuit as rose rabbi, of "the origin and course/Of love," the origin and course together making up the System, which is thus a purposive wandering. Since the poem opens with the statement that "The system was breaking down," the reader is prepared for the prose-poem's penultimate paragraph, that tells us "we are rescued by what we cannot imagine: it is what finally takes us up and shuts our story."

The account of the System begins in a charming vision too genial for irony, as though Aristophanes had mellowed wholly:

> From the outset it was apparent that someone had played a colossal trick on something. The switches had been tripped, as it were; the entire world or one's limited but accurate idea of it was bathed in glowing love, of a sort that need never have come into being but was now indispensable as air is to living creatures . . . if only, as Pascal says, we had the sense to stay in our room, but the individual will condemns this notion and sallies forth full of ardor and *hubris*, bent on self-discovery in the guise of an attractive partner who is *the* heaven-sent one, the convex one with whom he has had the urge to mate all these seasons without realizing it. . . .

This "glowing love" inevitably is soon enough seen as "muddle," and the first phase of quest fails: "Thus it was that a kind of blight fell on these early forms of going forth and being together, an anarchy of the affections sprung from too much universal cohesion." Rather than despair, or yield to apocalyptic yearnings, Ashbery consolidates upon his curious and effective passivity, his own kind of negative capability, becoming "a pillar of waiting," but Quixotic waiting upon a dream. As he waits, he meditates on "twin notions of growth" and on two kinds of happiness. One growth theory is of the great career: "a slow burst that narrows to a final release, pointed but not acute, a life of suffering redeemed and annihilated at the end, and for what?" This High Romanticism moves Ashbery, but he rejects it. Yet the alternative way, a Paterian "life-as-ritual" concept, the *locus classicus* of which we could find in the magnificent "Conclusion" to *The Renaissance*, he also turns from, or asserts he does, though I think he is more a part of this vision than he realizes. He fears the speed with which the soul moves away from others: "This very speed becomes a source of intoxication and of more gradually accruing speed; in the end the soul cannot recognize itself and is as one lost, though it imagines it has found eternal rest."

By evading both notions of growth, Ashbery rather desperately evades growth itself. Confronting two kinds of happiness, "the frontal and the latent," he is again more evasive than he may intend to be. The first is a sudden glory, related to the epiphany or Paterian "privileged moment," and Ashbery backs away from it, as by now we must expect, because of its elitism, he says, but rather, we can surmise, for defensive reasons, involving both the anxiety of influence and more primordial Oedipal anxieties. The latent and dormant kind he seeks to possess, but his long espousal of it seems to me the weakest sequence in *Three Poems*, despite a poignant culmination in the great question: "When will you realize that your dreams have eternal life?" I suspect that these are, *for Ashbery*, the most important pages in his book, but except for the lovely pathos of a dreamer's defense, they are too much the work of a poet who wishes to be more of an anomaly than he is, rather than the "central" kind of a poet he is fated to become, in the line of Emerson, Whitman, Stevens.

This "central" quality returns wonderfully in the last twenty pages of "The System," as the quest for love begins again. A passage of exquisite personal comedy, Chaplinesque in its profundity, climaxes in the poet's defense of his mask: "your pitiable waif's stance, that inquiring look that darts uneasily from side to side as though to ward off a blow——." Ashbery assimilates himself to the crucial Late Romantic image of the failed quester, Browning's Childe Roland, for the author of *Three Poems* now approaches his own Dark Tower, to be confronted there by every anxiety, as human and as poet, that he has evaded:

> It is only that you happened to be wearing this look as you arrived at the end of your perusal of the way left open to you, and it "froze" on you, just as your mother warned you it would when you were little. And now it is the face you show to the world, the face of expectancy, strange as it seems. Perhaps Childe Roland wore such a look as he drew nearer to the Dark Tower, every energy concentrated toward the encounter with the King of Elfland, reasonably certain of the victorious outcome, yet not so much as to erase the premature lines of care from his pale and tear-stained face. Maybe it is just that you don't want to outrage anyone, especially now that the moment of your own encounter seems to be getting closer.

This version of Childe Roland's ordeal is an Ashberyian transformation or wish-fullfillment, as we can be reasonably certain that Browning's quester neither wants nor expects a "victorious outcome." But Ashbery feels raised from a first death, unlike Childe Roland, who longs for any end, and lacks a "quiet acceptance of experience in its revitalizing tide." Very gently, Ashbery accomplishes, a Transcendental and open ending to "The System," complete with an Emersonian "transparent axle" and even an equivalent to the closing chant of Emerson's Orphic Poet in *Nature*, though Ashbery's guardian bard speaks to him in a "dry but deep accent," promising mastery. Insisting that he has healed the sadness of childhood, Ashbery declares his System-wanderings are completed, the right balance attained in "what we have carefully put in and kept out," though a lyric "crash" may impend in which all this will be lost again. But, for now:

> The allegory is ended, its coils absorbed into the past, and this afternoon is as wide as an ocean. It is the time we have now, and all our wasted time sinks into the sea and is swallowed up without a trace. The past is dust and ashes, and this incommensurably wide way leads to the pragmatic and kinetic future.

This Shelleyan conclusion, akin to Demogorgon's dialectical vision, offers hope in "the pragmatic" yet menaces a return of the serpent-allegory (whose name is Ananke, in Ashbery as in Stevens or Shelley) in the still "kinetic" future.

The Coda of "The Recital" is a wholly personal apologia, with many Whitmanian and Stevensian echoes, some of them involuntary. "We cannot interpret everything, we must be selective," Ashbery protests, "nor can we leave off singing" which would return the poet to the living death of an unhappy childhood. Against the enemy, who is an amalgam of time and selfishness, Ashbery struggles to get beyond his own solipsism, and the limits of his art. On the final page, an Emersonian-Stevensian image of saving transparence serves to amalgamate the new changes Ashbery meets and welcomes. This transparence movingly is provided by a Whitmanian vision of an audience for Ashbery's art: "There were new people watching and waiting, conjugating in this way the distance and emptiness, transforming the scarcely noticeable bleakness into something both intimate and noble." So they have and will, judging by the response of my students and other friends, with whom I've discussed Ashbery's work. By more than fifteen years of high vision and persistence he has clarified the initial prophecy of his work, until peering into it we can say: "We see us as we truly behave" and, as we see, we can think: "These accents seem their own defense."

ALFRED CORN

A Magma of Interiors

"To create a work of art that the critic cannot even talk about ought to be the artist's chief concern," John Ashbery has said (*Art News*, May 1972). This statement was made about painters, but there's every chance Ashbery would appropriate that concern for poetry as well. He said, in another review, "Poets when they write about artists always tend to write about themselves." The ambition to outdistance criticism can arise simply as a human dislike of being pinned down—"Is that all there is?"—but mainly indicates a commitment to innovation and evolution in art. A recurrent problem in the evolution of twentieth-century art is that so many writers, not content with being *absolument moderne*, have then supposed they ought to be futuristic; and what is more poignant than yesterday's imagination of the future? In practice, the will to innovation often produces works nobody can talk about, yes, but more to the point, works that nobody *cares* to talk about.

This does not apply to John Ashbery. His originality is, unmistakably, the kind that comes as a by-product of sincerity. One feels that Ashbery would consider it somehow "false" to write with any greater reliance on conventions of communications as they already exist—even if those conventions included some established by the early work of John Ashbery. In short, his achievement is a *surpassing* achievement.

All of Ashbery's books have been difficult to talk about, and *Self-Portrait in a Convex Mirror* resists analysis and evaluation as valiantly as the others. Still, the merit of his work now seems to be evident to just about everybody, at least, the work beginning with *The Double Dream of Spring*, including *Three Poems*, and culminating with the poems now

From *Parnassus* 1, vol. 4 (Fall/Winter 1975). Copyright © 1975 by Parnassus.

collected in this volume. In this climate of admiration and critical hesitation it's possible to conclude that some kind of corner has been turned in the movement—I don't say progress—of literature. Although Richard Howard, Harold Bloom, and David Kalstone have broken or are breaking important critical ground in Ashbery criticism, at present, and of necessity, it remains largely a project. What's most obvious to me now is simply the great pleasure, interest, and even the amazement *Self-Portrait* affords; and of course my assignment here is not an overall assessment, but rather the review of a book.

It's tempting to fall back on the methods of apophatic or "negative" theology and list everything the poems in this volume are *not*, but I think I'll plunge right in and say what they are, at least how the majority of them function for one reader. The poems seem to be imitations of consciousness, "meditations" about the present, including the moment of writing. Their ambition is to render as much of psychic life as will go onto the page—perceptions, emotions, and concepts, memory and daydream, thought in all of its random and contradictory character, patterned according to the "wave interference" produced by all the constituting elements of mind—a "magma of interiors," one of the poems puts it.

Ashbery's method is allusive, associative, and disjunctive, rather than logical, dramatic, or narrative. A typical extended poem will launch itself, or maybe wake up to find itself already in transit, throw out a fertile suggestion, make connections, go into reverse, change key, short-circuit, suffer enlightenment, laugh, nearly go over the edge, regard itself with disbelief, irony, and pathos, then sign off with an inconclusive gesture. The texture of many of the poems reminds me of Gaudí's mosaics in the Barcelona Parque Guell, where broken-up fragments of colored tile with all kinds of figuration—Arabic-geometrical, floral, pictorial—are carefully reassembled in a new and satisfying whole:

> Nathan the Wise is a good title it's a reintroduction
> Of heavy seeds attached by toggle switch to long loops leading
> Out of literature and life into worldly chaos in which
> We struggle two souls out of work for it's a long way back to
> The summation meanwhile we live in it "gradually getting used to"
> Everything and this overrides living and is superimposed on it
> As when a wounded jackal is tied to the waterhole the lion does come
> > ("Lithuanian Dance Band")

It's possible of course to consider this kind of poetry not simply an "imitation of consciousness" but rather a new synthetic kind of experience too underdetermined or maybe overdetermined to render consciousness accurately, and so existing on a purely contemplative, aesthetic plane.

Obviously, these two efforts overlap and blend: "imitation" in art is never duplication, and it always involves some synthesis; but nothing lifelike can be synthesized in art unless it can seem to belong to consciousness. In the measure, then, that an imitation becomes more stylized and synthetic, its resemblance to anyone's consciousness proportionately decreases—it becomes more purely artful. I don't see the poems in *Self-Portrait* as all occupying a fixed point on the spectrum that moves from direct representation of a stream of consciousness to a purely composed and synthetic experience. It's like the new mixed suiting materials—some are more synthetic than others. Nor would I assume that any of the poems were pure products of "automatic writing." If there's an automatic writer that can rap out phrases like the following, one wants the thing installed immediately:

> This was one of those night rainbows
> In negative color. As we advance, it retreats; we see
> We are now far into a cave, must be. Yet there seem to be
> Trees all around, and a wind lifts their leaves, slightly.
> ("Märchenbilder")

In a sense, all good writing is an "imitation of consciousness" insofar as that is compatible with the selectivity required for effective, beautiful communication. A special quality of consciousness as imitated by Ashbery, however, is its inclusiveness, or, more precisely, its magnification: into these poems come minute or translucent mental events that would escape a less acute gaze, an attention less rapt. It's the same degree of magnification, I think, used to apprehend the *tropismes* in Nathalie Sarraute's early fiction, though Ashbery lacks the fury and venom characteristic of her work. In this poetry, the unconscious—that misnomer—is in agreeable tension with the conceptual, composing mind; the free interweaving of the known and the about-to-be-known makes for a rich experiential texture in which guesswork, risk, and discovery contribute almost a tactile quality to the overall patterning.

Imitating consciousness, or the stream of consciousness, as a writing method is sown with thistles for any writer without genius or at least without a mental complexion as special and original as John Ashbery's. Zany, elegiac, informed—and sometimes interestingly deformed—by an acquaintance with arcane or demotic or technological subject matter, it's a sensibility one thread of which has been described by the narrator of *A Season in Hell*:

I liked idiotic paintings, carvings over doorframes, vaudeville drop-scenes, sign-boards, dimestore prints, antiquated literature, church Latin, pornographic books with bad spelling, novels by our grandmothers, fairy tales, children's books, old operas, silly lyrics, uncouth meters.

Cultural allusion in Ashbery goes high as well as low—classic and sometimes obscure works of music, painting, and literature come into mention, without, however, being presented as "letters of credit," as they sometimes are with insecure writers; so that it would be wrong to call Ashbery's poetry "literary." The charge more often than not is made disingenuously, by the way. No subject matter, I think, is safely out of poetry's reach, even literary subject matter. It strikes me as unnatural, even artificial, to proscribe literary or cultural allusion from poetry in the age of the paperback, the LP, and color reproduction. If recondite allusion is a fault, then it ought to be acknowledged that, at present, readers of poetry are more likely to have accurate perceptions and definite feelings about, say, the *Pastoral Symphony,* or *The Cherry Orchard,* or *The Twittering Machine,* than about the Snake River, the hornbeam tree, or the engine of a Diamond Reo. It's true that art can come to conceal the world around us and act as a filter to unmediated experience (not necessarily a bad thing—who would *always* take his experience unmediated?) so that too many people get described as looking like "Bronzinos," and too often office routines are summed up as "Kafkaesque"; but Ashbery avoids that kind of triteness—or any kind of creative abdication. I'd say the cultural allusions were brought in simply as part of an environment, the nuts and bolts of daily life in a cultural capital.

I haven't made a survey, but I believe most of the allusions in this volume have to do with music; in fact, many of the poems take their titles from music: "Grand Galop" (Liszt), "Tenth Symphony" (Mahler's unfinished one?), "Märchenbilder" (the Schumann Opus 113), and "Scheherazade," which could be Rimsky-Korsakov or possibly Ravel, if we allow for English spelling. The texts of the poems include many other musical allusions; and, in a published interview, Ashbery has stated that he often writes with music playing, as a stimulant. All of this ought to be a tip-off. The Symbolist (and Paterian) doctrine that all the arts aspire to the condition of music has been, implicitly, a point of departure for development of modernist art in this century and stands behind the two distinctive tendencies in that art—the drive toward abstraction and the absolute fusion of form and content.

Ashbery is something of an American Symbolist, and his poem "The Tomb of Stuart Merrill" is by way of an *hommage* to a not too well known American poet of the fin-de-siècle who expatriated, wrote in French, and enlisted in the Symbolist movement. (Incidentally, if mention of the French tradition always comes up in any discussion of Ashbery, nonetheless his Americanness remains obvious and inescapable, as Wallace Stevens' does. Ashbery only occasionally reproduces the formal restraint, sensuousness, and lucidity of characteristically French art; more often his work exhibits the sincerity, distrust of artifice, and studied awkwardness we associate with achievement in the American grain.)

Valéry, a good Symbolist and word-musician, said that content in art was only impure form, and Ashbery's poem "Soonest Mended," two books ago, suggested that meaning might be "cast aside some day / When it had been outgrown." Of course meaning is never outgrown—*magari*— until life is; nor can meaning ever be cast aside, really, because the act of doing so then becomes the "meaning" of a text. No, John Ashbery's poetry does retain content, a content, however, radically fused with form—the result is that paraphrases of the poems are more than usually lame, if not downright impossible. Anyway, I'd rather listen to the *Bagatelles* than read an account of them.

The poems in *Self-Portrait* don't attempt to resemble music by taking the false lead of "verbal music" and onomatopoeia in the manner of, say, Poe, or even of Stuart Merrill. Instead, they find a poetic equivalent of music—a kind of abstraction of argument and theme in which the reader follows a constantly evolving progression of mood, imagery, and tone, with sudden shifts and modulations, and a whole rainbow of emotive and conceptual sonorities; none of this logical or foreseeable and yet, at its best, embodying, in its engagement with chaos—as with Beethoven—an elusive, convincing necessity. Sounds improbable, but, in support, I offer this ancecdote: to someone not an expert in poetry I read several pages from *Self-Portrait*; his comment was, "It's like music."

Strangely enough, but rightly, the poems make their music mainly out of visual materials: they are crowded with images, colors, silhouettes. Ashbery has the intense gaze of the child, the divine, or simply the poet, whose vision so absorbs him that the line between the visible world and the self begins to dematerialize, subject to fuse with object. In Mae West's words, "I've been things and seen places."

> The shadow of the Venetian blind on the painted wall,
> Shadows of the snake-plant and cacti, the plaster animals,
> Focus the tragic melancholy of the bright stare
> Into nowhere, a hole like the black holes in space.
>
> ("Forties Flick")

I hope I haven't given the impression that these poems lack conceptual themes altogether. Argument, though not presented directly or logically, fuels and supervises the poetic proceedings, especially in the title poem. Because of the great ambiguity (surely more than seven kinds come into play) an Ashbery poem is likely to become a sort of *auberge espagnole*, to be furnished out in different schemes by every reader who stops with it; but that's usual even with less ambiguous poetry. My notion is that everyone ought, according to his lights and darknesses, forge ahead with interpretations—responsible and as little "forged" as possible, of course. Also, I'd suggest that it's better to talk about the general *area* of meaning being explored, rather than about hard and fast aphoristic conclusions. But back to our sheep.

The phrase "tragic melancholy" from the above lines sums up for me the prevailing tone of the book. The tragedy arises from dilemmas of epistemology and solipsism; and Ashbery's characteristic response to those dilemmas is neither rage nor despair, but melancholy—a melancholy well acquainted with terrible necessity but one whose most frequent gesture is a cosmic, valedictory shrug: things are like that, we have to move on. In good Pierrot fashion, Ashbery often transmutes melancholy into laughter; *Self-Portrait* is grandly comic. Anyone who has seen one of the old cartoons in which cat, coyote, or *luftmensch* walks over the edge of a cliff and navigates successfully until he perceives it was by blind faith alone knows that laughter may be metaphysical—and this scenario is one that occurs, varied and abstracted, in many of Ashbery's poems. Humor in *Self-Portrait*, if often crackerbarrel or camp, is also cosmic. To describe it, one wants to adapt Rilke's definition of beauty and say that, for Ashbery, laughter is the beginning of terror we're still just able to bear.

His last book, *Three Poems*, made a kind of secular religion out of necessity: random and hopeless as our experience is, this book says, we are nonetheless "saved," and, in some sense, whatever is is O.K. This benign vision has mostly been abandoned in the new book or temporarily supplanted by an agonized awareness of solipsism and radical uncertainty: Who or what is "I"? How is it that experience is nothing but ourselves and still, supremely, *not* ourselves? How can "I" be known to anyone else when "I" is already a conundrum to itself? To answer these questions is an unrealizable and therefore noble project. In a number of the new poems Ashbery performs the poetic equivalent of dead reckoning, whereby the subject moves from steppingstone to unsteady steppingstone, from bright, fading image to disembodied idea, from recollection to speculation, as if it all might lead to a conclusion, and not simply an ending. So much inconclusive striving, such a strenuous inertia, is very painful—all the more because the poems present the narrator as a kind of Tantalus who both believes and disbelieves in some final release, a privileged moment just about to occur in which all opposites will be united:

> The pageant, growing ever more curious, reaches
> An ultimate turning point. Now everything is going to be
> Not dark, but on the contrary, charged with so much light
> It looks dark, because things are now packed so closely together.
> We see it with our teeth. And once this
>
> Distant corner is rounded, everything
> Is not to be made new again. We shall be inhabited
> In the old way, as ideal things came to us,
> Yet in the having we shall be growing, rising above it
> Into an admixture of deep blue enameled sky and bristly gold stars.
> ("Voyage in the Blue")

Privileged moments such as this one are presented as evanescent; they solve nothing permanently and function largely to make us realize the abjection of ordinary, "underprivileged" consciousness.

When we come to the end of one of these poems we would feel dissatisfied, I think, at not having been provided with some kind of resolution or wisdom if it weren't for the poems themselves, which are, when good, enough. Two endings:

> The night sheen takes over. A moon of cistercian pallor
> Has climbed to the center of heaven, installed,
> Finally involved with the business of darkness.
> And a sigh heaves from all the small things on earth,
> The books, the papers, the old garters and union-suit buttons
> Kept in a white cardboard box somewhere, and all the lower
> Versions of cities flattened under the equalizing night.
> The summer demands and takes away too much,
> But night, the reserved, the reticent, gives more than it takes.
> ("As One Put Drunk into the Packet Boat")
>
> Yet we are alone too and that's sad isn't it
> Yet you are meant to be alone at least part of the time
> You must be in order to work and yet it always seems so unnatural
> As though seeing people were intrinsic to life which it just might be
> And then somehow the loneliness is more real and more human
> You know not just the scarecrow but the whole landscape
> And the crows peacefully pecking where the harrow has passed
> ("Lithuanian Dance Band")

So far I've avoided quoting from the title poem (which I take to be the greatest in the volume) because, well, partly because, like any great monument, it has to be approached with caution, you may stumble as you climb up to it. Extraordinary achievement is likely to be greeted with silence—you simply want to point, even though there's an element of rudeness in doing so. Let me try then to do a little more. "Self-Portrait in a Convex Mirror" is an extended poem (reminding one again that in recent years, for whatever reason, the best poems written in America are long poems), and takes its title and subject from an early work of the Mannerist Francesco Parmigianino. The self-portrait is an "anamorphic" painting, that is, one that distorts normal perspective rendering by reproducing either a slant view of the subject or mediating it through non-plane reflecting surfaces such as cylindrical, conic, or convex mirrors. Examples of "slant" rendering (imagine looking at a movie screen from the first row) are found in the notebooks of Leonardo, and they almost always come into play in the *trompe-l'oeil* effects in late-Renaissance and baroque ceiling frescoes. The first major treatise on anamorphic art was Jean Niceron's *La Perspective curieuse* (1638), which gives techniques for making paintings to be reconstituted in non-plane reflecting surfaces. Jan van Eyck's *Arnolfini marriage group* (1434) and other Renaissance paintings include a convex mirror as a detail in a larger decor, but Parmigianino's self-portrait is the first—as far as I know, the only—portrait in a convex mirror.

Why did he paint himself this way? Why has Ashbery chosen this painting as a subject for poetic meditation? Call it happy accident, and then simply applaud the results—a painting of extraordinary psychological richness and a poem with passages like the following:

> But there is in that gaze a combination
> Of tenderness, amusement and regret, so powerful
> In its restraint that one cannot look for long.
> The secret is too plain. The pity of it smarts,
> Makes hot tears spurt: that the soul is not a soul,
> Has no secret, is small, and it fits
> Its hollow perfectly: its room, our moment of attention.

When I read this poem I'm reminded of a slide projector with a button-operated focus. A picture appears, sharp in outline; then another replaces it, out of focus—the vague forms, as they ooze toward clarity, suggest numerous possibilities, but, no, the picture is something different from anything we'd imagined, though the final image now seems inevitable. The next picture is blurred, too, and so engaging in its abstract form, we're tempted to leave it; but, reluctantly, we bring it into focus. When the show is over we realize that all the pictures shared something—they recorded a summer in Italy, or a trip to the National Gallery, or the building of a bridge.

I don't understand every line in "Self-Portrait," nor do I mind much; the coming and going of understanding as managed here is an interesting, involving experience. And poetry is much more a matter of pleasure than it is of argument: we are more readily seduced than convinced, I think. In any case, the free-hand development of this poem's principal theme—that art is like a distorting mirror wherein we discover a more engaging, mysterious, and enduring image of ourselves than unmediated experience affords—is carried out with great assurance and variety; gradually, as one reads, the poem attains a supernatural, slow-motion grandeur seldom encountered in poetry in any language, or in art in any medium:

> A peculiar slant
> Of memory that intrudes on the dreaming model
> In the silence of the studio as he considers
> Lifting the pencil to the self-portrait.
> How many people came and stayed a certain time,
> Uttered light or dark speech that became part of you
> Like light behind windblown fog and sand,
> Filtered and influenced by it, until no part
> Remains that is surely you. Those voices in the dusk
> Have told you all and still the tale goes on
> In the form of memories deposited in irregular
> Clumps of crystals. Whose curved hand controls,
> Francesco, the turning seasons and the thoughts
> That peel off and fly away at breathless speeds
> Like the last stubborn leaves ripped
> From wet branches? I see in this only the chaos
> Of your round mirror which organizes everything
> Around the polestar of your eyes which are empty,
> Know nothing, dream but reveal nothing.

Or, finally:

> Is there anything
> To be serious about beyond this otherness
> That gets included in the most ordinary
> Forms of daily activity, changing everything
> Slightly and profoundly, and tearing the matter
> Of creation, any creation, not just artistic creation
> Out of our hands, to install it on some monstrous, near
> Peak, too close to ignore, too far
> For one to intervene? This otherness, this
> "Not-being-us" is all there is to look at
> In the mirror, though no one can say
> How it came to be this way. A ship
> Flying unknown colors has entered the harbor.

DAVID KALSTONE

"Self-Portrait in a Convex Mirror"

In 1972 John Ashbery was invited to read at Shiraz, in Iran, where for several years the Empress had sponsored a festival of music, art, and drama which was remarkable, even notorious, for its modernity: Peter Brook's *Orghast,* Robert Wilson's week-long production *Ka Mountain and GUARDenia Terrace,* Merce Cunningham's dances, the music of Stockhausen and John Cage. Ashbery and another visitor, David Kermani, reported that "to a country without significant modern traditions, still under the spell of its own great past, where a production of Shaw or Ibsen would count as a novelty, such an effort even might seem quixotic." Taking into consideration Iranian critics who demanded Shakespeare first or Chekhov first, Ashbery's own response was delighted and characteristic: "The important thing is to start from the beginning, that is, the present. Oscar Wilde's 'Take care of the luxuries and the necessities will take care of themselves' might well have been the motto of the festival, and its justification." That oversimplifies his view of tradition and modernism, this poet who has rich and felt connections, for example, to Traherne and Marvell as well as to recent poets like Wallace Stevens and Auden and Marianne Moore. But the present is always Ashbery's point of departure: "Before I read modern poetry, the poetry of the past was of really no help to me."

Familiar notions about a poet's development won't quite apply to Ashbery's work. He doesn't return to objects, figures and key incidents which, as the career unfolds, gather increasing symbolic resonance. Nor do his poems refer to one another in any obvious way. Ashbery writes autobiography only inasmuch as he writes about the widening sense of

---

what it is like to gain—or to try to gain—access to his experience. The present is the poem. "I think that any one of my poems might be considered to be a snapshot of whatever is going on in my mind at the time—first of all the desire to write a poem, after that wondering if I've left the oven on or thinking about where I must be in the next hour." Or, more tellingly, in verse ("And Ut Pictura Poesis Is Her Name," from Houseboat Days):

> The extreme austerity of an almost empty mind
> Colliding with the lush, Rousseau-like foliage of its desire to
>   communicate
> Something between breaths, if only for the sake
> Of others and their desire to understand you and desert you
> For other centers of communication, so that understanding
> May begin, and in doing so be undone.

Like Penelope's web, the doing and undoing of Ashbery's poems is often their subject: fresh starts, repeated collisions of plain talk with the tantalizing and frustrating promises of "poetry." The "desire to communicate" erodes, over a pointed line-break, into hasty beleaguered utterance. Nor does an accumulating personal history provide a frame for him with outlines guiding and determining the future: "Seen from inside all is / Abruptness."

> And the great flower of what we have been twists
> On its stem of earth, for not being
> What we are to become, fated to live in
> Intimidated solitude and isolation.
>   ("Fragment")

In his images of thwarted nature, of discontinuity between present and past, Ashbery has turned his agitation into a principle of composition. From the start he has looked for sentences, diction, a syntax which would make these feelings fully and fluidly available. When he used strict verse forms, as he did in much of his first book, Some Trees, it was always with a sense of their power to explore rather than to certify that he was a poet. There are three sestinas in Some Trees, and one, the remarkable "Faust," in his second book, The Tennis Court Oath.

> These forms such as the sestina were really devices at getting into remoter areas of consciousness. The really bizarre requirements of a sestina I use as a probing tool. . . . I once told somebody that writing a sestina was rather like riding downhill on a bicycle and having the pedals push your feet. I wanted my feet to be pushed into places they wouldn't normally have taken. . . .

Ashbery's rhyming, too, was restless. At the close of "Some Trees" his final rhymes create a practically unparaphraseable meaning, the two words inviting overtones they wouldn't have in prose:

> Placed in a puzzling light, and moving,
> Our days put on such reticence
> These accents seem their own defense.

There were other, drastic attempts to get at "remoter areas of consciousness," some of them in *The Tennis Court Oath* close to automatic writing. "Europe," a poem Ashbery now thinks of as a dead end, was "a way of trying to obliterate the poetry that at the time was coming naturally" to him. Exploding any notion of continuity, it consisted of "a lot of splintered fragments . . . collecting them all under a series of numbers." The "French Poems" in *The Double Dream of Spring* were first written in French, then translated "with the idea of avoiding customary word-patterns and associations." In *Three Poems*, his fifth book, long prose pieces were a way to overflow the "arbitrary divisions of poetry into lines," another way to an "expanded means of utterance."

What I am getting at is that a great deal of Ashbery's writing is done in an atmosphere of deliberate demolition, and that his work is best served not by thinking about development, but by following his own advice: beginning at the beginning, "that is, the present." *Self-Portrait in a Convex Mirror* (1975) is the present with which I want to begin. The long title poem of that volume is in every sense a major work, a strong and beautiful resolution of besetting and important problems. Ashbery had already broached these problems in *The Double Dream of Spring*, in which he characteristically approached the world as a foreigner, sometimes in the role of explorer, sometimes as a pilgrim, and almost always as someone bewildered by the clutter of a situation which, wryly phrased, "could not be better." The world of that book is often divided, out of bristling necessity, between inside and outside, between *we* and a dimly identified *they* as in "The Task": "They are preparing to begin again: / Problems, new pennant up the flagpole / In a predicated romance." Access to the present was more peremptorily barred than it was to be in *Self-Portrait in a Convex Mirror*.

The Double Dream of Spring had looked at alternatives with grim amusement. In "Definition of Blue" the cant words of social engineers, historians and broadcasters—*capitalism, romanticism, impetuses*—drain away, with their tripping rhythms, into colorless sentences, while the imaginative eye, seeking out materials for escape, finds only that "erosion" has produced:

> . . . a kind of dust or exaggerated pumice
> Which fills space and transforms it, becoming a medium
> In which it is possible to recognize oneself.

This comic decay of language and the laws of perspective allows us "A portrait, smooth as glass, . . . built up out of multiple corrections / And it has no relation to the space or time in which it was lived." The joke is on us, especially the grammatical joke that it is the portrait which lives, fragments of personality out of touch with anything but the mirroring tricks which make it seem to be a likeness. Meanwhile

> . . . the blue surroundings drift slowly up and past you
> To realize themselves some day, while, you, in this nether
>   world that could not be better
> Waken each morning to the exact value of what you did and
>   said, which remains.

The separation of "nether world" from the independent and inaccessible world of plenitude, the blue surroundings which drift past us and "realize themselves," is a source of frustration and mockery.

> There is no remedy for this "packaging" which has
>   supplanted the old sensations.
> Formerly there would have been architectural screens at the
>   point where the action became most difficult

Yet Ashbery also takes a rueful "pop" pleasure in the vocabulary of "packaging," allowing it to deflate itself, as in the double-take of a "world that could not be better." The feelings here are not totally resolved, nor are they meant to be. Ashbery once said that he was willing for his poems to be "confusing, but not confused."

> It seems to me that my poetry sometimes proceeds as though an argu-ment were suddenly derailed and something that started out clearly suddenly becomes opaque. It's a kind of mimesis of how experience comes to me: as one is listening to someone else—a lecturer, for instance—who's making perfect sense but suddenly slides into something that eludes one. What I am probably trying to do is to illustrate opacity and how it can suddenly descend over us, rather than trying to be willfully obscure.

"Definition of Blue" is, on the surface, laconically faithful to expository syntax, the *sinces* and *buts* and *therefores* which lash explanations together. The logical bridges lead into eroded territory, and then unexpectedly back again; the poem moves in and out of focus like a mind bombarded with received ideas. So—"mass practices have sought to submerge the personality / By ignoring it, which has caused it instead to branch out in all directions." Or, with deadpan determination—"there is no point in looking to imaginative new methods / Since all of them are in constant use." Just at the point when imagination seems reduced to novelty, an overloaded switchboard, we learn that this "erosion" with its "kind of dust or exaggerated pumice" provides "a medium / In which it is possible to recognize oneself." A serious challenge peeps through: how far are we responsible for, dependent upon, these denatured senses of identity?

"Each new diversion," Ashbery tells us, "adds its accurate touch to the ensemble." Mischievous saboteur that he is, Ashbery's pun on *diversion* shows how much he enjoys some of the meandering of unfocused public vocabularies and the "accurate touches" they supply (as a wardrobe?). But, basically, our sense is of someone bristling, boxed in by a maze of idioms, frustrated and diminished by his presence there. Only the mirrored portrait lives "built up out of multiple corrections." Or, to be more exact, in a petrifying shift to a past tense and the passive voice: "it has no relation to the space or time in which it was lived"—a disaffected vision of personality if there ever was one. The world of "packaging" appears to have robbed him of a life, of his access to power and vision.

I have chosen this example, more extreme than some of the others in *The Double Dream of Spring,* because it is so energetically answered and refigured by Ashbery's long poem "Self-Portrait in a Convex Mirror." In that more recent, more encompassing work, the poet takes charge of the emerging self-portrait rather than suffering it as he had in "Definition of Blue." He tests an identity captured by art against the barrages of experience which nourish and beset it. He is sparked by a Renaissance painting, Parmigianino's self-portrait, alongside which he matches what proves to be his own: a mirror of the state of mind in which the poem was written, open to waves of discovery and distraction, and aware of the unframed and unframeable nature of experience.

> Today has no margins, the event arrives
> Flush with its edges, is of the same substance,
> Indistinguishable.

Parmigianino's work is itself problematic, and haunting, done on the segment of a halved wooden ball so as to reproduce as closely as possible the painter's image in a convex mirror exactly the same size. That Renaissance effort, straining to capture a real presence, touches off in Ashbery a whirling series of responses, visions and revisions of what the painting asks of *him*.

I

"Self-Portrait" begins quietly, not overcommitted to its occasion, postponing full sentences, preferring phrases:

> As Parmigianino did it, the right hand
> Bigger than the head, thrust at the viewer
> And swerving easily away, as though to protect
> What it advertises. A few leaded panes, old beams,
> Fur, pleated muslin, a coral ring rung together
> In a movement supporting the face, which swims
> Toward and away like the hand
> Except that it is in repose. It is what is
> Sequestered.

A lot could be said about Ashbery's entrance into poems and his habit of tentative anchorage: "As on a festal day in early spring," "As One Put Drunk into the Packet Boat" (title: first line of Marvell's "Tom May's Death"). Such openings are reticent, similes taking on the identity of another occasion, another person—a sideways address to their subject or, in the case of "Self-Portrait," a way of dealing with temptation. The speaker in "Self-Portrait" appears to "happen" upon Parmigianino's painting as a solution to a problem pondered before the poem begins. At first glimpse the glass of art and the face in the portrait offer him just the right degree of self-disclosure and self-assertion, the right balance of living spirit and the haunting concentrated maneuvers of art. The judicious give-and-take appears to him: thrust and swerve; toward and away; protect and advertise. (This is, by the way, one of the best descriptive impressions of a painting I know.) That balanced satisfaction never returns. What at first comforts him, the face "in repose," prompts an unsettling fear: "It is what is / Sequestered." This is the first full sentence of the poem—brief, shocked and considered, after the glancing descriptive phrases. An earlier draft of the lines was weaker: "protected" rather than "sequestered" and the word placed unemphatically at the end of the line, as if some of the menace to be sensed in the finished portrait hadn't yet surfaced.

From then on the poem becomes, as Ashbery explains it in a crucial pun, "speculation / (From the Latin *speculum*, mirror)," Ashbery's glass rather than Francesco's. All questions of scientific reflection, capturing a real presence, turn instantly into the other kind of reflection: changeable, even fickle thought. The whole poem is a series of revisions prepared for in the opening lines, where in Parmigianino's receding portrait he imagines first that "the soul establishes itself," then that "the soul is a captive." Finally, from the portrait's mixture of "tenderness, amusement and regret":

> The secret is too plain. The pity of it smarts,
> Makes hot tears spurt: that the soul is not a soul,
> Has no secret, is small, and it fits
> Its hollow perfectly: its room, our moment of attention.

In an earlier draft of the poem it was not quite so clear why such strong feeling emerges:

> . . . that the soul
> Has no secret, is small, though it fits
> Perfectly the space intended for it: its room, our attention.

Rewriting those lines Ashbery allowed more emphatic fears to surface. "The soul is not a soul." Acting on an earlier hint that Parmigianino's mirror chose to show an image "glazed, embalmed," Ashbery sees it in its hollow (overtones of burial) rather than in the neutral "space intended." "Our moment of attention" draws sparks between the glazed surface of the portrait and the poet's transient interest which awakens it, and places notions like the *soul* irredeemably in the eye of the beholder. When the poet looks at this ghostly double, alive in its mirroring appeal, the emerging fear comes across like Milly Theale's (*The Wings of the Dove*) in front of the Bronzino portrait resembling her, "dead, dead, dead."

Throughout "Self-Portrait in a Convex Mirror" the poet speaks to the portrait as in easy consultation with a familiar, but with an ever changing sense of whether he is addressing the image, trapped on its wooden globe, or addressing the free painter standing outside his creation, straining to capture a real presence, restraining the power to shatter what may become a prison: "Francesco, your hand is big enough / To wreck the sphere, . . ." An explosion has been building from the start as Ashbery returns over and over, puzzled by that hand which the convex mirror shows "Bigger than the head, thrust at the viewer / And swerving easily away, as though to protect / What it advertises." At first that defensive posture in a work of art attracts him, an icon of mastery. But, a little later, feeling the portrait as "life englobed," he reads the hand differently:

> One would like to stick one's hand
> Out of the globe, but its dimension,
> What carries it, will not allow it.
> No doubt it is this, not the reflex
> To hide something, which makes the hand loom large
> As it retreats slightly.

The hand returns not in self-defense, but

> . . . to fence in and shore up the face
> On which the effort of this condition reads
> Like a pinpoint of a smile, a spark.
> Or star one is not sure of having seen
> As darkness resumes.

Philosophic questions mount, but always apprehended through gestures, new expressions glimpsed as one stares at the painting—here a glint of self-mockery, as the painter absorbed with prowess finds himself trapped by his medium after all. "But your eyes proclaim / That everything is surface. . . . / There are no recesses in the room, only alcoves." The window admits light, but all sense of change is excluded, even "the weather, which in French is / Le temps, the word for time." The opening section of "Self-Portrait" winds down, the poet bemused but his poetry drained of the emotional concentration which had drawn him to the painting; a glance at the subject's hands sees them as symbolically placed, but inexpressive:

> The whole is stable within
> Instability, a globe like ours, resting
> On a pedestal of vacuum, a ping-pong ball
> Secure on its jet of water.
> And just as there are no words for the surface, that is,
> No words to say what it really is, that it is not
> Superficial but a visible core, then there is
> No way out of the problem of pathos vs. experience.
> You will stay on, restive, serene in
> Your gesture which is neither embrace nor warning
> But which holds something of both in pure
> Affirmation that doesn't affirm anything.

This is not Ashbery's final reading of the portrait's gesturing hand. But it launches a series of struggles with the past, with "art," with the notion of "surface," with the random demands of the present—struggles which are not only at the heart of this poem but a paradigm of Ashbery's work. Parmigianino's portrait has to compete with the furniture of the mind confronting it: the poet's day, memories, surroundings, ambitions, distractions. The solid spherical segment becomes confused, in the Wonderland of the mind, with other rounded images, toys of attention—a ping-pong ball on a jet of water, and then, at the start of the second section, "The balloon pops, the attention / Turns dully away." There is a rhythm to reading this poem, however wandering it may seem. We experience it as a series of contractions and expansions of interest in the painting, depending upon how much the poet is drawn to its powers of foreshortening and concentration, and alternately how cramped he feels breathing its air. The transitions between sections are marked as easy shifts in inner weather, opposed to the weatherless chamber of Parmigianino's portrait:

> The balloon pops, the attention
> Turns dully away.
>
> As I start to forget it
> It presents its stereotype again
>
> The shadow of the city injects its own
> Urgency:
>
> A breeze like the turning of a page
> Brings back your face.

The painting occurs to him at times as a ship: first, a "tiny, self-important ship / On the surface." In mysterious relation to it the enlarged hand in the distorted portrait seems "Like a dozing whale on the sea bottom." Threatening? Or a sign of throbbing vitality, an invisible part of its world? Later the portrait

> . . . is an unfamiliar stereotype, the face
> Riding at anchor, issued from hazards, soon
> To accost others, "rather angel than man" (Vasari).

Toward the end of the poem, the ship sails in to confirm some sense of

> . . . this otherness
> That gets included in the most ordinary
> Forms of daily activity, changing everything
> Slightly and profoundly, and tearing the matter
> Of creation, any creation, not just artistic creation
> Out of our hands, to install it on some monstrous, near
> Peak, too close to ignore, too far
> For one to intervene? This otherness, this
> "Not-being-us" is all there is to look at
> In the mirror, though no one can say
> How it came to be this way. A ship
> Flying unknown colors has entered the harbor.

Self-important and tiny? Issued from hazards? Flying unknown colors? Through contradictory senses of the ship, Ashbery judges the portrait's relation to risk and adventure, to the mysterious otherness of "arrival" in a completed work of art.

What happens, for example, when we start to imagine the life of cities behind the surface of a work of art, in this case the sack of Rome which was going on where Francesco was at work; Vienna where Ashbery saw the painting in 1959; New York where he is writing his poem? These are ways Ashbery has of summoning up the countless events which nourished the painting and his response to it. That outside life, again imagined in terms of risk, adventure, voyages, can be profoundly disturbing—a life not palpable in a "finished" work.

> . . . a chill, a blight
> Moving outward along the capes and peninsulas
> Of your nervures and so to the archipelagoes
> And to the bathed, aired secrecy of the open sea.

Such images focus the problem of how much life is lived in and outside a work of art. There is no point in disentangling what is hopelessly inter-twined. The images flow toward and counter one another, and the reader accumulates a bewildering sense of what it is to be both fulfilled and thwarted by his own grasped moments of vision (all attempts at order, not just artistic creation, Ashbery tries to remind us). Francesco's portrait has the capacity to make us feel at home; we "can live in it as in fact we have done." Or "we linger, receiving / Dreams and inspirations on an unas-signed / Frequency." But at another moment the portrait seems like a vacuum drawing upon *our* plenty, "fed by our dreams." If at one point the mind straying from the conical painting is like a balloon bursting, not much later the straying thoughts are imagined as wayward, even sinister progeny of the painting: the balloon has not burst at all. "Actually / The skin of the bubble-chamber's as tough as / Reptile eggs."

Struggling with the past, with art and its completeness, Ashbery is also struggling with the impulses behind his own writing at the very moment of writing.

> . . . you could be fooled for a moment
> Before you realize the reflection
> Isn't yours. You feel then like one of those
> Hoffmann characters who have been deprived
> Of a reflection, except that the whole of me
> Is seen to be supplanted by the strict
> Otherness of the painter in his
> Other room.

The threat is pressed home by a shift from an impersonal "you" to an endangered "me." The finished work of art is like "A cloth over a birdcage," and the poet wary of its invitations:

> Yet the "poetic," straw-colored space
> Of the long corridor that leads back to the painting,
> Its darkening opposite—is this
> Some figment of "art," not to be imagined
> As real, let alone special?

By the closing pages of the poem two irreconcilable views of "living" have proposed themselves. Parmigianino's appears to be a "Life-obstructing task." ("You can't live there.") More than that, the portrait exposes the poet's own efforts in the present:

> Our time gets to be veiled, compromised
> By the portrait's will to endure. It hints at
> Our own, which we were hoping to keep hidden.

When "will to endure" and "life-obstructing" are identified with one another, as they are here in describing our daily fiction-making activities, the psychological contradictions are themselves almost unendurable. Imagining is as alien and miraculous as the ambivalent image he finds for it: "A ship / Flying unknown colors has entered the harbor." Our creations, torn out of our hands, seem installed "on some monstrous, near / Peak, too close to ignore, too far / For one to intervene." Another way of looking at it: "the way of telling" intrudes "as in the game where / A whispered phrase passed around the room / Ends up as something completely different."

An alternative? Though the poem is always pressing us out of the past, it has no unmediated language for the present, which is as hard to locate as other poets' Edens. Where poets describing unknown worlds have always "liken'd spiritual forms to corporal," Ashbery must perform some of the same *likening* to enter the corporal present itself. He knows the present only from before and after, seen as through a terrifying hourglass:

> . . . the sands are hissing
> As they approach the beginning of the big slide
> Into what happened. This past
> Is now here.

Four of these five monosyllables—"This past is now here"—point to the present with all the immediacy of which English is capable, and *past* disarms them all. There is no comfort in the provisional, in being open to the rush of things. In fact, one of the most devastating contemporary critiques of randomness in poetry comes in the final moments of Ashbery's poem. Yet it is critique from within, in a poem open to the vagaries of mind—and from a writer deeply committed to describing the struggles we undergo in describing our lives. This is his unique and special place among contemporary poets. The blurring of personal pronouns, their often indeterminate reference, the clouding of landscapes and crystal balls, are all ways of trying to be true not only to the mind's confusions but also to its resistance of stiffening formulations.

In the distorting self-portrait of Parmigianino, Ashbery found the perfect mirror and the perfect antagonist—a totem of art and the past caught in the act of trying to escape from itself. Parmigianino's work of art confirms the poet in a vocation which refuses to be rescued by art, except in the moment of creation.

> Hasn't it too its lair
> In the present we are always escaping from
> And falling back into, as the waterwheel of days
> Pursues its uneventful, even serene course?

This is a difficult dialectic to which he submits. Francesco is the indispensable partner in a continuing conversation; yet Ashbery's final reading of the painterly hand in the self-portrait is the boldest stroke of all:

> Therefore I beseech you, withdraw that hand,
> Offer it no longer as shield or greeting,
> The shield of a greeting, Francesco:
> There is room for one bullet in the chamber:
> Our looking through the wrong end
> Of the telescope as you fall back at a speed
> Faster than that of light to flatten ultimately
> Among the features of the room, . . .

The pun on *chamber*, the dizzying transformations of rounded room into telescope and gun barrel, are triumphant tributes to all the contradictions of this poem and the hard-won struggle to be free of them. It would be a shallow reading which sees this poem as a modernist's dismissal of the past. Ashbery translates that *topos* into radical and embracing human terms. The elation we feel comes from the writer's own unwillingness to take permanent shelter in his work. Any work of art—not just those of the distant past—has designs on us, exposes for what it is our "will to endure." Ashbery builds the awareness of death and change into the very form of his work. It is the old subject of Romantic lyric—of Keats's *Ode on a Grecian Urn*—but here without undue veneration for the moments out of time. Ashbery admits into the interstices of his poem a great deal of experience—confusion, comedy, befuddlement, preoccupation—in which he takes as much joy as in the "cold pockets / Of remembrance, whispers out of time," which he also celebrates. His withdrawal from the privileged moments is never as regretful or as final as Keats's from his "cold pastoral." Nor is it as rueful as Ashbery's own sense of desertion in "Definition of

Blue" where "you, in this nether world that could not be better / Waken each morning to the exact value of what you did and said, which remains." In that earlier poem Ashbery feels diminished and powerless before a "portrait, smooth as glass, . . . built up out of multiple corrections," which "has no relation to the space or time in which it was lived." In the spaciousness of "Self-Portrait in a Convex Mirror" Ashbery radiates a new confidence in his ability to accommodate what is in the poet's mind: the concentrated poem and its teeming surroundings. In its achieved generosity and fluidity, in its stops and starts and turns, Ashbery's long poem dispels some of the frustrations of language and form, or assimilates them more closely into the anxieties and frustrations of living.

II

I said before that "Self-Portrait in a Convex Mirror" answers problems posed by Ashbery's poetic past and helps refigure it.

> Every moment is surrounded by a lot of things in life that don't add up to anything that makes much sense and these are part of a situation that I feel I'm trying to deal with when I'm writing.

Ashbery said this to an interviewer in 1972, as if anticipating the free and flexible voice he found for "Self-Portrait in a Convex Mirror." That year he had published the long prose pieces he entitled *Three Poems*, a work which evidently released him into an "expanded sense of utterance":

> . . . the idea of it occurred to me as something new in which the arbitrary divisions of poetry into lines would get abolished. One wouldn't have to have these interfering and scanning the processes of one's thought as one was writing; the poetic form would be dissolved, in solution, and therefore create a much more—I hate to say environmental because it's a bad word—but more of a surrounding thing like the way one's consciousness is surrounded by one's thoughts.

However odd or puzzling that last phrase may be, we can sense the pressure behind its deliberate, almost involuntary awkwardness. In both quotations Ashbery uses the word "surrounded" to suggest the number of seemingly unrelated "thoughts" or "things" at any given moment pressing behind the little that is articulated. This tension is the point of departure for *Three Poems*:

> I thought that if I could put it all down, that would be one way. And next the thought came to me that to leave all out would be another, and truer, way.
>
> clean-washed sea
>
> The flowers were.

> These are examples of leaving out. But, forget as we will, something
> soon comes to stand in their place. Not the truth, perhaps, but—yourself.
> It is you who made this, therefore you are true.

We are dealing with rich polarities in Ashbery's work. The impulse
to "leave all out" can be felt as early as a poem like "Illustration" from his
first book, *Some Trees*. The protagonist of that poem is a nun about to
leave behind the irrelevancies of the world by leaping from a skyscraper.
As this droll hierophant remarks: " 'I desire / Monuments . . . I want to
move / Figuratively, as waves caress / The thoughtless shore.' " The
narrator, too, is convinced: "Much that is beautiful must be discarded / So
that we may resemble a taller / Impression of ourselves." That was one
way of saying it, the way of concision and foreshortening.

But then there is another way to have it, as in "And *Ut Pictura
Poesis* Is Her Name" a more recent poem (1975):

> You can't say it that way any more.
> Bothered about beauty you have to
> Come out into the open, into a clearing.
> And rest . . .
>
>   Now
> About what to put in your poem-painting:
> Flowers are always nice, particularly delphinium.
> Names of boys you once knew and their sleds,
> Skyrockets are good—do they still exist?
> There are a lot of other things of the same quality
> As those I've mentioned. Now one must
> Find a few important words, and a lot of low-keyed,
> Dull-sounding ones.

A difference in approach makes all the difference. "Illustration" proposes
a "taller / Impression of ourselves," an epigrammatic and visionary avoid-
ance of ordinary "beauty," "*Ut Pictura*" makes space for a flustered, fuller
and meandering version of self. Vision is invited by coming out into a
clearing and taking a relaxed view of the surroundings. The poet finds "a
few important words" and "a lot of low-keyed, / Dull-sounding ones."

Though these poems come from different periods in Ashbery's
career, I don't want to suggest that one voice or approach replaces the
other. But with *Three Poems* Ashbery rounded a critical corner. Its *perpetuum mobile* style prepared him, when he returned to verse, for a new
fluidity, a way to re-admit the self to his poetry. Alive in its present, and
determined as a Jack-in-the-box, that self pops up when any moment of
poetic concision threatens to falsify or obliterate it. The discovery comes
as a relief, not so much a calculation as a necessity. Leaving things out,

"forget as we will, something soon comes to stand in their place. Not the truth, perhaps, but—yourself."

I am talking, then, about complementary gifts or voices in Ashbery's poetry. He has his own deadpan way of putting it: "In the last few years I have been attempting to keep meaningfulness up to the pace of random-ness . . . but I really think that meaningfulness can't get along without randomness and that they somehow have to be brought together." No wonder that the long "Self-Portrait in a Convex Mirror" stands as a centerpiece to his work in the early 1970s; no single short poem could handle such a copious problem. It would be a mistake to see this merely as an aesthetic question, a poet talking about poetry, about the relative virtues of condensed vision and expansive randomness. The emotional coloring that Ashbery gives this conflict, especially in his long poem, suggests psychological dimensions and stresses. Art "leaving things out" involves a sense of melancholy and sacrifice, a restlessness, a threat to vitality.

The Double Dream of Spring is shadowed by such feelings; the short poems of *Self-Portrait in a Convex Mirror* often counter them. Together these two books, five years apart, with their different moods, give a sense of the range and playfulness and boldness of Ashbery's emerging work. There are some poems, of course, which might be in either book. Still, certain characteristic titles belong to one and not the other: in *Double Dream*, "Spring Day," "Summer," "Evening in the Country," "Rural Objects," "Clouds"; in *Self-Portrait*, "Worsening Situation," "Absolute Clearance," "Mixed Feelings," "No Way of Knowing," "All and Some." The latter pick up colloquial ways of describing the emotional weather of the moment. Titles from *Double Dream* tend toward the generic and the pastoral. (Not that any Ashbery title is more than a clue or a point of departure, less a summary and more a key signature for the poem.)

In *The Double Dream of Spring* Ashbery seems absorbed in the forms that lie just behind an experience; the day's events, in "Years of Indiscretion," as "Fables that time invents / To explain its passing." Common phrases are challenged; buried meanings are coaxed out of them so that they surprise us with a life of their own, or chastise us for a sleepy acceptance of the "phraseology we become." Ashbery wants to push past the hardening of life into habit, the way it congeals into patterned phrases, the metaphysician's equivalent of "You are what you eat." I don't know whether "Young Man with Letter" is touched off by yet another appearance of a golden, well-introduced youth into the city which will absorb him. But the impulse of the poem quickly becomes something else: to awaken the "fable" sleeping behind a phrase like "making the rounds."

> Another feeble, wonderful creature is making the rounds again,
> In this phraseology we become, as clouds like leaves
> Fashion the internal structure of a season
> From water into ice. Such an abstract can be
> Dazed waking of the words with no memory of what happened before,
> Waiting for the second click. We know them well enough now,
> Forever, from living into them, tender, frivolous and puzzled
> And we know that with them we will come out right.

The cliché ("making the rounds") is teased alive by the strange sad comparison with the seasons. Ashbery performs what he then identifies, "dazed waking of the words," eventually "living into them." Many of the poems in *Double Dream* act out such discoveries, satisfied with nothing merely accidental, nothing less refined than "Fables that time invents / To explain its passing." Still, having gone beyond gossip in "Young Man with Letter," having absorbed a single bit of tattle into a large melancholy sense of natural cycles, Ashbery is left with some nagging questions. Once he has sidestepped the "corrosive friends" and "quiet bickering" in this poem, there is still something distant and unreal about the "straining and puffing / . . . commas produce":

> Is it not more likely that . . .
>   . . .   this ferment
> We take as suddenly our present
> Is our waltzing somewhere else, down toward the view
> But holding off?

The frustration and self-mockery, the sense of being deprived of the present, are inescapably twinned with the discoveries made in such poems. The mood is odd and disquieting; however gratifying the visionary insight, the poet also seems to feel experience being taken out of his hands. Hence, the way fresh hopes verge into nightmares in the long suspended sentence at the opening of "Spring Day":

> The immense hope, and forbearance
> Trailing out of night, to sidewalks of the day
> Like air breathed into a paper city, exhaled
> As night returns bringing doubts
> That swarm around the sleeper's head
> But are fended off with clubs and knives, so that morning
> Installs again in cold hope
> The air that was yesterday, is what you are.

In this supple maze of syntax things seem over, exhausted, before they begin; "immense hope" turns into "cold hope" in "the air that was yesterday."

Again, a sense of pleasure in natural cycles is slowly withdrawn in "Years of Indiscretion."

> Whatever your eye alights on this morning is yours:
> Dotted rhythms of colors as they fade to the color,
> A gray agate, translucent and firm, with nothing
> Beyond its purifying reach. It's all there.
> These are things offered to your participation.
>
> These pebbles in a row are the seasons.
> This is a house in which you may wish to live.
> There are more than any of us to choose from
> But each must live its own time.

The experience offered here, beginning in random pleasures of the eye, seems at first to belong to us, to *our* wishes and choices. And yet "participation" suggests limits to our control, and the ambiguous "its" in the last line shadows independent processes in which we "participate" but do not endure. The grave diction soon removes us into an atmosphere refined and impersonal, our lives roles rather than improvisations. "There ought to be room for more things, for a spreading out, like," Ashbery says of the generalizing screen which stands between us and details of the landscape ("For John Clare"). "Alas, we perceive them if at all as those things that were meant to be put aside—costumes of the supporting actors or voice trilling at the end of a narrow enclosed street."

In one of his best short poems, "Summer," Ashbery imagines the winter latent in summer branches: "For the time being the shadow is ample / And hardly seen, divided among the twigs of a tree." Winter's poverty emerges later in a full-blown reminiscence of Stevens: "and winter, the twitter / Of cold stars at the pane, that describes with broad gestures / This state of being that is not so big after all." I am struck by the frequency with which Ashbery returns in *Double Dream* to myths of the seasons, as to photographic negatives, for the true contours governing experience—and what's more important, he is looking not for myths of rebirth but for myths of diminution. In "Fragment" we learn that

> Summer was a band of nondescript children
> Bordering the picture of winter, which was indistinct
> And gray like the sky of a winter afternoon.

In the poem "Summer," "Summer involves going down as a steep flight of steps / To a narrow ledge over the water."

Ashbery takes his title *The Double Dream of Spring* from de Chirico and so puts us on warning that we are stepping through the looking glass into those deep perspectives and receding landscapes of the mind. He leads us, once we are prepared to follow, to yearned-for, difficult states, free of casual distraction.

> To reduce all this to a small variant,
> To step free at last, minuscule on the gigantic plateau—
> This was our ambition: to be small and clear and free.
> ("Soonest Mended")

Does the present exist principally "To release the importance / Of what will always remain invisible?" he asks, with some urgency, in "Fragment." *The Double Dream of Spring* seems to answer that question in the affirmative. It is Ashbery's most successfully visionary book, however sad its tone. Unlike *Self-Portrait in a Convex Mirror*, which struggles to include and authenticate the present, *Double Dream* finds the most striking images in its glimpses of the fables behind our lives, and it most yearns for the state which is both free and deathlike, diminished.

> The welcoming stuns the heart, iron bells
> Crash through the transparent metal of the sky
> Each day slowing the method of thought a little
> Until oozing sap of touchable mortality, time lost and won.

"Soonest Mended"—so goes the title of one of the best of these poems, illustrating a point we can scarcely grasp until we supply the first half of a proverb which has been mimetically suppressed: "least said; soonest mended." *Double Dream* calls for tight-lipped irony as well as yearning for visionary release. In "Soonest Mended" comic self-awareness and proverbial wisdom are the ways Ashbery finds to deal with the deposits of history and hazard which determine the course of life:

> They were the players, and we who had struggled at the game
> Were merely spectators, though subject to its vicissitudes
> And moving with it out of the tearful stadium, borne on
>   shoulders, at last.

It is entirely in keeping with the tone of this poem that we are left uncertain as to whether we are borne out of the stadium triumphant or dead. Or both. Just as, at the end of "Soonest Mended," action is described as

> . . . this careless
> Preparing, sowing the seeds crooked in the furrow,
> Making ready to forget, and always coming back
> To the mooring of starting out, that day so long ago.

The brave carelessness here is licensed by some certainty that no matter how many mistakes we make, no matter what happens, we *do* return to the "mooring of starting out." We can also read this as helplessness. The tone is partly elegiac, owning up to the futility of our efforts, with "mooring" sounding as much like death as a new life. The entire poem has this doubleness of feeling. Its long breathy lines shift quickly from one historical hazard to another; it doesn't take long to get from the endangered Angelica of Ariosto and Ingres to Happy Hooligan in his rusted green automobile. Caught up in a whirligig of historical process, the self has no chance to recover balance, and above all, no conceptual means, no language to do so. Still, the energetic lines breathe the *desire* to assert ego and vitality. The poem sees the world as so full of bright particulars that no rules of thumb can keep up with them; and so it is fairly bitter about standard patterns of history and learning, sees them only as shaky hypotheses. "Soonest Mended" doesn't yet pretend pleasure in the present, a pleasure Ashbery *does* experience in later poems; and yet the poem doesn't entirely fall back on dreams of another world. Falling back, not with too much conviction, on the proverbial wisdom of the title, Ashbery has found a middle diction: ready to improvise, yielding to but not swamped by randomness.

III

I have talked about complementary voices and attitudes in Ashbery's work—alternatives between which "Soonest Mended" seems poised—the ways of concision and copiousness. Before *Three Poems* Ashbery was strongly attracted to foreshortening, "leaving all out," moving figuratively: discarding things so that we "resemble a taller / Impression of ourselves." It is easy to forget how fierce and compelling that desire was:

> . . . groping shadows of an incomplete
> Former existence so close it burns like the mouth that
> Closes down over all your effort like the moment
> Of death, but stays, raging and burning the design of
> Its intentions into the house of your brain, until
> You wake up alone, the certainty that it
> Wasn't a dream your only clue to why the walls
> Are turning on you and why the windows no longer speak
> Of time but are themselves, transparent guardians you
> Invented for what there was to hide.

Something has happened between that fevered vision from "Clepsydra" and the more relaxed, but still yearning, close of "Self-Portrait in a

Convex Mirror": the Parmigianino portrait recedes, virtually assassinated
by the poet; it becomes

> . . . an invitation
> Never mailed, the "it was all a dream"
> Syndrome, though the "all" tells tersely
> Enough how it wasn't. Its existence
> Was real, though troubled, and the ache
> Of this waking dream can never drown out
> The diagram still sketched on the wind,
> Chosen, meant for me and materialized
> In the disguising radiance of my room.

Both this passage and the one from "Clepsydra" acknowledge a
constellation of dreams perhaps more "real" than "real life" ("the certainty that it / Wasn't a dream"). But the version in "Self-Portrait" is
wistful, rather than driven: Ashbery seems open to the varieties of experience, registers more pleasurably the ache of the veiled and ineluctable
dream. He makes his bow to an ironic view of the visionary self ("the 'it
was all a dream' / Syndrome") before returning to a hidden truth behind
colloquial language ("the 'all' tells tersely / Enough how it wasn't"). The
present *disguises* the tempting dream behind Parmigianino's portrait, but
disguises it in the "radiance" of the poet's room. No need to choose
between the present and the unseen—and in the pressured light of the
passing of time, no *way* to do so.

It is the jumble of everyday pleasures and frustrations that we hear
most often in the fluid style of some of the shorter poems of *Self-Portrait in
a Convex Mirror*. Even the longer poem "Grand Galop" is almost literally
an attempt to keep the poem's accounting powers even with the pace of
inner and outer events. Naturally it doesn't succeed. The mind moves in
several directions at once, and the poem is partly about the exhaustions
and comic waste carried along by the "stream of consciousness":

> The custard is setting; meanwhile
> I not only have my own history to worry about
> But am forced to fret over insufficient details related to large
> Unfinished concepts that can never bring themselves to the point
> Of being, with or without my help, if any were forthcoming.

At the start of the poem, the mind moves on ahead of some lists of names
(weigela, sloppy joe on bun—the end of the line for Whitman's famous
catalogues) and then the poem says we must stop and "wait again."
"Nothing takes up its fair share of time." Ashbery calls our attention
repeatedly, and with frustration rather than exultation, to the fact that
the poem's time is not actual time.

"Grand Galop" also laments the generalizing and pattern-making powers which intervene and block our experience of particulars:

> Too bad, I mean, that getting to know each just for a
>   fleeting second
> Must be replaced by imperfect knowledge of the featureless
>   whole,
> Like some pocket history of the world, so general
> As to constitute a sob or wail unrelated
> To any attempt at definition.

Imperfect and *featureless* fall with deadpan accuracy in lines which expose the hazards of "aping naturalness." Ashbery's "A Man of Words" finds that

> All diaries are alike, clear and cold, with
> The outlook for continued cold. They are placed
> Horizontal, parallel to the earth,
> Like the unencumbering dead. Just time to reread this
> And the past slips through your fingers, wishing you were there.

Poetry can never be quite quick enough, however grand the "galop," however strong the desire to "communicate something between breaths." This explains some of the qualities of Ashbery's style which trouble readers. What seems strange is not so much *what* he says as the space between his sentences, the quickness of his transitions. "He" will become "you" or "I" without warning as experiences move close and then farther away, photographs and tapes of themselves. Tenses will shift while the poem refers to itself as part of the past. We feel as if something were missing; we become anxious as if a step had been skipped. So does the poet who, in several of the shorter poems, describes himself as a dazed prologue to someone else's play. In "As One Put Drunk into the Packet Boat," he longs for a beautiful apocalypse:

> . . . for a moment, I thought
> The great, formal affair was beginning, orchestrated,
> Its colors concentrated in a glance, a ballade
> That takes in the whole world, now, but lightly,
> Still lightly, but with wide authority and tact.

There are moments when Ashbery takes perilous shelter in the world of fable and dream, as in "Hop o' My Thumb," whose speaker, a kind of Bluebeard, imagines possessing his sirens ("The necklace of wishes alive and breathing around your throat") in an atmosphere at once hothouse and *Lost Horizon:*

> There are still other made-up countries
> Where we can hide forever,

> Wasted with eternal desire and sadness,
> Sucking the sherbets, crooning the tunes, naming the names.

Yet these worlds, while drawing out some gorgeous imaginings, generate as much restlessness as the confusing world of daytime plenty. We may share the moment in "Märchenbilder" when "One of those lovelorn sonatas / For wind instruments was riding past on the solemn white horse." With it goes impatience, the desire to escape, a very rich and suggestive ambivalence. The fairy tales

> . . . are empty as cupboards.
> To spend whole days drenched in them, waiting for the next
>   whisper,
> For the word in the next room. This is how the princes must have
>   behaved,
> Lying down in the frugality of sleep.

The third of the exotic poems in this volume, "Scheherazade," suggests what Ashbery is after in such works. He doesn't retell the story of the Sultan and the ideal storyteller, but he does explore with evident interest and desire the condition of that inventive lady. She is part of a world of dry lands, beneath which are rich hidden springs. "An inexhaustible wardrobe has been placed at the disposal / Of each new occurrence." She loves the "colored verbs and adjectives,"

> But most of all she loved the particles
> That transform objects of the same category
> Into particular ones, each distinct
> Within and apart from its own class.
> In all this springing up was no hint
> Of a tide, only a pleasant wavering of the air
> In which all things seemed present.

That love of detail and rich ability to cope with it, an experience of the world without anxiety, without being overwhelmed by plenitude, is rarely felt in Self-Portrait, and therefore to be envied in the world of "Scheherazade." Is it available in the randomness of daily life in America? Ashbery has an affectionate eye and an especially affectionate ear for the comic and recalcitrant details of American life: "sloppy joe on bun" stands not too far from the weigela which "does its dusty thing / In fire-hammered air." In "Mixed Feelings" several young girls photographed lounging around a fighter bomber "circa 1942 vintage" summon up a sense of the resistant particulars which tease the imagination. The fading news-shot flirts with the poet's curiosity. He names the girls of that period affectionately—the Ruths and Lindas and Pats and Sheilas. He wants to know their hobbies. "Aw nerts, / One of them might say, this guy's too much for me." Each side has its innings: the girls are imagined as wanting to dump the poet and go off to the garment center for a cup of coffee; the poet, laughing at their "tiny intelligences" for thinking they're in New York, recognizes that their scene is set in California. What's delightful about this poem is the relaxed exchange of imagining mind with imagined objects, a kind of seesaw in which each is given independent play. Though the girls are dismissed, he is fully prepared to encounter them again in some modern airport as "astonishingly young and fresh as when this picture was made."

One of the most engaging things about Ashbery's book is his own susceptibility to American sprawl, while understanding its impossible cost. There is a serious undertone—or is it the main current?—in a poem called "The One Thing That Can Save America."

> The quirky things that happen to me, and I tell you,
> And you instantly know what I mean?
> What remote orchard reached by winding roads
> Hides them? Where are these roots?

Along with a healthy love of quirkiness, Ashbery expresses a bafflement that any individual radiance is ever communicated from one person to another. The "One Thing" that can "Save America" is a very remote and ironic chance that

> . . . limited
> Steps . . . can be taken against danger
> Now and in the future, in cool yards,
> In quiet small houses in the country,
> Our country, in fenced areas, in cool shady streets.

The poem reaches a political point which it would be oversimplifying, but suggestive, to call "populist."

The enemy, over and over again, is *generality*. The generalizing habit, he tells us in "All and Some," draws us together "at the place of a bare pedestal. / Too many armies, too many dreams, and that's / It." I don't mean that *Self-Portrait in a Convex Mirror* gets down to cracker-barrel preaching. There is too much self-mockery for that.

> Do you remember how we used to gather
> The woodruff, the woodruff? But all things
> Cannot be emblazoned, but surely many
> Can, and those few devoted
> By a caprice beyond the majesty
> Of time's maw live happy useful lives
> Unaware that the universe is a vast incubator.

What I am getting at is that Ashbery's new variety of tone gives him access to many impulses unresolved and frustrated in *The Double Dream of Spring*.

Whitman's invitation for American poets to loaf and invite their souls can't have had many responses more mysterious, peculiar, searching and beautiful than Ashbery's recent poems. Where he will go from here there is, to use one of his titles, "no way of knowing." What *is* important is that Ashbery, who was on speaking terms with both the formalism of the American 1950s and the unbuttoned verse of the 1960s, is now bold and beyond them. His three most recent books have explored apparently contradictory impulses—a melancholy withdrawal and a bewildered, beguiling openness—which stand in provocative tension with one another. Older readers have tended to find the poems "difficult"; younger readers either do not experience that difficulty or see past it, recognizing gestures and a voice that speak directly to them. Perhaps it is reassuring to them: a voice which is honest about its confusions; a voice which lays claim to ravishing visions but doesn't scorn distraction, is in fact prey to it. Ashbery does what all real poets do, and like all innovators his accents seem both too close and too far from the everyday, not quite what we imagine *art* to be. He mystifies and demystifies at once.

HAROLD BLOOM

The Breaking of Form

I turn to a proof-text, Ashbery's long poem, *Self-Portrait in a Convex Mirror*. It would not have been thought a long poem by Browning, but five hundred and fifty-two lines is a long poem for our damaged attention-spans these days. Ashbery, like Stevens, is a profoundly Whitmanian poet, frequently despite appearances. Throughout Ashbery's career, he has centered upon full-scale poems, the great successes being *Fragment*, *The Skaters*, the prose *Three Poems*, *Fantasia on "The Nut-Brown Maid,"* and above all *Self-Portrait*. They are versions or revisions of *Song of Myself*, in some of the same subtle ways that Stevens wrote revisions of Whitman in *The Man with the Blue Guitar* and *Notes toward a Supreme Fiction*. Necessarily, Ashbery also revises Stevens, though more overtly in *Fragment* and *Fantasia* than in the very Whitmanian *Skaters* and *Three Poems*. Both Stevens and Whitman are ancestral presences in *Self-Portrait*, and so is Hart Crane, for the language of the poem engages, however covertly and evasively, the central or Emersonian tradition of our poetry.

Angus Fletcher, in his studies of Spenser, Milton, Coleridge, and Crane, has been developing a liminal poetics or new rhetoric of thresholds, and I follow Fletcher both in my notion of the topoi of "crossings" as images of voice, and in my account of the final revisionary ratio of *apophrades* or reversed belatedness, which is akin to the classical trope of *metalepsis* or transumption and to the Freudian "negation" (*Verneinung*) with its dialectical interplay of the defenses, projection and introjection. I will re-expound and freshly develop these Fletcherian ideas in the reading of Ashbery that follows.

Ashbery divides *Self-Portrait* into six verse-paragraphs, a happy division which I shall exploit, naming them by my apotropaic litany of evasions or revisionary ratios. Swerving easily away from Whitman and from Stevens, Ashbery begins his *clinamen* from tradition by a brilliant description of the painting that gives him his title:

> As Parmigianino did it, the right hand
> Bigger than the head, thrust at the viewer
> And swerving easily away, as though to protect
> What it advertises. A few leaded panes, old beams,
> Fur, pleated muslin, a coral ring run together
> In a movement supporting the face, which swims
> Toward and away like the hand
> Except that it is in repose. It is what is
> Sequestered.

This abrupt opening is itself evasive, the "As" being one of Stevens' "intricate evasions of as." The hand's defensive gesture is a reaction formation or rhetorical *illusio*, since what is meant is that the hand acts as though to advertise what it protects. Here a swerve is another mode of repose, so that defense does not so much protect as it sequesters, a word whose Late Latin antecedent had the meaning "to give up for safekeeping." Ashbery quotes Vasari's description of the halved wooden hall upon which Parmigianino painted what the poet calls the face's "receiving wave/of arrival." Unspoken is each wave's ebbing, but the absent image of departure informs the poem's countersong, which thus makes its initial entrance:

> The soul establishes itself.
> But how far can it swim out through the eyes
> And still return safely to its nest? The surface
> Of the mirror being convex, the distance increases
> Significantly, that is, enough to make the point
> That the soul is a captive, treated humanely, kept
> In suspension, unable to advance much farther
> Than your look as it intercepts the picture.

The poignance of the extreme dualism here will be almost constant throughout the poem. Such dualism is a surprise in Ashbery, yet the pathos is precisely what we expect from the self-portraitist of *Fragment* and *Three Poems*. Certainly the anguish of *Self-Portrait* has an intensity to it that marks Ashbery, yet generally not to this degree. I will suggest that *Self-Portrait*, though meditation rather than lyric, is a poem closely related to the *Ode on a Grecian Urn* and to Stevens' version of Keats's *Ode*, *The Poems of Our Climate*. Three reveries upon aesthetic distance and poetic coldness share a common sorrow, and manifest almost a common glory.

The soul is a captive, but art rather than the body appears to be the captor.

> The soul has to stay where it is,
> Even though restless, hearing raindrops at the pane,
> The sighing of autumn leaves thrashed by the wind,
> Longing to be free, outside, but it must stay
> Posing in this place. It must move
> As little as possible. This is what the portrait says.
> But there is in that gaze a combination
> Of tenderness, amusement and regret, so powerful
> In its restraint that one cannot look for long.
> The secret is too plain. The pity of it smarts,
> Makes hot tears spurt: that the soul is not a soul,
> Has no secret, is small, and it fits
> Its hollow perfectly: its room, our moment of attention.

We can remark that the actual painting looks rather like the actual Ashbery, and that this poet's characteristic expression could not be more accurately described than as "a combination/Of tenderness, amusement, and regret . . . powerful/ In its restraint." The secret *is* irony, is the strong presence that is an abyss, the palpable absence that is the poet's soul. Times and places come together in the *attention* that makes the painter's and the poet's room into the one chamber. But this attention is a Paterian music, surpassing both painting and poetry:

> That is the tune but there are no words.
> The words are only speculation
> (From the Latin *speculum*, mirror):
> They seek and cannot find the meaning of the music.

Angus Fletcher, in his seminal study of "Threshold, Sequence and Personification in Coleridge," reminds us that while numerology suggests a timeless ontology, the *poetics* of number accept our time-bound duration. Poetry, as St. Augustine conceived it, is "the mirror or *speculum* of the world," a mirror that "temporalizes and historicizes number." Ashbery, as a rider of poetic motion, labors at the fiction of duration, but his evident ruefulness at becoming what Stevens' *Asides on the Oboe* called "the human globe" or "the man of glass" is strongly emphasized. The *clinamen* is away from Stevens' celebration of Emersonian centrality, or praise for "the man who has had the time to think enough," and towards a lament for the confinements of art and artist:

> We see only postures of the dream,
> Riders of the motion that swings the face
> Into view under evening skies, with no
> False disarray as proof of authenticity.
> But it is life englobed.
> One would like to stick one's hand
> Out of the globe, but its dimension,
> What carries it, will not allow it.
> No doubt it is this, not the reflex
> To hide something, which makes the hand loom large
> As it retreats slightly.

A representation conveyed only as a mode of limitation; this irony is the peculiar mark of the poem's initial movement of *clinamen*, its swerve away from its origins, which truly are not so much in Parmigianino as in Stevens, particularly in the Whitmanian Stevens of *Poem with Rhythms*, written just after *Asides on the Oboe*, a poem where "The hand between the candle and the wall/Grows large on the wall." The painter's hand as seen by Ashbery must stay within aesthetic limitation:

> There is no way
> To build it flat like a section of wall:
> It must join the segment of a circle . . .

Stevens, like the Whitman of *The Sleepers*, whom he echoes earlier in *Poem with Rhythms*, breaks the limitation by an act of will, by the hyperbole of a Sublime power:

> It must be that the hand
> Has a will to grow larger on the wall,
> To grow larger and heavier and stronger than
> The wall; and that the mind
> Turns to its own figurations and declares,
> *"This image, this love, I compose myself*
> *Of these. In these, I come forth outwardly.*
> *In these, I wear a vital cleanliness,*
> *Not as in air, bright-blue-resembling air,*
> *But as in the powerful mirror of my wish and will."*

A mind that can turn to its own figurations and constitute an ego by love of those figurations, is a Whitmanian, transcendentalizing mind of summer. Such a mind is also that of Freudian Man, since Freud defines narcissism as being the self's love of the ego, a love that by such cathexis veritably *constitutes* the ego. The *speculum* or convex mirror of Ashbery precisely is not the powerful mirror of his wish and will, and in this inclination away from his fathers, the palpable Stevens and the ghostly

Whitman, Ashbery establishes his true *clinamen*. But the cost is severe, and Ashbery accurately observes that his own "pure affirmation," like the painter's, "doesn't affirm anything." Or, to illuminate this properly ironic affirmation by using Fletcher's terms, Ashbery affirms only his own perpetual liminality, the threshold stance that he shares with Hart Crane and with the more delicate, fragile nuances of Whitman's more antithetical moments. Fletcher, writing on Coleridge, seems to be describing the first part of Ashbery's poem:

> While epic tradition supplies conventional models of the threshold, these conventions are always subject to deliberate poetic blurring. . . . poets have wished to subtilize, to dissolve, to fragment, to blur the hard material edge, because poetry hunts down the soul, with its obscure passions, feelings, other-than-cognitive symbolic forms. . . .

Ashbery hunts down the soul, following Parmigianino, and finds only two disparate entities, a hand "big enough/To wreck the sphere," and an ambiguous hollow, a room without recesses, only alcoves, a chamber that defeats change, "stable within/Instability," a globe like our earth, where "there are no words/For the surface, that is,/No words to say what it really is."

A threshold is a crossing, and at the close of this first verse-paragraph Ashbery deliberately fails to negotiate a first crossing, and so fails to get over a threshold of poetic election. The disjunction is from the artist's "pure/Affirmation that doesn't affirm anything" to "The balloon pops, the attention/Turns dully away." Since the attention is the memory that the soul's only room was "our moment of attention," the balloon's pop dislodges the earlier "ping-pong ball" of the painting's stable instability. A failed crossing of election leaves the poet helpless (by choice) as experience threatens to engulf his sense of his own pathos. Ashbery's second verse paragraph is his poem's *tessera,* its antithetical completion which fails all completion. The poet, necessarily unsure of his poethood's survival, is only the synecdoche for voices that overwhelm him:

> I think of the friends
> Who came to see me, of what yesterday
> Was like. A peculiar slant
> Of memory that intrudes on the dreaming model
> In the silence of the studio as he considers
> Lifting the pencil to the self-portrait.
> How many people came and stayed a certain time,
> Uttered light or dark speech that became part of you
> Like light behind windblown fog and sand,
> Filtered and influenced by it, until no part
> Remains that is surely you.

There is an affinity between this peculiar slant of memory's light, and Dickinson's oppressive certain slant of light that imaged death. Both are synecdoches of a kind that belongs to Coleridge's wounding sense of symbol or to Anna Freud's defense mechanism of turning against the self. Anna Freud said of a patient that "by turning her aggressive impulses inwards she inflicted upon herself all the suffering which she had formerly anticipated in the form of punishment by her mother." What I call the revisionary ratio of *tessera* is the poetic transformation of such turning against the self. Ashbery, *as poet*, is compelled to present himself as being only a mutilated part of a whole already mutilated. Why most strong poems in our tradition, from Wordsworth on, manifest this masochistic impulse of representation, *even as they strive to pull away from initial ironies*, is beyond my present capacity to surmise. Yet Ashbery's contribution to this necessity of representation clearly joins the Wordsworthian "enchantment of self with self":

> In the circle of your intentions certain spars
> Remain that perpetuate the enchantment of self with self:
> Eyebeams, muslin, coral. It doesn't matter
> Because these are things as they are today
> Before one's shadow ever grew
> Out of the field into thoughts of tomorrow.

Fletcher remarks that, in the context of poetic thresholds, " 'sequence' means the process and the promise that something will follow something else." Such process begins spatially, Fletcher adds, but ends "on a note of temporal description," perhaps because sequence in a poem is a mode of survival, or fiction of duration. I have experienced my own defensive emotions concerning the sequence of revisionary ratios that I find recurrent in so many poems, quite aside from the defensive reactions I have aroused in others. But the sequence is *there* in the sense that image and trope tend to follow over-determined patterns of evasion. Thus, Ashbery's poem moves on to a third verse paragraph that is a *kenosis*, an isolating defense in which poetic power presents itself as being all but emptied out:

> Tomorrow is easy, but today is uncharted,
> Desolate, reluctant as any landscape
> To yield what are laws of perspective
> After all only to the painter's deep
> Mistrust, a weak instrument though
> Necessary. Of course some things
> Are possible, it knows, but it doesn't know
> Which ones. Some day we will try

> To do as many things as are possible
> And perhaps we shall succeed at a handful
> Of them, but this will not have anything
> To do with what is promised today, our
> Landscape sweeping out from us to disappear
> On the horizon.

This "today" seems not so much uncharted as non-existent. Ashbery displaces "today" by "possible," "promises" or "dream" throughout his third verse-paragraph. A sequence of "possible," "possible," "promised," "promises" and "possibilities" in lines 151–168 is replaced by seven occurrences of "dream" or "dreams" from lines 180–206, where the section ends. All these are metonymies for, reductions of "today," and perform the self-emptying action of *kenosis*: "out from us." Brooding on aesthetic forms, Ashbery attains to a poignant and characteristic sense of "something like living":

> They seemed strange because we couldn't actually see them.
> And we realize this only at a point where they lapse
> Like a wave breaking on a rock, giving up
> Its shape in a gesture which expresses that shape.

Kenosis is Ashbery's prevalent ratio, and his whole poetics is one of "giving up/Its shape in a gesture which expresses that shape." What but the force of the past, the strength of his own poetic tradition, could drive Ashbery on to his next threshold, the disjunctive gap or crossing of solipsism that he leaps between his poem's third and fourth verse paragraphs? The transition is from "a movement/Out of the dream into its codification" to the angelic or daemonic surprise of the face of Parmigianino/Ashbery. The Uncanny or Sublime enters both through repression of the memory of the face, and through a return of the repressed by way of what Freud termed Negation:

> As I start to forget it
> It presents its stereotype again
> But it is an unfamiliar stereotype, the face
> Riding at anchor, issued from hazards, soon
> To accost others, "rather angel than man" (Vasari).
> Perhaps an angel looks like everything
> We have forgotten, I mean forgotten
> Things that don't seem familiar when
> We meet them again, lost beyond telling,
> Which were ours once.

The great modern critic of Negation, foreshadowing the Deconstruction of Derrida and even more of de Man, is Walter Benjamin. I do not believe that Ashbery cites Benjamin here, but it is inevitable that any fresh Sublime should remind us of Benjamin, who joins Freud as the century's theorist of the Sublime. Ashbery's tentative formula "Perhaps an angel looks like everything/We have forgotten" is very close to Benjamin's meditation upon his angel:

> The angel, however, resembles all from which I have had to part: persons and above all things. In the things I no longer have, he resides. He makes them transparent.

This is Benjamin's *aura* or light of the Sublime, truly visible only in the shock of its disappearance, the flight of its repression. Ashbery has lost, he goes on to say, "the whole of me" to the strict otherness of the painter. Yet the loss becomes the Emersonian-Stevensian *surprise*, the advent of power, in a passage that plays against Stevensian images:

> We have surprised him
> At work, but no, he has surprised us
> As he works. The picture is almost finished,
> The surprise almost over, as when one looks out,
> Startled by a snowfall which even now is
> Ending in specks and sparkles of snow.
> It happened while you were inside, asleep,
> And there is no reason why you should have
> Been awake for it, except that the day
> Is ending and it will be hard for you
> To get to sleep tonight, at least until late.

Even the accent suggests very late Stevens, the perception of "Transparent man in a translated world,/In which he feeds on a new known." But instead of the Stevensian "clearness emerging/From cold," with a power surpassing sleep's power, Ashbery opts for a lesser pathos, for an uneasiness, however Sublime, rather than a transcendence. As always, Ashbery represses his own strength, in his quest to maintain an evenness of tone, to avoid climax-impressions. This results in a spooky Sublime, indeed more canny than uncanny, and the reader of Ashbery more than ever has to cultivate a patience for this limpid style, this mode of waiting without seeming to wait. "The surprise, the tension are in the concept/ Rather than its realization." Yet even the concept is hidden, buried deep in the image of depth in this daemonic verse paragraph: "the face/Riding at anchor, issued from hazards." Throughout the poem, the painting is imaged as a ship, appearing to us "in a recurring wave/Of arrival," but still a "tiny, self-important ship/On the surface." Towards the close of the poem, in lines 478–89, a transumption of these earlier tropes will be

accomplished with mysterious urgency, when "A ship/Flying unknown
colors has entered the harbor." The portrait as ship suggests the peril of
poetic art from Spenser to Stevens, but to Ashbery's reader it seems
another version of the oxymorons that concluded his magnificent earlier
meditation, *Soonest Mended,* where the poet speaks of

> . . . learning to accept
> The charity of the hard moments as they are doled out,
> For this is action, this not being sure, this careless
> Preparing, sowing the seeds crooked in the furrow,
> Making ready to forget, and always coming back
> To the mooring of starting out, that day so long ago.

Parmigianino's self-portrait is another "mooring of starting out,"
and such an oxymoron (with its quasi-pun on "morning") is for Ashbery a
characteristic sublimation of unfulfillable poetic desires. A greater sublimation comes in the poem's *askesis,* its fifth verse-paragraph, where Ashbery
perspectivizes against both the painter and his own poetic self. The
perspectives are bewildering, as the "outside" cities and landscapes are
played off against the inner space of painting and of poem:

> Our landscape
> Is alive with filiations, shuttlings;
> Business is carried on by look, gesture,
> Hearsay. It is another life to the city,
> The backing of the looking glass of the
> Unidentified but precisely sketched studio. It wants
> To siphon off the life of the studio, deflate
> Its mapped space to enactments, island it.

If the soul is not a soul, then the inside/outside, mind/nature
metaphor is rendered inadequate, aside from its built-in inadequacies of
endless perspectivism. Ashbery boldly sets out to rescue the metaphor he
has helped to bury. A cold wind of aesthetic and vital change rises to
destroy Ashbery's kind of urban pastoral, and the painter, as the poet's
surrogate, is urged to see and hear again, albeit in a necessarily illusory
present:

> Your argument, Francesco,
> Had begun to grow stale as no answer
> Or answers were forthcoming. If it dissolves now
> Into dust, that only means its time had come
> Some time ago, but look now, and listen. . . .

But though Ashbery goes on to urge the normality and correctness
of metaphor, such a rescue operation must fail, reminding us perhaps that

the prestige of metaphor and of sublimation tends to rise and fall together in cultural history. A third and most crucial threshold-crossing takes place as Ashbery moves reluctantly away from metaphor and into the giant *metalepsis* or ratio of *apophrades* that concludes and is the glory of his poem. The long final sixth verse-paragraph (ll. 311–552) begins with a surprised sense of achieved identification, introjecting both the painting and the poet's death:

> A breeze like the turning of a page
> Brings back your face: the moment
> Takes such a big bite out of the haze
> Of pleasant intuition it comes after.

Before describing this crossing and the superb section it introduces, I digress again into Fletcher's theories of threshold, sequence and personification, as they were my starting-point for thinking about transumption. Coleridge credited Spenser with being the great inventor in English poetry of the "land of Faery, that is, of mental space." Fletcher follows Coleridge in relating such mental space to daemonic agency, personification and topical allusion. What Fletcher's grandest innovation does is to alter our understanding of personification, by compounding it both with transumption and the pun. Complete projection or introjection is paranoia, which means, as Fletcher says, that "madness is complete personification." But most strong poets avoid this generative void, though all pause upon its threshold. John Hollander, following Fletcher, has traced the figurative power of poetic echo and its link to the Post-Romantic transformations of *metalepsis* or transumption, transformations which based themselves upon Milton's transumptive use of similes:

> . . . the peculiar quality of Miltonic simile, by which, as Dr. Johnson put it, he "crowds the imagination," is a mode of transumption—the *multitudinousness* of the Satanic legions in Book I is like that of autumn leaves, but unclaimed manifestly for the comparison are the other likenesses (both are fallen, dead) whose presence is shadowed only in the literalizing of the place name of Vallombrosa.

Hollander cites the mythographic commentary by George Sandys on Ovid's story of Echo, where Sandys quotes Ausonius and then adds that "the image of the voice so often rendred, is as that of the face reflected from one glasse to another, melting by degrees, and every reflection more weake and shady than the former." This, Hollander implies, is the predicament that Milton and his heirs escaped by making their images of voice transumptive. And this is precisely the predicament that Ashbery evades in *Self-Portrait,* and particularly in its sixth or transumptive section to which I now return.

The breeze whose simile is a page's turning, and that brings back the self-portrait, returns more than two hundred lines later in the closing passage of the poem:

> . . . the ache
> Of this waking dream can never drown out
> The diagram still sketched on the wind,
> Chosen, meant for me and materialized
> In the disguising radiance of my room.
>
> The hand holds no chalk
> And each part of the whole falls off
> And cannot know it knew, except
> Here and there, in cold pockets
> Of remembrance, whispers out of time.

The wind transumes the breeze, returning the self-portrait to an introjected earliness, an identification of poet and painter. The pockets of remembrance, though cold as painting and poem are cold, remain the winds whispering *out of* time, in a multiple play upon "out of," which refers us back to Keats' cold pastoral that teased us out of time, as did eternity. The echo of the *Grecian Urn* reinforces the echo of the *Nightingale*'s "waking dream." Death, as in Keats' odes, is what the figurations defend against, quite directly. So, going back to the start of the sixth verse paragraph, the page-turning similitude is necessarily followed directly by the introjection of death, in a Crossing of Identification that links not only painter and poet, but also the tragic Alban Berg and *Cymbeline.* Reflections upon the common mortality of artists lead to earlier presages of aesthetic whispers out of time:

> I go on consulting
> This mirror that is no longer mine
> For as much brisk vacancy as is to be
> My portion this time. And the vase is always full
> Because there is only just so much room
> And it accommodates everything. This sample
> One sees is not to be taken as
> Merely that, but as everything as it
> May be imagined outside time—

The vase, emblem both of Keats' *Ode* and Stevens' *The Poems of Our Climate,* is as full as the poet's own time is briskly vacant, the oxymoron strengthening Ashbery's own recovery of strength in the poem.

A meditation upon Ashbery's familiar "permanent anomaly," a certain kind of erotic illumination, leads on to a new sense of earliness, a metaleptic reversal of the poem's ironic opening:

> All we know
> Is that we are a little early, that
> Today has that special, lapidary
> Todayness that the sunlight reproduces
> Faithfully in casting twig-shadows on blithe
> Sidewalks. No previous day would have been like this.
> I used to think they were all alike,
> That the present always looked the same to everybody
> But this confusion drains away as one
> Is always cresting into one's present.

What shadows this freshly achieved earliness is the doubt that still more art is needed: "Our time gets to be veiled, compromised/By the portrait's will to endure." Creation being out of our hands, our distance from even our own art seems to become greater. In this intensification of estrangement, Ashbery's meditation gradually rejects the paradise of art, but with enormous nostalgias coloring farewell. A sublime pun, fulfilling Fletcher's vision of threshold rhetoric, is the climax of this poignant dismissal, which reverberates as one of Ashbery's greatest passages, majestic in the aesthetic dignity of its mingled strength and sadness:

> Therefore I beseech you, withdraw that hand,
> Offer it no longer as shield or greeting,
> The shield of a greeting, Francesco:
> There is room for one bullet in the chamber. . . .

The chamber, room of poet's and painter's self-portraits, room as moment of attention for the soul not a soul, fitting perfectly the hollow of its tomb, is also the suicide (or Russian roulette?) of a self-regarding art. Ashbery's poem too is the shield of a greeting, its defensive and communicative functions inextricably mixed. Yet Ashbery's reading of his tradition of utterance, and my reading of Ashbery, are gestures of restitution. Achieved dearth of meaning is exposed as an oxymoron, where the "achieved" outweighs the "dearth." The antithetical critic, following after the poet of his moment and his climate, must oppose to the abysses of Deconstruction's ironies a supermimesis achieved by an art that will not abandon the self to language, the art of Ashbery's earlier *Fragment:*

> The words sung in the next room are unavoidable
> But their passionate intelligence will be studied in you.

DOUGLAS CRASE

The Prophetic Ashbery

W e are used to hearing of poets so private they speak for us all. We are not used to hearing, however, that
John Ashbery is among them. Anyone who has ever been baffled by
Ashbery's work will understand the temptation to conclude that here we
have a poet so private he is truly private, so difficult he is truly inaccessible. But to arrive at that dead end is exasperating, if only because the
reputation leads one to expect much more. Why shouldn't people expect
access to a poetry so widely honored for what it is doing with their
language? Why shouldn't they expect the poet, as Emerson promised, to
apprise us "not of his wealth, but of the commonwealth"? These are not
retrograde or feeble expectations, and because I think they are powerfully
met in the work of John Ashbery I would champion him not as our most
private poet, but as our most public one. The difficulty with Ashbery is
that his poetry is *so* public, so accurately a picture of the world we live in,
that it scarcely resembles anything we have ever known. Just so, the
present is indeed a world none of us has ever known, because the words to
describe it can be put together only after the fact. When the poet does put
them together the combination comes as a shock. Understandably, one
may at first regard that combination as hermetically private. Only gradually do we realize that it describes the public world we were living in just
moments ago—that some prophet has arrived with news of the commonwealth.

I suppose "prophet" sounds as though I am claiming a generous
role for the poet when anyone ought to know that the current audience

---

for poetry is limited first in size and second in its willingness to suspend not disbelief, but irony. I would guess also that readers of poetry are even more disaffected than most when it comes to the commonwealth. They are not an audience to whom a poet as savvy as John Ashbery would innocently address Emersonian prophecies. True enough, but let me offer a proposition that should not be very surprising: the audience that reads his poetry is not always the one for which the poet writes. The events that produce a poet are many and various, but one of them is surely not his first contact with an English professor or his first reading at the local poetry project. The audience he would love to reach is more likely "the fair-sheaved many" who do not give a hoot for poetry. It will include the father he could never please, the mother bewildered by her strange offspring, the younger brother who died at the age of nine. It is made up, in other words, of all the unreachable people, the ones who appear in Ashbery's "Melodic Trains" as figures on the station platform while the poet watches them from the standing train. Though he identifies them as "my brothers," it is precisely their remoteness that accounts for the plaintive tone in which he continues.

> If I were to get down now to stretch, take a few steps
>
> In the wearying and world-weary clouds of steam like great
> White apples, might I just through proximity and aping
> Of postures and attitudes communicate this concern of mine
> To them? That their jagged attitudes correspond to mine,
>
> That their beefing strikes answering silver bells within
> My own chest . . . ?

No, he could not communicate his concern, at least not in poetry. If they are reading at all, his brothers probably are occupied with the latest manual on how to get more out of life, and poetry will be far down the list of recommended exercises. One knows this, but it does not lessen the insistent wish to reach them. Instead, one dresses the wish in any number of disguises—ironic or even slapstick. In this way you can prophesy to your brothers all you want without fear of looking foolish before the worldly audience that comes to your readings. You release a little horse that "trots up with a letter in its mouth" or in Hollywood fashion you direct a butler to enter "with a letter on a tray/Whose message is to change everything" or you send some fool "shouting into the forest at nightfall . . . / News of some thing we know and care little of." The poetry audience laughs at the joke, but the regularity with which Ashbery returns to the device makes me believe that, though he too is laughing, he is hopefully serious about the prophecy's having arrived.

Arrival is not the same as being understood, however, and we are told that the former Quiz Kid was at first hurt by the baffled response to his work. By now he may enjoy being a mystery, having confirmed his suspicion that it is the "mystery" part of truth that makes it marketable. But why does he remain so mysterious? There are two reasons, and the first is his style. By itself, his style is so beguiling or so outrageous, depending on your point of view, that the transfixed reader is powerless to get beyond it. The beguiled explain their condition by saying Ashbery does not "work" or "mean" like other poetry. The outraged assert that it is not poetry at all, or, if it is, then its essential ingredient must be obscurity. But no prophet sets out to be permanently obscure—where is the immortality in that? And no master stylist is after a result that fails to "work" its magic. With some effort, and some willingness too, I think we ought to be able to find his style out. The second reason Ashbery remains mysterious is his choice of subjects or, it would be better to say, his context. We are accustomed to pinched poetry, the kind whose context is one Incan rock, and we know how to deal with that. In Ashbery we encounter a poet who, as his friend Frank O'Hara wrote, "is always marrying the whole world." Readers who prefer their Incan rock may agree with the reviewer who complained of Ashbery that "you can't possibly quote anything 'out of context' since there is never a context." But every poet marks out his subject matter, and it is not possible for him to write independent of that context. It is simply that the Ashbery context is so wide open that it takes a great deal of reading before you can visit its boundaries. Until then, you may understandably feel that the signs along the way point in all directions and nowhere in particular.

Style and context do not occur separately in a poem, and the one is ultimately meaningful only as it is enfolded in the other. Much foolishness can be produced by trying to consider them as things apart. But this essay is not a poem, and so there is no alternative. I must try to untangle them, doing as little violence to their connections as possible, so that when they are reunited we may have some idea of how they came to make a coherent whole in the first place. I am going to begin with context—the context of a poet who married the world.

John Ashbery announced his engagement in the opening line of his first major book: "We see us as we truly behave." The strictness and the generosity are in that "truly." The strictness is that we will not see us as we might have behaved or as we ought to behave. The generosity is that we are going on a tour of the world as it might look on "a day of general honesty," knowing there is nothing larger or more extraordinary. It will be a vast excursion, and we can expect the itinerary to be recalcitrant even as we follow it: "As laughing cadets say, 'In the evening/ Everything has a schedule, if you can find out what it is.' "

One way to learn the schedule is to go along with it; in retrospect it is easier to see what it was. If this sounds too spineless, think of it as a version of Keats's negative capability. It takes a strong constitution to live into the present so ruthlessly available to whatever is waiting there. And I do not think it exaggerates to say that, of the poets I know, Ashbery is most ruthlessly available to the present. In our time, that present is largely to be found in the curricula of the city and its sophisticated outposts. Arguably, the present has been there longer than this; yet we have grown up with a literature that would look energetically in almost any other direction—to the frontier, the sea, to Walden, or to a room in Amherst—in order, as it claims, to front the essential facts of life. Though he started life on a farm in upstate New York, Ashbery has done his "fronting" in the great metropolis—Boston, Paris, New York, and their suburbs—and a list of his cultural entanglements and cultured acquaintances would be stag-gering, many times longer than the lists of names he in fact included in the pages of *The Vermont Notebook*. Larry Rivers, Alex Katz, Willem de Kooning, Harold Rosenberg, Elaine de Kooning, James Schuyler, Jane Freilicher, Kenneth Koch—just a few names from these lists are enough to stand for the enormous and "timely" experiences that were there when Ashbery was. Nor are we star-struck if we insist on the importance of such a constellation. We are not star-struck to note that Mannerist painters Pontormo, Rosso, and Parmigianino, say, were all in Rome before the Sack of 1527 and that Rosso and Parmigianino worked side by side there for four years. It is important that, one with the other or one against the other, they worked toward a "timely" style that, unclear as it may have been to them, is now timelessly clearer to us. In making my case, I do not mean to suggest the Hamptons today equals Rome before the Sack. But I would not insist on the differences either. So much as John Ashbery has moved in a timely world, just so much is he able to make that world available to us.

Just so much, as long as we remember that negative capability was to be our guide. "The mind / Is so hospitable, taking in everything / Like boarders," says the title poem from *Houseboat Days*. Wallace Stevens reports that his mind was similarly commodious; yet I think he was choosier than Ashbery when it came to which boarders to take in. Stevens, we remember, proposed to "live in the world, but outside of existing conceptions of it." Ashbery not only lives very much in the world, he seems to live by all existing conceptions of it simultaneously, regardless of how contradictory the lot may be. How else would it be possible to bring over accurately into language the ripe complexity of us as we truly behave in this almost "terminally sophisticated" society? When you put his capacity for taking in boarders together with the timely milieus in which the man has moved, the result is a brilliant, and thus dense, mingling of attitudes and their languages. Just as all colors together equal no color, so what looked to the reviewer like no context is instead many contexts. Or, to use another illustration, it is many contexts tangled into one another like parts of a score—interesting in themselves, perhaps, but best all at once:

> The conductor, a glass of water, permits all kinds
> Of wacky analogies to glance off him, and, circling outward,
> To bring in the night. Nothing is too "unimportant"
> Or too important, for that matter. The newspaper and the
>   garbage
> Wrapped in it, the over, the under.

I hope I am not taken to mean that negative capability makes Ashbery timely, and headed for timelessness, because it prints out a rebus only for the painters, poets, and culturati who have been his friends. No, in the city one also sees a great many "real" people, most of them strangers. They come and go as types; one sees their faces and hears their news, and, as the poem I just quoted puts it: "Nothing is too 'unimportant' / Or too important, for that matter." The papers are on the stands, the radio is plugged in, films arrive at the movie theater, and all are filled with suggestive abstractions. To the extent that the city includes the past, it is alive with all the suggestions of our culture: "Rome where Francesco / Was at work during the Sack . . . / Vienna where the painting is today . . . / New York / Where I am now, which is a logarithm / Of other cities." With your Keatsian apparatus, you can be as big as the city you live in. But, unless we think this must be a painless way to gain an empire, you can also be as small, as passion-strewn, as constantly slapped up or yanked down—in other words, at civil war. "Is not a man better than a town?" asked Emerson, implying that the two were different. The question could hardly occur to Ashbery: "Whatever the villagers / Are celebrating with less conviction is / The less you."

A good deal is said about the impenetrable solipsism of this poet who is so private he is truly private. It is said in exasperation and as an excuse to quit reading, and its best authority is the poet himself, who will tell us, as he does in *Three Poems*, that his "elaborate veiw" really comes from "looking inside." If he is so solipsistic, how can he mean anything? But grant that Keats was right, that there is such a thing as negative capability, and you have begun to answer the question yourself. For if Keats was right, then the elaborate landscape of the city and of the poet's timely entanglements in it may indeed be found, in their contrariness, by "looking inside." At one time or another, the mind will believe every squabbling part of itself, the poem mean everything it says. So the trick is turned: How can it be solipsism if he means everything?

> Everything is landscape:
> Perspectives of cliffs beaten by innumerable waves.
> More wheatfields than you can count, forests
> With disappearing paths, stone towers
> And finally and above all the great urban centers, with
> Their office buildings and populations, at the center of which
> We live our lives, made up of a great quantity of isolated
>   instants
> So as to be lost at the heart of a multitude of things.

It has become a cliché to note that the quantity of information in the world has exploded while space has collapsed, and the cliché does not make it less real. But to say we have turned into a global village is inaccurate. "Global" is a nod in the right direction, but "village" is a bow to nostalgia. Our culture is nothing so simple or settled as a village. It is more of a stellar explosion caught in an earthly jar, a revolving explosion of needs and demands and diversions, and in the midst of this tumult we take our chances on "daily life." *This* is the context of John Ashbery, because only in this reality can we see us as we "truly" behave. While he was living in Paris, Ashbery wrote in praise of Raymond Roussel a line that might have been written prospectively for himself: "it is no longer the imaginary world but the real one, and it is exploding all around us like a fireworks factory in one last dazzling orgy of light and sound." To be aware of this context is an immense help to knowing the poems. For example, if a fireworks of attitudes competes for the same pen (or typewriter in this case), won't they cross, won't they comment on one another? Yes, they will, sometimes in the poem itself and sometimes from offstage. So to have missed the context is also to miss this commentary—commentary that provides some of the best moments, playful and rueful, that Ashbery can offer.

There are good precedents for such serious play, though probably more in English poetry than our own. I am thinking especially of the "influence" who peeps out at us over two Ashbery titles ("The Picture of Little J. A. in a Prospect of Flowers," and "As One Put Drunk into the

Packet-Boat")—and that is Andrew Marvell. Like Ashbery, Marvell saw a lot of the "timely" world and, like Ashbery, seems to find a single point of view impossible, not even desirable. The masterly example is "The Garden," and a masterly reading of it is the one by Joseph Summers. The extravagant first stanza has begun, and what Summers says of it strikes me as exactly right: "The outrageous suavity and the calculated rationality . . . of the lines invite us to smile and warn us of extravagances to come. The poem is going to claim *everything* for a life of infinite leisure in the garden; but the ways in which it makes its claim reveal the urbanity of the poet who created this fictional voice, his recognition of values beyond those which he pretends to dismiss and those which he pretends exhaust all the pleasant and virtuous possibilities of human life." I have quoted this remark because it goes directly to the point I am talking about. Consider the opening of John Ashbery's "Definition of Blue," which has caused its share of trouble.

> The rise of capitalism parallels the advance of romanticism
> And the individual is dominant until the close of the
>   nineteenth century.
> In our own time, mass practices have sought to submerge the
>   personality
> By ignoring it, which has caused it instead to branch out in all
>   directions
> Far from the permanent tug that used to be its notion of
>   "home."

Robert Pinsky writes in his recent book that this opening is too funny for us "to take any subsequent idea quite seriously." If I read him right, he is disappointed because the poem therefore "fails to convince" us of the value advanced in its lovely last lines. But we do not ask to be convinced of the argument in "The Garden." On the contrary, the "outrageous suavity and the calculated rationality of the lines invite us to smile and warn us of extravagances to come." Like Marvell, Ashbery is eating his cake and having it too, being serious and having fun. To know the wide context in which this is possible is to be let in on both seriousness and fun ourselves.

If we have decided, then, to give up our grumpiness and go along with the play, we will find it necessary to break out of the confines of the single poem. One attitude heckles another from poem to poem or forgives it from collection to collection. You can trace this in the recurrent appearance of the American garden suburb, whose boredom and beauty make for one of Ashbery's dearest subjects, much as another kind of garden became one of Marvell's. *A Nest of Ninnies*, the novel written in collaboration with James Schuyler (which Auden called a minor classic), is about some nice people who live on Long Island, read Proust, go out for drinks at Howard Johnson's, and escort their European guests on a tour of the Walt Whitman Shopping Plaza. Then there is "Farm Implements and Rutabagas in a Landscape," where the very form—the troubador's sestina— becomes a deft satire because of its content. The envoy ends roughly: "Popeye chuckled and scratched / His balls: it sure was pleasant to spend a day in the country." But the roughness is charmed in the same collection by the graceful "Evening in the Country," though we can hear Mr. Offstage Attitude still sniping away in the wings. One has to read twice the last phrase in these lines: "things eventually take care of themselves / With rest and fresh air and a good view of things." In "Pyrography" the theme hangs on: "At Bolinas / The houses doze and seem to wonder why . . . / Why be hanging on here?" But again it is both more fun and more poignant if we read this back against its echo in "The One Thing That Can Save America." That earlier poem begins fed up with the "overgrown suburbs, / Places of known civic pride, of civil obscurity"; yet it closes with an elegiac and mixed affirmation brought by another of those pro- phetic messages, this one telling of danger,

> . . . and the mostly limited
> Steps that can be taken against danger
> Now and in the future, in cool yards,
> In quiet small houses in the country,
> Our country, in fenced areas, in cool shady streets.

Realism, nostalgia, goofiness, and even a shred or two of the American Dream—in Ashbery's suburbia they all are available at once.

There are more complicated examples of serious play in Ashbery than this approach-avoidance bout with the suburbs. Yet this gentle contest can serve as a manageable illustration of how one mixes the wit and the sadness, the transport and the debunking, because the world is so contradictory that there is no single attitude clean enough to live life straight through. It is not always easy to keep many outlooks in the air at once, but it has been done. "I contain multitudes," said the Whitman who seems to have divided his time in Manhattan equally among going to the opera, drinking at Pfaff's, and stalking the trolleys. It is not one's first impression of him, but in the context of the real city he lived in his statement suggests a certain savoir faire. To repeat, the world is very much bigger now, in terms of all the information blazing into one man-size neocortex. To contain multitudes—the fireworks of experience, language, and belief—must now require an even greater, more elastic savoir faire.

Something strange is creeping across me.
La Celestina has only to warble the first few bars
Of "I Thought about You" or something mellow from
Amadigi di Gaula for everything—a mint-condition can
Of Rumford's Baking Powder, a celluloid earring, Speedy
Gonzales, the latest from Helen Topping Miller's fertile
Escritoire, a sheaf of suggestive pix on greige, deckle-edged
Stock—to come clattering through the rainbow trellis
Where Pistachio Avenue rams the 2300 block of Highland
Fling Terrace.

That is only the beginning of Ashbery's "Daffy Duck in Hollywood," which contains more multitudes to come: the Fudds' garage, the Gadsden Purchase, the Princesse de Clèves and the Wallets (including Skeezix); bocages, tanneries, and water meadows; London and St. Petersburg. We cannot reduce this to the still privilege we once expected from poetry. This is the exploded culture in which we truly behave, and it is no help to cry "No context!" because we cannot find one small enough to suit us. Here is no Incan rock but an avalanche—no still point in a turning world but the turning world itself, and it is exploding all around us like a fireworks factory in one last dazzling orgy of light and sound.

To fit the context of the turning world he lives in, Ashbery made the style we call "Ashbery." In fact, having named it "Ashbery" has apparently released some readers from the worry of whether it is also English. In one fundamental way, of course, it isn't English at all—it is American. But, whichever, it represents our language in the sense Wallace Stevens meant when he said a poet's dialect was analogous to common speech and yet not that speech. A poet's dialect is our language gone a little screwy, and it is the screwy part that gives us back the odd things we ordinarily say and do, only they come back a little odder. This is why screwiness may signify "Prophet Speaking." On the other hand, it may also signify a fake.

People in this country are notoriously leery of fakes, regardless of their being regularly taken in by them. And those of us who read poetry are no exception to this national virtue. One test many Americans use to identify fakery in a poet these days is the test of diction. If the suspect moves haltingly from word to word, if those words are tight little Anglo-Saxon islands, each one surfacing after obvious struggle in the depths, then the speaker is ipso facto cleared, his authenticity and our integrity proved. But if his words flow like the sea itself, if they alternately recede in demotic eddies and advance in Latin swells, then we turn away from him, secure in knowing we met temptation and were not weak. For poetry this makes a curious test. Yet it was current long before its current proponents took it up. I haven't read Bronson Alcott's *Psyche* (not poems, though surely meant to be poetic). Still, I can sympathize with the abashed Alcott, who received from the hand of Emerson these shalts and shalt nots, via the United States mail: "To the prophetic tone belongs simplicity, not variety, not taste, not criticism. As a book of practical holiness, this seems to me not effective. This is fanciful, playful, ambitious, has a periphrastic style & masquerades in the language of scripture. . . . The prophet should speak a clear discourse straight home to the conscience in the language of earnest conversation." When it comes to virtuosity, we are a nation of prigs. Fanciful, playful, ambitious, periphrastic, a masquerade—what an indictment! And not one count on which we could acquit John Ashbery.

Even Ashbery's titles are playful, periphrastic, a masquerade—taking "As One Put Drunk into the Packet-Boat" from an index of first lines is hardly straight home to the conscience—and they deserve their fraction of credit for whatever confusion the Ashbery style stirs up. These titles are like the hand that looms forward in Francesco Mazzola's self-portrait, each one "thrust at the viewer / And swerving easily away, as though to protect / What it advertises." In fact, "Self-Portrait in a Convex Mirror" is a good example because it is so frequently read as if Emerson's commandment held, as if this had been written straight home to the conscience. Why shouldn't it read as it seems to read? Here is the painter's self-portrait, here is the poet looking at the painter's self-portrait, and here, therefore, is the poet's self-portrait. The whole thing is commonly referred to now as "Self-Portrait," revealing our bias toward the private. Unquestionably, that is one way to read "Self-Portrait in a Convex Mirror." What troubles me is that we should fasten doggedly on the seeming straightforwardness of one title and one poem in the midst of a canon we know is everywhere else artful and foxy. What troubles me is that we should ignore the hint, there in the first four lines, that things are being simultaneously protected and advertised. What troubles me is that we have indeed swerved away with the hand thrust at us—"Self-Portrait"—and left the protected remainder of the title very much alone. What does it signify, "in a Convex Mirror"?

Since there is no answer that is not manifold and suspect, I may as well brave it and offer my own. On the poem's evidence I take the convex mirror to stand for at least three things beyond that physical object it actually is. One is the imagination, the convex brain, the thing called negative capability: "And the vase is always full / Because there's only just so much room / And it accommodates everything." Two is the city, especially New York, which provides the imagination with its raw material: "We have seen the city; it is the gibbous / Mirrored eye of an insect. All things happen / On its balcony and are resumed within." And, three, the one I want to focus on now, is the poet's style—for how else does an artist make himself an example if not in his own style? And what better way for Ashbery to describe his own style than by reference to this Mannerist painter whose work is in many ways a tantalizing parallel to his own?

> The consonance of the High Renaissance
> Is present, though distorted by the mirror.
> What is novel is the extreme care in rendering
> The velleities of the rounded reflecting surface
> (It is the first mirror portrait),
> So that you could be fooled for a moment
> Before you realize the reflection
> Isn't yours.

Mannerism is almost a synonym for virtuosity and, true to our priggishness, we are apt to shun it as vulgar and inauthentic. But the idea of *maniera* in early art criticism implied almost the opposite. It was borrowed from the literature of manners, where it was something to boast about. If you had *maniera*, you had style. You had grace, sophistication, savoir faire. So when it was applied to the work of Parmigianino, say, it originally meant much the same thing: here was grace, here was elegance, here was "the stylish style." So stylish was his style that Parmigianino eventually became a verb, *imparmiginare*, "to submerge expression of the subject in elegance and delicacy." I cannot make a verb so sonorous from "Ashbery," but the meaning of *imparmiginare* suggests what parallels are being dangled before us. To submerge the subject in an elegance that knows just where and how far it is breaking the rules—this is not the mannerism we speak of when we want to say someone is "affected." This is Mannerism given its due capital, the style of the savoir faire.

Getting back to poetry, there is a pleasurable symmetry to be had from thinking that the same times that produced Mannerism in painting would also produce it in her sister, poetry—the same times, if for English we allow for a cultural lag long enough to include the author of "To His Coy Mistress." In his book on Renaissance style, Wylie Sypher makes a nice case for this lag and for the similarities at either end of it. Of the "Coy Mistress" he writes: "Marvell's sharp but unsustained attack—brilliant, sensitive, private—is like the loose and surprising adjustment and counter-adjustment of figure to figure in Parmigianino's paintings, with their evidence of subject stress." Isn't it another pleasant symmetry that the prize-winning *Self-Portrait in a Convex Mirror* begins with just this Marvell peeping over its first title and ends with just this Parmigianino reflected in its last? Of course, the idea of guilt by association is something of an outrage (though less outrageous, one sees, in criticism), and it would be a tenacious conspiracy that could span centuries to include Ashbery, Marvel, and Mazzola. Yet the choice of titles was Ashbery's, not ours, and one has as evidence against him his remarks on the arbitrary titles of Tanguy's pictures: "Yet the fact that most of them are titled implies that a choice has been made, and that the purpose of this choice is to extend the range of the picture's meaning by slanting it in a certain direction."

Now in poetry there are a number of figures that are likely to be found in a stylish style. Not surprisingly, they are also found in "the sublime." Not surprisingly, because only so far as these figures are reckless with the sublime will they betray a subjective stress analogous to the self-consciousness of Mannerism—as Mannerism betrayed its stress by recklessness with the High Renaissance. Longinus named these figures with some big words, and, because it is more convenient in discourse to name a thing than to have to describe it over and over, I am going to introduce them by their big names and perpetuate the error, in a way.

1. First is *periphrasis,* who himself likes to name things. But periphrasis is never able to land on a name outright; instead he goes at it around Robin Hood's barn, and arriving at one haystack of the thing he names *that.* Therefore periphrasis is especially good at naming unnameable things, like attitudes.

> . . . a kind of fence-sitting
> Raised to the level of an esthetic ideal.

2. Periphrasis has a cousin, *apophasis,* who names things by unnaming them. Apophasis is like Peter being interrogated; his denials prove a great deal.

> the soul is not a soul

3. Third is that rogue *paranomasia,* who likes to make fun of the things he names. We know him most often as pun, but he is agile in a variety of circumstances.

> You walk five feet along the shore, and you duck
> As a common heresy sweeps over.

4. Another prankster is *polyptoton.* He likes to keep us in the dark as to your pronouns, so one cannot be sure if I will be doing the talking, let alone what tense we might have been in.

> But I was trying to tell you about a strange thing
> That happened to me, but this is no way to tell about it, . . .
>
> And one is left sitting in the yard . . .
>
> As though it would always happen in some way
> And meanwhile since we are all advancing
> It is sure to come about in spite of everything
> On a Sunday, where you are left sitting
> In the shade.

5. *Hyperbole* is a show-off. He more than names, he swaggers—and therefore he sometimes gets mixed up. Longinus thought the better hyperboles would conceal themselves, but what fun is it getting all dressed up if you can't go to town?

> . . . you my friend
> Who saved me from the mill pond of chill doubt
> As to my own viability, and from the proud village
> Of bourgeois comfort and despair, the mirrored spectacles of grief.

6. But the real virtuoso is *hyperbaton,* mad for taking chances—the most reckless of them all. Hyperbaton will mix words that should never be mixed, like someone who invites rival lovers to the same cocktail party just to watch the sparks fly. Even more exhilarating, he will climb a great slide of words and let go, sure as gravity that chance will bring him out to truth at the bottom.

> They all came, some wore sentiments
> Emblazoned on T-shirts, proclaiming the lateness
> Of the hour, and indeed the sun slanted its rays
> Through branches of Norfolk Island pine as though
> Politely clearing its throat, and all ideas settled
> In a fuzz of dust under the trees when it's drizzling:
> The endless games of Scrabble, the boosters,
> The celebrated omelette au Cantal, and through it
> The roar of time plunging unchecked through the sluices
> Of the days, dragging every sexual moment of it
> Past the lenses: the end of something.

His recklessness makes hyperbaton a public danger. Longinus says, "He carries his audience with him to share in the dangers of his long inversions." But like other public dangers he is powerfully convincing, since his conclusions seem not thought up but passionately wrung from him, almost against his will.

In addition to these six, there are other figures, or near-figures, that lack such elegant and accurate names. They are likewise more interesting as they are twisted away from the ideal. Longinus took up one of them, diction, but the chapters in which he discussed it are largely lost, so we will have to continue on our own.

7. *Diction* can be a matron or a streetwalker, depending on how she decides to dress. At her most vulgar she could hook even Emerson. This girl is adept with clichés, and she can arrange them to put out a stinging accuracy.

> We hold these truths to be self-evident:
> That ostracism, both political and moral, has
> Its place in the twentieth-century scheme of things.

8. *Irony* is getting to be a brat. She may be forthright as satire or burlesque, but, since she is often timid in the nature of brats, she also likes to sow her discord on the sly. One of her amusements might be called *épater les critiques,* including Harold Bloom (as in "The Other Tradition"), Ruskin ("The Gazing Grain"), or even Horace ("And *Ut Pictura Poesis* Is Her Name"). Nor is irony above biting the hand that writes her, as when she prompts Daffy Duck in Hollywood to despair of his own avian self-portrait in a convex mirror.

> I scarce dare approach me mug's attenuated
> Reflection in yon hubcap.

9. *Surrealism* is an ingenious housewife, forever rearranging the furniture, and she is also fed up with being thought French. She knows her Emerson ("Bare lists of words are found suggestive, to an imaginative and excited mind") and she can squeeze an analogy out of the barest list. She had a field day in *The Vermont Notebook,* but often she gets stuck in the house, where she understandably insists on the sad variety of woe.

> And a sigh heaves from all the small things on earth,
> The books, the papers, the old garters and union-suit buttons
> Kept in a white cardboard box somewhere.

Last will come prophecy, but before we can consider her without interruption we have to take time out so those two laggards, parergon and paralipomenon, can make their appearance.

10. *Parergon* likes to enter from offstage or even to speak offstage when you least expect it—as if to imply that it is by no means settled who are the principals and who the walk-ons in the play. Being ornamental enough to attract attention, parergon also likes to turn up in unlikely locations so you will question where the real action is taking place.

> A few black smudges
> On the outer boulevards, like squashed midges
> And the truth becomes a hole, something one has always known,
> A heaviness in the trees, and no one can say
> Where it comes from, or how long it will stay—

11. *Paralipomenon* has never been easy to keep track of either and is continually being neglected or overlooked. When recovered as a supplement, however, paralipomenon gets its revenge—because the whole rest of the text is now characterized as much by what it left out, and may have left out still, as by what it included. Paralipomenon may come at the beginning, midsection, or end, but the revenge is sweetest when it comes as an afterthought.

> My wife
> Thinks I'm in Oslo—Oslo, France, that is.

12. Now on to *prophecy*, who enters sometimes as parergon or paralipomenon, but who also appears in so many other shapes we will have to extend her gender, Tiresias fashion. He and she are almost a summary of the other figures, but a summary never quite in the picture, and they are therefore sad with yearning. No matter how deeply she may yearn to influence the action, he also knows they must remain forever outside that action, emblematic only, like the prophetic figures who appear in the background of *The Marriage of St. Catherine* or the *Madonna of the Long Neck* (both by Parmigianino).

> Wait by this
> Mistletoe bush and you will get the feeling of really
> Being out of the world and with it.

So, although prophecy never gives up the attempt, his or her voice arrives oddly anomalous to its source or object, as letters on trays or as fools shouting into the night.

> . . . words like disjointed beaches
> Brown under the advancing signs of the air.

By introducing these dozen figures in such an offhand manner, I do not mean to imply that we are to take them lightly. When they are brought into play, it is usually because there is some serious work for them to do. The elegance of combining many refined figures, and of stretching each of those in a way that would shiver the woodlots in Concord, is that it makes possible the reproduction in poetry of a world very much like the one in which the poet lives—a world where no attitude can hide from another, but all are revealed and commented on at once. It is largely the abundance of these dozen that makes the Ashbery style exasperating to some readers and makes them fear they are being taken in. But when the playful figures are for serious work, and when an abundance of them appears in one poem, then that may be a very serious poem indeed. One would not like to see this indulgence extended to poets across the board. But when we turn to a book like *Houseboat Days* we see how high is the high seriousness of which the stylish style is capable.

We should not leave the matter of John Ashbery's style without some mention of his unabashed borrowings from all over the place. These do not seem to annoy people very much; no one expects honor among thieves. On the contrary, people who are otherwise baffled may pick out the borrowings with pleasure. They are like the people one sees in a museum who have just come into the gallery, spied a famous picture whose reproduction they have seen many times, and are now congratulating each other on its presence, saying, "It's here! It's here!" This is good fun; we have all enjoyed it, and we can extend it to poetry. Take "Melodic Trains," where we have been waiting in the station and are suddenly asked, "How do they decide how much / Time to spend in each?" Now that question is a nugget of wonder, and nuggets of that kind have been polished to such perfection by James Schuyler that one finds it hard to resist pocketing them for himself. If this one was borrowed from Schuyler it is only one example of how the New York School is quarried for Ashbery's poetry, though Ashbery would not find such a comment very meaningful. Nor do I, in terms of the long-range meanings in his work that I am after today. But his New York School friendships and collaborations with Schuyler, Frank O'Hara, and Kenneth Koch are factual and momentous. Had you collected Pontormo and Parmigianino around a table in 1525 and informed them of their Mannerist fellowship, they probably would have responded, "Not very meaningful." They would have been right, and so would you.

Ashbery's affinities for certain European writers, writers in the big lump known as surrealism, are also fact. His "Into the Dusk-Charged Air," with its Rousselian list of every river in the encyclopedia, was published in the same summer as his translation of the first chapter from Roussel's *Impressions of Africa.* He has also translated from another favorite, Giorgio de Chirico, the painter who can make sentences that sound remarkably Ashberian. It was from de Chirico that Ashbery borrowed the title *The Double Dream of Spring.* But we could go on like this at length, citing Hesiod, the Book of Common Prayer, "An Ordinary Evening in New Haven," even the books for which he once wrote jacket copy at Oxford

University Press—among them Henry Steele Commager's *Freedom, Loyalty, Dissent* and an edition of Schumpeter's *History of Economic Analysis.* After all, if there is a disposition called negative capability that will take in a host of attitudes, it will take in a host of other writers too. In an interview Ashbery was asked: "What types of diction are you aware of incorporating into your poetry?" The answer was: "As many kinds as I can think of."

CHARLES BERGER

Vision in the Form of a Task:
"The Double Dream of Spring"

By now John Ashbery has become a
firm pattern in the contemporary mind and ear. We know the feel of his
poems, the figures they cut, although we may be less certain about what
they mean. This circumstance is partly due, I think, to a reluctance on
the part of even his greatest admirers to read Ashbery as they would, say,
Stevens. He is so radical and experimental a voice that one wishes to
suspend the normal procedures of interpretation in his presence. After a
while, however, the interpretive faculty cries out for its own assuagement
and we yield to that impulse. We then respond to Ashbery with our full
intellect, having first been convinced through the ear that the quest for
meaning will be rewarded.

Our contemporaries come to us poem by poem, volume by volume,
as a series of shocks. This sequence is a great blessing, for we are free to
deal with each poem on its own terms and not as preparation for what
comes next. Yet as the oeuvre builds we can hardly ignore its internal
coherence. We need to be alive both to the individual poem and to the
poet's larger shaping will: that impulse to give his career a form, an
emblematic outline. And, especially with poets of our moment, we cannot
fail to see how intensely self-allusive the career often becomes. James
Merrill is a case in point. With Ashbery the poems (and prose pieces) come
tumbling out at us, at least four rich volumes in the last decade. A future
Collected Poems (depressing thought!) very likely will erode the bound-

From *Beyond Amazement*, edited by David Lehman. Copyright © 1980 by Cornell University
Press.

aries between volumes altogether and simply render the poems chronologically. Such an edition would certainly help readers discern the relations between poems, but at the cost of losing a sense of where the crossings came, those moments in which the poet's meta-will stood out most clearly.

No volume of Ashbery's is more crucially transitional than *The Double Dream of Spring* (1970). There are some poems in *Rivers and Mountains* (1966) that could have found a place in the later book: "These Lacustrine Cities" and "A Blessing in Disguise," to name two. But *The Double Dream of Spring* as a whole inaugurates a style, a mode of discourse—meditative, less harshly elliptical—that sets it off from the earlier volumes and creates a rhetoric for the subsequent poems to continue, but also to violate. (The poems of *Houseboat Days* [1977] seem to indicate an intention on Ashbery's part to complicate the style in the direction of a return to the elliptical mode.) More important, *The Double Dream of Spring* assumes a stance that Ashbery's later books have not repudiated—that of the poet of high imagination, the visionary. The stance is crossed with obliquity, no doubt: but its presence is undeniable and still astonishing to witness. We can say that in the densely charged lyrics of *The Double Dream*, and especially in its magnificent long poem "Fragment," Ashbery comes into his own and into his inheritance. My scrutiny of this volume attempts to establish the precise terms of this stance, another way of saying that I hope to bring out the full coherence of Ashbery's poetic grammar. Holding hard to the orders of this crucial volume will bring added revelations about Ashbery's whole career to date.

The opening lyrics of Ashbery's books tend to share a common approach to the volumes they inaugurate. Each of these remarkably crystalline lyrics truly *opens* space for the other poems to inhabit: they come first by necessity. Ashbery likes to open his books with prophetic and proleptic lyrics, brief but encompassing. "The Task," at the head of *The Double Dream of Spring* is perhaps the most overtly inaugural poem Ashbery has written. It is close in spirit to a traditional beginning piece such as Frost's "The Pasture" or Whitman's "By Paths Untrodden" in its deliberate gesture of placing the poet in space—Ashbery shrinks the spot to "here"—and in its ironically understated way of characterizing the poet's enterprise: "I plan to stay here a little while / For these are moments only, moments of insight."

The reduced scope of such a plan is attractive in its very insouciance: we think of Whitman lounging, inviting the reader to come along with him. After all, the poet will make no great demands; his poems are "moments only." This casual, indeed deprecating, pose is wholly American. No sooner has Ashbery done with this bit of masquerade than he begins to describe the ensuing volume as a journey, the goal of which turns out to be a possible cure for angst. This is the other side of the American poet's stance toward his works, a view in which art is substitute for religion and other forms of psychic healing: "there are reaches to be attained, / A last level of anxiety that melts / In becoming, like miles under the pilgrim's feet."

Much of the difficulty readers have with Ashbery stems from problems in gauging his tone. The difficulty intensifies when it becomes a question of determining whether or not he is parodying a traditional literary *topos.* This way of posing the reader's alternatives sets up the question in a misleading way, although I think that many readers do pose these terms in oppositional fashion. I think that seasoned readers of Ashbery learn not to demand of his poems that they move in a univocal direction: he can both parody and mean "seriously" at the same time, he both sees and revises simultaneously. At times he appears to war against the very idea of received tradition, even while acknowledging, by his refusal to give them up, that the old tropes embody a storehouse of poetic wisdom still alive for us today.

This problem bears upon the opening of "The Task." On the one hand, there is Ashbery's explicit refusal to use the first-person pronoun here at the beginning. "They are preparing to begin again"; whether "they" refers to the Muses or whatever force seems to sponsor and survive the individual singer, the process is started outside the self. *They* pull the strings, initiating the new claim to attention. Although the new romance is a predicated one, even "they" recognize the need for new beginnings, opening outward and away from the origin of things. "Fragment," the last poem in *The Double Dream,* opens with a line that translates this opening and repeats its dialectic of endings and beginnings: "The last block is closed in April."

Once the necessity of a new start is realized, the quester is sent out on his mission, at which point Ashbery breaks into an uneasy, hyperbolic rhetoric that both inflates "the task" and blanks out the voyager. He becomes an Everyman, a too-programmatic fulfillment of the shibboleth that the lyric poet never speaks in propria persona but always *imperson-*ally. This Everyman moves westward as all the great questers do, in search, like Aeneas, of the fugitive lands. There may be hidden autobiographical irony in this, if we consider that *The Double Dream* is composed of poems written after Ashbery returned to America from his self-imposed "exile" abroad. So the exile, or fugitive, is really moving *back* toward home and "that time / In whose corrosive mass he first discovered how to breathe." "First" should be stressed here, since it tends to confirm the drift of the lines back to an origin. Learning "how to breathe" is a striking trope for discovering poetry, here imaged as a *breathing* exercise.

Just as "The Task" enacts a move westward, or homeward again after exile, so it moves from impersonal pronouns toward the discovery of an "I," withheld until the last six lines. We have explored the shifting strategy of self-representation in these lines but have not discussed the mysterious transitional moment that opens the final stanza: "Just look at the filth you've made,/ See what you've done." Part of the mystery here is due to Ashbery's fruitfully imprecise use of the second-person pronoun. Are these words meant to be spoken by one part of the self to another part, or do they come from "outside"? If the latter, who speaks them? The entrance of children into the poem just after these words, coupled with their tone of rebuke, leads us naturally to the mother; exactly why she is upbraiding the poet-child is the reader's surmise. The words are harsh and abrupt, as they doubtless were to the child, and yet they do not really interrupt the round of supper, play, and "promise of the pillow . . . to come." Ashbery sees the parental injunction in perspective, just as he will view all later moments of possible guilt and shame with a kind of steady tolerance and self-forgiveness. Even the moment of transgression has its part in the whole cycle: the mother wounds by day, heals by night.

The reprimand might also issue directly from the poet as an evaluation of his works and days, in the same spirit as Whitman at ebb-point surveying his shattered corpus. The poet's own judgment upon himself would then be an echoing, a repetition of the parental judgment. The seamlessness of "The Task" inclines one to choose all options for interpretation, uniting them to reveal an extraordinary instance of Ashbery touching upon a source, a seemingly random event that goes on meaning, especially when repeated by the adult poet. It is at this level that Ashbery's autobiographical tendencies should be discussed: autobiography is a most complex structure for him, involving little in the way of direct personal reminiscence. It is worth paying close attention to the carefully modulated "descent" of "The Task," in order to discover the place of the "personal" I. The poem slowly drops downward in a countersublime, descendental gesture: from the sun and Everyman as wandering Jew, we drop to the children playing after supper, while the poem ends with a pilgrim touching earth yet intent on the "reaches."

"The Task," then, presents us with a voice that threatens to disrupt, or at least to interrupt. But the poem incorporates that voice by revealing it to be as much an inner as an outer thing. Ashbery's sense of inclusiveness pervades *The Double Dream of Spring* and is sometimes mistaken for homogeneity of tone, as though his poems were not sufficiently differentiated. Metrically speaking, this is surely not true. Ashbery works in a remarkable variety of line lengths, and he is committed to a continual alternation of stanza patternings. We, as readers, sometimes tend to homogenize all poets, contemporary or traditional: the great name is invoked as though it meant one thing, one way of writing, one occasion for the birth of the poem.

Prosodic variation is the most obvious way of marking the differences in a poet's repertoire of voices. Within each Ashbery poem, the reader must always be on guard to catch the subtle shifts of perspective, the putting on of different inflections, in order to gather the full range of voice. Before *The Double Dream of Spring*, Ashbery indulged more openly in outrageous ellipses, sharp transitions from one mode of discourse to another. All this is toned down somewhat in *The Double Dream*, making the reader's task even more challenging, for it becomes more difficult to locate crucial moments of vocal scene-changing. Ashbery has never been what we would call a dramatic poet, and the voices he draws into his poems, no matter how far-fetched, are always versions of an elusive but central speaker. With the poems of *The Double Dream*, these competing voices become more strongly perceived as possible modes of self-presentation, within a range extending from the sublime to more natural, perhaps even colloquial measures. And the outrageous poem has hardly disappeared from the volume: "Farm Implements and Rutabagas in a Landscape" may be Ashbery's wildest parody.

"Spring Day," the second poem in *The Double Dream of Spring*, reveals Ashbery at his most cunning. The poem crosses internal boundary marks incessantly, and yet the flow of the whole, like "a river breaking through a dam," seems barely to pause as the different streams emerge and dissolve. "Spring Day" is precisely located in time: it is set at the moment of awakening, the lyric time of *aubade*—only here we find the self engaged in monologue. (The more one reads Ashbery the clearer his poetic time frames become.) The situation of the early riser experiencing the freshness of dawn as "cold hope," where cold is a trope of power, is similar to that in Stevens's "The Latest Freed Man." The first two stanzas of "Spring Day" engage cyclicity, the raising and deflating of immense hope, but the tone is not one of exhaustion. After all, night is over and the mind has achieved respite, fending off nightmares. Here I must disagree with David Kalstone even while admiring his eloquence. Kalstone describes the opening stanzas of "Spring Day" in the following way: "Fresh hopes verge into nightmares in the long suspended sentence at the opening of 'Spring Day.' . . . In this supple maze of syntax things seem over, exhausted, before they begin; 'immense hope' turns into 'cold hope' in the 'air that was yesterday.' " Were this true, I do not see how the poem could achieve the cadence of its magnificent close. My disagreement centers on the value of "cold hope"; I read this, again, as a sign of power, to be compared with Stevens's "refreshment of cold air." Kalstone's reading nevertheless exerts a powerful counterpull on more optimistic interpretations of the poem.

Any characterization of "Spring Day" must take its *two* speakers into account. The poem cannot be said to oppose voices so much as blend them, though it acknowledges a different strain of voice by enclosing one of its speeches in quotation marks. Who speaks here: " 'They were long in coming' "? We *are* told that: "The giant body relaxed as though beside a stream / Wakens to the force of it and has to recognize / The secret sweetness before it turns into life." This giant, introduced by the poem's other voice, may be seen as the sleeping Albion within us all, ear attuned to the stream of primordial desire for freedom and release, a river that speaks only at the first breaking of day and then goes underground, like Arnold's buried stream. The giant's speech upon these barely repressed heights deserves to be called sublime. Ashbery concurs by marking off the speaking mountain's sermon for the day, much as Emerson distinguished his radical chant of freedom in *Nature* by inserting quotation marks and assigning the sublime speech to a certain "Orphic Poet." Ashbery's Orphic self begins by declaring that we must break through the shell of custom and tradition:

> "They were long in coming,
> Those others, and mattered so little that it slowed them
> To almost nothing. They were presumed dead,
> Their names honorably grafted on the landscape
> To be a memory to men. Until today
> We have been living in their shell.
> Now we break forth like a river breaking through a dam,
> Pausing over the puzzled, frightened plain,
>
> And our further progress shall be terrible,
> Turning fresh knives in the wounds
> In that gulf of recreation, that bare canvas
> As matter-of-fact as the traffic and the day's noise."

Some of these lines are written in the mode of self-conscious epic simile: the puzzled, frightened plain is a wonderful imitation, not a parody, of Vergilian style. Yet this epic speaker, this giant of the self caught " 'twixt wake and sleep," also acknowledges the need to hold tight to the commonplaces. It is a program both sweet and terrible, as the sublime should be, modulating at the close, while day nears, into an appreciation of the reality principle.

"The mountain stopped shaking"; its Vesuvian speech, as Dickinson would put it, is over, and the poem moves toward the accents of day and inevitable "contradiction." But first there is a last glimpse of the stars, at the moment of fade-out:

> . . . far from us lights were put out, memories of boys and girls
> Who walked here before the great change,
>
> Before the air mirrored us,
> Taking the opposite shape of our effort,
> Its inseparable comment and corollary
> But casting us further and further out.

The constellations are viewed here as the surviving fragments of the mythopoeic imagination, from a time before the turn toward self-consciousness and its attendant dualisms. The trace that man left in the sky, as sign of his myth-making faculty, was not a mark of difference but grew rather out of the sense that man and nature were united. The human image was seen within nature, not apart from it. But then a "great change" came about (itself, of course, a heuristic myth): an age of reflection rather than vision took over, and man saw his image everywhere, but at the cost of losing his ability to see anything else. When he now looked into nature, he saw only himself, distorted. Nature became a commentary upon our traces; while we thought we were attracting the world to us, we were actually alienating ourselves in the service of a remorseless consciousness of self.

There is a touch of play here, for this whole dialectic has grown so familiar that even to repeat it requires somewhere a saving touch of irony. Ashbery achieves it with the reference to the starry images of lost heroes and heroines as "boys and girls," a playfully reductive touch that helps us put the whole argument in perspective. (Stevens startles us at a similar moment in "Notes toward a Supreme Fiction" when he declares that "Adam / In Eden was the father of Descartes.") And we should also remember that Ashbery's Orphic speaker actually strikes out against the myth of unity and its avatars with their "names grafted on the landscape" (of the sky?), urging instead a kind of violence against nature in order to achieve desire.

We are, then, confronted with a double dream upon the dawning of this spring day. One is the remoter dream of lost unity, of a time before the fall into the "great change." There is also the giant's dream, half-slumbering Albion's vision of breaking the chains, even the chains of past myths of freedom. In this sense Ashbery, at his most visionary, does not look backward as Blake does to "ancient times" as a paradigm for restoration. Both these dreams begin to fade at the moment when the sun and the natural self rise from sleep. Ashbery shows this native self rubbing its eyes, so to speak, and gazing around him: "Wha—what happened?" Has the sun ever been less ceremoniously greeted? The rebound is quick, however, and a truly uncanny voice now emerges as day takes over, but a day now informed by the dream of early morning (those dreams Dante calls the truest). The self that now appears also wants to be healed, but not through any violation of nature. Rather, innocence and beauty are to be attained by becoming at one with "The orange tree," emblem of all that is vital and earthly:

>   You are with
> The orange tree, so that its summer produce
> Can go back to where we got it wrong, then drip gently
> Into history, if it wants to.

History is not abjured but becomes an option for the embowered self; it will be engaged on the gentlest of terms. Some readers may find retreat in this, preferring the more strenuous and violent vision of the Orphic speaker. The compensation for such cultivation of the inner forest is the flowering of a tone of remarkable civility and ceremony at the poem's close. One thinks of "A Prayer for My Daughter" when listening to the end of "Spring Day," and yet Ashbery's pastoral precinct shows no trace of social conservatism. There is, rather, an abiding respect for the "growing thing" and an implicit abhorrence of violence—even in the service of vision—that Yeats, alas, did not share:

> No use charging the barriers of that other:
> It no longer exists. But you,
> Gracious and growing thing, with those leaves like stars,
> We shall soon give all our attention to you.

No rhetorical figure could better have described the locus of Ashbery's concern than his phrase "leaves like stars." The skybound or sublime constellations and their vestiges of mythic union have disappeared, to be replaced by earthly coordinates, the aim of the natural quester. It is a deeply moving emblem upon which to end a poem: we are entreated to care for the earth's own sublimity.

The threshold moment of sunrise is one that Ashbery faces throughout *The Double Dream of Spring.* "Sunrise in Suburbia," despite its title (which may refer to an inner sense of being stranded outside the city proper) faces "the coming of strength out of night: unfeared" on urban ground. The poem calls itself a "woven city lament," an elegy either for the city as it now is, or for the self at bay in such a metropolis. Courage *is* certainly what is needed to face the coming day, as Ashbery conceives it in this poem, for the advent of sunrise creates a "morning holocaust, one vast furnace, engaging all tears." Holocaust and furnace are potential opposites here, one standing for destruction by fire, the other for a creative welding of elements. "Tears," a trope for lament, are somehow *engaged* by this early morning fire; the expression moves us away from the threat of being *consumed.* Yet no explanation can fully deflect the poet's strenuous and violent conception of lethal powers arrayed against him. "How quick the sunrise would kill me," Ashbery says along with Whitman— and though both poets send bolts out of themselves as a defense, the danger remains real. The final vision of "Sunrise in Suburbia" can be tempered only by another poem of the threshold moment and its combative harnessing of such energy: "Evening in the Country."

That poem is also oddly titled, unless its speaker proleptically addresses the "sign of being / In me that is to close late, long." However this may be, the poem is surely situated at dawn, ending at the instant of sunrise, monumentally represented. "Evening in the Country" closes with a vision of the sun as an "unblinking chariot," a rhetorical figure that captures both the sun's power (it is a great engine) and its "knowledge" (its eye never shuts, like the world it illumines it is a "vast open"). What is the speaker's stance with regard to this great force?

> We may perhaps remain here, cautious yet free
> On the edge, as it rolls its unblinking chariot
> Into the vast open, the incredible violence and yielding
> Turmoil that is to be our route.

Lines such as these point to a kind of timidity found elsewhere in *The Double Dream:* "It is probably on one of the inside pages/ That the history of his timidity will be written." The quotation comes from "French Poems," a sequence in which Ashbery appears to accuse himself of essential cowardice. But we should be wary of taking this pose as the whole truth. "On the edge" is a loaded phrase, filled with traces of the center/ periphery dialectic found so often in American poetry. To declare oneself "marginal" may only be another way of saying that the center shifts to where the poetic self happens to be. There is no center except where the central speaker takes up his or her stance. Whitman, in the opening poem of *Calamus,* seems to exile himself to the margin only to then evolve a new version of centrality. We must also remember that the sun is both center and periphery at once. Ashbery's path will become the same as the sun's, for by the end of the poem he is able to call its arc "our route." He does not, it is true, make the logical next connection—that he is at the reins of the sun chariot—but he does not really need to, having summoned all that power into his poem, performed his ritual magic on the sun's own rising.

"We may perhaps remain here" is an equally gnomic phrase, pointing both to exile and to centrality. If we search within the poem for a strongly contrasting "there," we find it in the vision of the city "back there," presumably abandoned by the poet in his retreat:

> But if breath could kill, then there would not be
> Such an easy time of it, with men locked back there
> In the smokestacks and corruption of the city.

"Here" becomes, by contrast, a provincial center away from the lethal *urbs*. The fatal breath Ashbery evokes is more than simple industrial pollution; "breath," as we have seen in "The Task," can stand as a trope for poetry, though we should not forget that it can also refer to "fallen" speech. In either case, breath is threatening, whether it carries the serious rivalry of poetic competition or the malice of common defamation. This sense of the mysterious *other* as a backdrop against which Ashbery plays out his own liberation, yet toward which he experiences ambivalence and guilt, is given full treatment in "Soonest Mended" and "Clouds."

"Here" can also be a gesture indicating the ground upon which the lyric poem always takes it stand—so it was used in "The Task." That ground is always central, the poet hopes, however physically "exiled" it might be. All the community necessary for the poet in this form of exile is provided by versions of his own being: this is one reason why "Evening in the Country" plays with a variety of personal pronouns. A related question concerns where the self begins and ends, especially in its relation to the things of nature:

> Now as my questioning but admiring gaze expands
> To magnificent outposts, I am not so much at home
> With these memorabilia of vision as on a tour
> Of my remotest properties.

The pose is reminiscent of an earlier parody of exile, in the Oriental mode, found in the latter sections of "The Skaters." But "Evening in the Country" complicates the question by also treating avatars of the self as remote, first, then as *propre*. We are never quite sure what "I" stands for: Does it indicate a unified or a fragmentary self? Does the ability to say "I" necessarily exclude other states of being? The poem's opening line seems to imply this sort of reductive stability: "I am still completely happy." This static opening should have halted the poem right there, the statement's self-sufficiency reinforced by its containment within one line, the only such "whole" sentence in the poem. The self as still center—it is hard not to supply a comma after "still"—prevails and moves off center only to the extent of indulging in "motionless explorations."

But this stillness belongs only to the moment of threshold. As the sun begins to stir, so does a more active, larger being within, a *second* person requiring, quite naturally, the second-person pronoun:

> Have you begun to be in the context you feel
> Now that the danger has been removed?
> . . . has the motion started
> That is to quiver your head, send anxious beams
> Into the dusty corners of the rooms
> Eventually shoot out over the landscape
> In stars and bursts? For other than this we know nothing
> And space is a coffin and the sky will put out the light.
> I see you eager in your wishing it the way
> We may join it, if it passes close enough.

The two versions, I and you, blend into "we." "I see you," despite its touch of hide-and-seek, has great force at this point, presaging a greater inward visibility as the sun begins its climb. The anxious "I" who has survived a night of threat by drawing in his defenses can now respond as a central man would, tracing his own orbit and drawing the circle as he goes.

I would not want to leave "Evening in the Country" without paying homage to its tone, a mixture of rapture and urbanity, self-composure and ecstasy. The volumes after *The Double Dream of Spring* have only deepened Ashbery's commitment to this tone and the stance it conveys. His urbanity, like Shelley's, somehow furthers the intensity generated by moments of high imaginative "kindling," a favorite word of Shelley's and one that Ashbery invokes at the center of the companion piece to "Evening in the Country," the more severe lyric "Parergon."

Once again we find an opening gambit of achieved self-contentment: "We are happy in our way of life." "Parergon," however, immediately displays a sense of restlessness; it is from the beginning a more troubled poem than "Evening in the Country," more haunted by the urge to reach out to the "others" and communicate one's Orphic wisdom. It is tempting to regard this poem as picking up where "Evening in the Country" left off, a night piece to the other's hymn of the sun, a Penseroso dream-vision to set beside the less searing visions of day. Three lines from its end we are told that the lesson of the poem "eddied far into the night," and throughout there is a sense of heightened dream. The opening pronoun only furthers the temptation to link the two poems: "*We* are happy" seems to pitch us into a space where the disparate selves, having come together as one, now discover the urge to break the stasis of achieved satisfaction. Yet there is no direct movement toward "the others"; rather, the stasis deepens, as "our entity pivots on a self-induced trance / Like sleep." This pivot, or center, gradually discloses itself as a deep desire to speak prophetically to these unreachable others, to be a *vox clamantes*. Ashbery seems to require distance between himself and this desire, a distance attained, first, by confining the straying prophetic voice to the purlieus of dream and then encasing the cry in quotation marks. The effect of the latter has already been seen in "Spring Day." It is open to each reader's judgment to decide how effective is this distancing (I would not call it parody or irony). And how are we to read what follows the address, the passage beginning, "As one who moves forward from a dream"? Have we awakened, or have we simply moved from dream to dream, in a deeper piercing of the darkness?

　　" 'O woebegone people!' " the voice begins, contrasting its own crying with that in the streets:

> "O woebegone people! Why so much crying,
> Such desolation in the streets?
> Is it the present of flesh, that each of you
> At your jagged casement window should handle,
> Nervous unto thirst and ultimate death?
> Meanwhile the true way is sleeping."

The last line can be read two ways: more simply, the true way is obscured; but the line might also imply that the true way exists within the sleep of this Orphic dreamer and visionary preacher, who assures us that "it is always time for a change." Ashbery as preacher? We might recall that one of the poems in *Rivers and Mountains* was entitled "The Ecclesiast"; there are many moments in his poetry when he becomes a Stevensian orator who "chants in the dark / A text that is an answer, although obscure." Besides, beneath the surface esprit, some of the poems in *The Double Dream* are unabashedly didactic: "Sortes Vergilianae" and "Some Words" immediately come to mind. The Orphic crier ends on a note of deep irony, however, when he declares, from the vantage of sleep, " 'We need the tether/Of entering each other's lives, eyes wide apart, crying.' " Only in dream can we do so, and will the people listen to our savage cry of assuagement.

The fantasy deepens and we pass from the oracle to the god proper. These terms may seem hyperbolic, but Ashbery casts off restraint as he sends his quester forward into the visionary night. "Parergon" approaches that sacred circle of apotheosis staked out in "Kubla Khan":

> As one who moves forward from a dream
> The stranger left the house on hastening feet
> Leaving behind the woman with the face shaped like an
>   arrowhead,
> And all who gazed upon him wondered at
> The strange activity around him.
> How fast the faces kindled as he passed!

What is especially remarkable in this final movement is not only the breakthrough or admission of prophetic fantasy but the context in which we find it. For the "strange activity," or spectacle of the self draws its inevitable spectators, one of whom may be the poet's ordinary consciousness standing off to one side and observing the "stranger." "Weave a circle round him thrice," Coleridge cautioned the onlookers in "Kubla Khan." Ashbery's dangerous stranger reposes, for a moment, in "the enclosure of some court," some common space now sanctified by his presence. The worshipers are necessary, if only to pay homage to the difficulty of the quest, and to the fact that only one figure can bear it:

> Yet each knew he saw only aspects,
> That the continuity was fierce beyond all dream of enduring,
> And turned his head away.

The glow is too bright. Certainly the closing movement is hyperbolic, but its rhetoric of poetic elevation is one that great poets have not shied away from. The sense of "continuity," as Ashbery uses it, involves a kind of apostolic succession of seers. The dream of poetic divinity, of undying joyousness, extracts a harsh price from the poet who bears it—he is "caught in that trap," as the poem's last words tell us, surrounded by the "others."

For too long Ashbery has seemed to readers—especially professional readers—a poet more often casual than relentless about establishing meaning. His mask of insouciance has managed to remain intact, despite the writing of poem after difficult poem, and the evidence is that each new effort has been aimed hard at getting his subject right—not fixing it forever, but bringing the moment's wisdom and the moment's ephemerality together. Too often, critics have stressed the latter and ignored the former. A myth grew up around Ashbery: he had somehow discovered new dimensions to the poetic act, or a new kind of writing machine, capable of generating poems in the absence of the usual anxieties about subject—more remarkably, poems free from worry about the traditional criteria of greatness. Ashbery has contributed to this myth in subtle ways, but supporters and critics have gone even further, sometimes suggesting that Ashbery had willed himself to be a minor poet, inhabitor of a necessarily diminished sphere. They seize on lines such as the following: "To step free at last, miniscule on the gigantic plateau— / This was our ambition: to be small and clear and free."

These lines come from "Soonest Mended," one of Ashbery's most popular poems. It is a poem written firmly in the middle voice and one which seems to erect an aesthetic credo out of holding to the middle range in all things: "a kind of fence-sitting / Raised to the level of an aesthetic ideal." The poem needs to be quizzed on this advocacy, however, if it does not indeed already question itself. One reason "Soonest Mended" is so well liked, aside from its wrought gracefulness and measured tone of loss, is that it gives an image of the poet many readers would like Ashbery to be: casual, urbane, resigned to "an occasional dream, a vision."

Now the poems we have been considering—"The Task," "Spring Day," "Evening in the Country," "Parergon"—are hardly what we would call conversational, although "Evening in the Country" comes closest perhaps to "Soonest Mended" in its use of the long line as a way of achieving flexibility of voice. Yet the conversational measure tightens toward the close of "Evening in the Country," and even though Ashbery keeps to an urbane pitch he manages to ascend the chariot of poetic deity. Readers are probably coming to realize that Ashbery has almost unobtrusively mastered the long line—the line of more than ten syllables— and now uses it as powerfully as anyone before him in the twentieth century. From *Double Dream* to *Houseboat Days* his power over this measure has only grown. The long line is also the visionary line, the mode of Whitman and Blake, and Ashbery has not been reluctant to use it in this task. The lengthened line, however, can trail away from the poet, as it does in "As I Ebb'd with the Ocean of Life," creating an effect of dispersed power and draining strength. Or the line can seem to hover in a kind of fruitful suspension, a creative sense of drift and repose. This feeling steals over one at times in reading Keats's odes, where the lines seem to grow longer than ten syllables as the Keatsian patience spreads its wings. "Soonest Mended" fulfills this last use of the long line almost perfectly, but it is worth noting that the poem is sui generis and not "vintage" Ashbery. More often, Ashbery will begin with a sense of drift but then gather toward some point of vision. The first poem in *Houseboat Days* is a perfect illustration. "Street Musicians" sees rising signs of drift but looks beyond them to what it perceives as a possible source, an "anchor": "Our question of a place of origin hangs / Like smoke."

"Barely tolerated, living on the margin," is something between a boast and a lament. The margin, once again, does not necessarily lead to marginality: it may be the true center. Yet "Soonest Mended" is less sure than other Ashbery poems of the poet's power to be the center wherever he falls out, on the "brink" or what not. I would still argue that even as the poem's seemingly limpid lines crystallize with time and repeated readings, so its sense of marginality inches toward the center. Indeed, the movement is already there in the poem however one interprets it, for the margin of the poem's opening line becomes a "mooring" at the end. The precarious present yields to a sense of origins: the self is where it is as a result of an original event or choice. Our exile to the margin is self-willed. We started out from the margin-as-mooring; we are always placing ourselves by necessity at the brink of a new beginning, a making ready. Only when we lose the trace of the tether back to this site do we regard ourselves as weakly marginal. So the poem will move back through personal memory to an event *in illo tempore*, or sacred time, when the poet's true chronology began.

"Soonest Mended" remains striking within the Ashbery oeuvre not so much for its return at the end to a sense of origination—other poems certainly enact this course—as for its planned, haphazard course *to* that end. David Kalstone has written beautifully of this trajectory. He speaks of the poem's "brave carelessness" and points out, rightly, that "the tone is partly elegiac." Ashbery's suppression of mimesis only partly obscures the clear fact that "Soonest Mended" is, as Harold Bloom calls it, a lament for "Ashbery's generation." Writing at the level he does throughout *The Double Dream of Spring* inevitably means that Ashbery will feel deep ambivalence toward this comically helpless "generation" and toward his own early self. But I must disagree with Kalstone when he says that " 'mooring' sounds as much like death as a new life." He tends to be more concerned with how the poem "shifts quickly from one historical hazard to another," while "the energetic lines breathe the *desire* to assert ego and vitality." As a stylistic description of the poem this cannot be surpassed.

"Historical hazard" is something Ashbery does not often open his poems to; the randomness of the ordinary is not quite the same thing. Such randomness can be organized and redeemed by the solitary eye; but history, or life within the community, can become far more oppressive to the poet. Ashbery's detractors would argue that he closes himself off to what he cannot organize, despite an appearance of the erratic within his poems, and this is hard to dispute. "Soonest Mended" gives us a somewhat coded account of community and offers reasons why this poet must find it dissatisfying. Another poem in the volume, "Clouds," will deal more severely with the need to break away, artistically speaking, from even the most nourishing community. "Soonest Mended" does not quite enact such a break, turning its gentler scrutiny on the poignant inability of any enclave whatsoever to satisfy the desire for true speech. This pathos comes through in a key passage where Ashbery sets the sign of disillusionment against the undeniably sweet faces of the others:

> This is what you wanted to hear, so why
> Did you think of listening to something else? We are all talkers
> It is true, but underneath the talk lies
> The moving and not wanting to be moved, the loose
> Meaning, untidy and simple like a threshing floor.

The powerful enjambment at the end of the third line in this quotation expresses all of Ashbery's ambivalence. "Underneath the talk lies"—so he might wish to leave it, until a softening sets in and he admits that beneath the deceit of social "talk" there hides the shifting forms of desire. The last line in this passage echoes the muse/mother's reprimand in "The Task"—"Just look at the filth you've made"—and here, too, the scatterings wait to be gathered into meaning. This vision of the others, the desired but not "extinct" community, will never fully betray or renounce the spirit of that time and place. It is enough to point, once, to the inevitable wounds that arise when we give and take in mere "talk." About this (least said), soonest mended.

Beyond conversation and beneath the colloquial texture of the poem lies the deep meaning of poetic language:

> Night after night this message returns, repeated
> In the flickering bulbs of the sky, raised past us, taken away
>   from us,
> Yet ours over and over until the end that is past truth,
> The being of our sentences, in the climate that fostered them,
> Not ours to own, like a book, but to be with, and sometimes
> To be without, alone and desperate.

This is the credo that holds the haphazard aesthetic course together, and it is a credo Ashbery is willing to share. He does not astonish the others as he did in "Parergon." In fact, "Soonest Mended" ends with several attempts to register halting progress, so unlike the streaming movement at the close of "Parergon," as though Ashbery were trying to blend defeat with triumph. Does this, in the context of the poem, amount to a version of survivor guilt? Thus, the visionary moment becomes a "hard dole," "action" turns to uncertainty, preparation is "careless." And yet no degree of restraint can fully quell the sense of triumph and power attendant upon recovering the spot of origin at the poem's close. "That day so long ago," the day of poetic inauguration, does not belong to the time frame of memory. It belongs to a greater sequence. To understand the resonances of such a "day" it would help to look at the preceding poem in *The Double Dream*, "Plainness in Diversity." This lesser-known poem abbreviates the course traveled by "Soonest Mended" but moves in a remarkably similar direction. Once again it is the emptiness of "talk" that brings the truth home to the poetic quester; his place is elsewhere:

> Silly girls your heads full of boys
> There is a last sample of talk on the outer side
> Your stand at last lifts to dumb evening
> It is reflected in the steep blue sides of the crater,
> So much water shall wash over these our breaths
> Yet shall remain unwashed at the end. The fine
> Branches of the fir tree catch at it, ebbing.
> Not on our planet is the destiny
> That can make you one.
> To be placed on the side of some mountain
> Is the truer story.

The second stanza continues to construct an outline of the journey myth, as it uses "the sagas" to discover a fitting point of origin and a worthy end to the quest:

> There is so much they must say, and it is important
> About all the swimming motions, and the way the hands
> Came up out of the ocean with original fronds,
> The famous arrow, the girls who came at dawn
> To pay a visit to the young child, and how, when he grew up
>   to be a man
> The same restive ceremony replaced the limited years
>   between,
> Only now he was old, and forced to begin the journey to the
>   stars.

"Plainness in Diversity" locates us in myth more firmly than "Soonest Mended" chooses to do; but the gesture of starting out with which the latter concludes is also, surely, a version of heroism.

Another account of this truer—that is to say, more severe—poetic autobiography comes in the mysterious poem "Clouds," a terse lyric of bounded quatrains, gnomic and revealing at the same time. The poem tells something of the same story as "Soonest Mended," but its voice is

wholly different. "Clouds"—the title becomes clear only in the last line—
has none of the evasive charm of "Soonest Mended." It judges the
generation out of which Ashbery emerged with harsher accuracy and
claims expansive, indeed Dionysian, powers for its own speaker. (Semele,
upon whom the poem devolves at the close, was the mother of Dionysus.)
The opening quatrain can hardly be matched elsewhere in Ashbery's
writing for its uncanny mixture of power and prophecy, on the one hand,
tranquillity and reverie on the other:

> All this time he had only been waiting,
> Not even thinking, as many had supposed.
> Now sleep wound down to him its promise of dazzling peace
> And he stood up to assume that imagination.

These lines might stand as epigraph to *The Double Dream of Spring*,
the volume in which Ashbery first truly stands up to assume the task of
poethood. What distinguishes "Clouds" from other such moments of declaration is its preoccupation with what came before. Both "Parergon" and
"Evening in the Country" showed glimpses of the *others*, the dark background against which Ashbery measures the intensity of his own flare.
Here the poet broods more penetratingly on the character of these others—
the poets, let us say, with whom Ashbery started out. The names of this
generation are well known. Ashbery schematizes the setting in "Clouds"
and leaves us with a strong, if intentionally vague, impression only of an
avant-garde enclave worrying problems of continuity and rupture. Ashbery
turns to judge them, sounding like an abstract version of Yeats assessing
the poets of the nineties:

> There were others in the forest as close as he
> To caring about the silent outcome, but they had gotten lost
> In the shadows of dreams so that the external look
> Of the nearby world had become confused with the cobwebs
>   inside.

"They had gotten lost": *he*, on the other hand, has been found.
"Clouds" gives itself over to declaring this difference, which amounts to
declaring its speaker greater than the others—"He shoots forward like a
malignant star," as the poem later puts it—while at the same time holding
him true to the poetic program of this early coterie. "Clouds" emblematizes the conflict in Ashbery's crossing from the early phase of *Some Trees*
and *The Tennis Court Oath* to *Rivers and Mountains* and *The Double Dream
of Spring*. We might choose to see the promise of this early phase as
fulfilled in the poems of *The Double Dream*—yet how can one fulfill the

experimental, the tentative? And how can one establish continuity with a phase that was itself commited to personal and historical discontinuity?

> How can we outsmart the sense of continuity
> That eludes our steps as it prepares us
> For ultimate wishful thinking once the mind has ended
> Since this last thought both confines and uplifts us?

This stana, the ninth of fourteen, marks the point of transition in the poem. The preceding stanzas turned over the question of continuity, of resisting what the poem calls "joining," even while acknowledging the need to forge "separate blocks of achievement and opinion." "Clouds" scatters penetrating kernel descriptions of avant-gardism, none of which is more striking than the following:

> And the small enclave
> Of worried continuing began again, putting forth antennae
> into the night.

> How do we explain the harm, feeling
> We are always the effortless discoverers of our career,
> With each day digging the grave of tomorrow and at the same
> time
> Preparing its own redemption, constantly living and dying?

The poem's "sestet," its final five or six stanzas, grants that we can never "outsmart the sense of continuity," but it does not take this as a sign of defeat. Rather, Ashbery drops any note of elegiac helplessness and strikes out, in a remarkable evocation of animal vitality. No more worried continuing, no more sleek antennae:

> He was like a lion tracking its prey
> Through days and nights, forgetful
> In the delirium of arrangements.

The conceit is striking and outrageous. We hunt down "continuity," even devour it at moments, but we cannot extinguish the concept or the species itself: we are tied to our prey. The circle of tracking and destruction is obsessive, a "delirium of arrangements." We waste the present in this *quest for* a present uncontaminated by the past. We locate ourselves on the outer rim of this devastation, pushing farther into the brake:

> The birds fly up out of the underbrush,

> The evening swoons out of contaminated dawns,
> And now whatever goes farther must be
> Alien and healthy, for death is here and knowable.
> Out of touch with the basic unhappiness

He shoots forward like a malignant star.
The edges of the journey are ragged.
Only the face of night begins to grow distinct
As the fainter stars call to each other and are lost.

Day re-creates his image like a snapshot. . . .

The glory and the sorrow of the avant-garde are acted out here, in the flight outward and the inevitable return to habitual nature: our image rendered by someone or something else.

"Clouds" is a powerfully condensed poem, ascetically framed and argued. Vision is not deflected as it is in "Soonest Mended"; there is no pretense of lassitude, no effort to mask the true desires of the poetic self. In fact the poem is so clear about how it places its speaker that we, as readers, perhaps search for evasions that simply are not there. This is one of the more curious reactions Ashbery inspires in his audience. But even if we pay homage to the obliquity of presentation in "Clouds," we cannot fail to recognize the poem's true prey as it emerges with the abrupt invocation of Semele, the mother of Dionysus. If the god is about to be born at the end of the poem, he is about to be born again, into poetry, at the poem's opening. The shock of these terms is itself instructive: it cautions us against reading Ashbery too casually.

On the way toward "Fragment" and away from these charged lyrics, we might think about some poems in The Double Dream of Spring that seem to exist for the sheer sake of performance. Intended to elude interpretation, these poems never become nonsensical. Instead, they end as parodies where, more often than not, the matter of parody can be located in the "serious" poems of the volume. The place of texts such as "Variations, Calypso and Fugue on a Theme of Ella Wheeler Wilcox," "Farm Implements and Rutabagas in a Landscape," "Some Words," "Sortes Vergilianae," is crucial: nearly every line, every moment from these variously wild poems can be "related" to more coherent structures of meaning elsewhere in The Double Dream. These poems mock interpretation on their own ground—they mean, but mean elsewhere, anywhere else but within their own boundaries. A residual trace of guilt can be found in Ashbery toward the whole enterprise of false coherence, and this is why he makes his readers collaborate so strenuously in the hermeneutic process of coming upon meaning. He seems at times deliberately to mar his poems, although I would argue that this occurs more often in Houseboat Days than in The Double Dream of Spring. His bad conscience at approximating the "traditional" poem with its criteria of lucidity and comprehensibility is somewhat appeased by the overtly experimental poems in his volumes: these disperse meaning as much as other poems concentrate it. It is not that the experimental poem in *The Double Dream*, for instance, is formless; on the contrary, this kind of poem is overdetermined by form. Meaning goes along for the ride. What these experimental poems do best is to exaggerate and hypostatize thematic concerns and prosodic patterns that exist everywhere in *The Double Dream*. The volume is extraordinarily well-knit and, in a sense, it is these willful, seemingly unbounded pieces that most remind us of this fact. Such experimentation is *vitally* parasitic; it is alive in itself but also needs the preexistence of texts found elsewhere: a bit of doggerel from Ella Wheeler Wilcox, the "Popeye" cartoon, a French text by Arthur Cravan, the notion of a privileged "sacred" text that exists as pure anteriority (Vergil). For a poem that stands alone we must turn to the deeper experimentalism of a true masterpiece: "Fragment."

The title at first leads us to expect jaggedness in the poem's lines—frequent and sharp transitions—certainly not the overt symmetry of fifty ten-line stanzas, parodically reminiscent of stately Renaissance pageantry. Yet, if we look closer, is there not a sense of completion in the title's emphasis on the singular: "Fragment," not "Fragments"? (Suppose Pound had called his epic *Canto?*) So, even if the poem stands in synecdochic relation to some external whole, it completely embodies its own partiality. It is a whole fragment. There are, not surprisingly, many tag lines, emblematic moments in the poem, that help us to parse the title: "The stance to you / Is a fiction, to me a whole" is one such moment in which Ashbery flatters his song. A later passage turns against this self-flattery and broods about the poem's possible incompleteness:

> . . . the externals of present
> Continuing—incomplete, good-natured pictures that
> Flatter us even when forgotten with dwarf speculations
> About the insane, invigorating whole they don't represent.

Insane, invigorating: Is the whole worth capturing? Deciding this is as difficult as trying to locate the poem's transitions, which are everywhere and nowhere. We are tricked by the title and by an earlier mélange like "The Skaters" into readying ourselves for a tour de force of ellipsis. Yet the poem flows and flows, somehow running over its points of switchover, eliding its own elisions in a credible portrait of continuity. The lines, however seemingly discontinuous, are held together by a metrical or rhythmic hum, a buzzing undertone of similitude and relationship.

Whether it opens on a note of closure or aperture, "Fragment" clearly *does* begin with a marked point of departure. It is also worth noting that the poem's last stanza seems to be a clear end-sign. This is a good reminder to the reader not to ignore sequence entirely, even at moments of exasperation (or release), when the thread of continuity appears most strained. Invoking April as it does, "Fragment" pays homage to the hallowed starting ground for the long poem in English, from Chaucer to Eliot. And indeed, the poem's first six lines are among the most densely and richly allusive Ashbery has yet written. The poem opens by seeming to deny the possibility of further openings: "The last block is closed in April." Whatever "block" may mean, from building metaphor to cell block, the overt sense in the line moves toward grim, monosyllabic finality. Yet the force of "April" as a point of origin or place of aperture overrides any terminus, impelling the line as a whole to say: "The last block is closed in aperture"; we move toward a new opening even as we shut down or shut out the past (the last).

The focus on "her face" in the poem's second line introduces a series of concentric circles of reference, where "she" comes to stand for the beloved in all her avatars: lover, mother, muse, earth itself. Ashbery's cynosure is about as readily identifiable as Keats's Moneta or Stevens's female imago figures. And, indeed, the powerful apostrophe in stanza two—"your face, the only real beginning,/ Beyond the grey of overcoat" —links Ashbery to these two, especially on that mysterious and crucial ground where the origins of Eros and the lyric are intertwined. Ashbery's overt strategy of invocation by repetition and difference does not end here, however; we need to confront the shade of Eliot as well, summoned by the proximity of "memory" to "April," and by the figural substitution for the missing word in the Eliotic triad: April, memory . . . *desire*. Desire, indeed, is the key to the whole of the poem's magnificent opening. It is the "intrusion" that "Clouds over" the beloved's countenance; it is the dream of "older / Permissiveness," as the stanza goes on to call it, a shrewd way of troping upon the erotic storehouse of childhood and adolescence. And desire helps us to understand why the budding forsythia extend a present sympathy to us, in opposition to the "recondite" or buried past, return to which can only involve a lethal falling backward:

> You
> See the intrusions clouding over her face
> As in the memory given you of older
> Permissiveness which dies in the
> Falling back toward recondite ends,
> The sympathy of yellow flowers.

(I do not read "The sympathy of yellow flowers" as being in apposition to "recondite ends." I place a mental ellipsis between lines five and six in the opening stanza.) Here Ashbery separates himself from Eliot, who viewed his Waste Land flowers as anything but sympathetic tokens. For Ashbery, however, the forsythia bloom as an emblem of "a moment's commandment," to use the clarion phrase upon which he closes this first "block" of words. They stand as sign of openness, of potential: Who is equal to imagine them? The second half of this dense inaugurating stanza finds a credo to withstand the intrusion of the past and release the stanza as a whole from its brooding density. The credo centers on "Space not given and yet not withdrawn / And never yet imagined: a moment's commandment." The rest of "Fragment" will explore that space in an attempt to merit the muse/moment's injunction.

"Fragment" is a poem that endlessly emblematizes itself; its primary point of reference is itself as an ongoing process of opening out, creating new imaginative routes, new patterns among the old hieroglyphs. This preoccupation of the poem with the poem is linked to the dilemma of the ghostly "author" who can love only himself:

> . . . that this first
> Salutation plummet also to the end of friendship
> With self alone. And in doing so open out
> New passages of being among the correctness
> Of familiar patterns.

An unwary reader might assume that here, in the poem's second stanza, Ashbery freely acknowledges the perils of solipsism, the rigor mortis of self-love, hoping for a release from both narcissism and "familiar patterns" (with the latent pun on familiar brought to the surface). A reading such as this would make for good conventional advice: open yourself to others and release the creative force within you, and so forth. Yet the clear sense of wishing to end "friendship / With self alone" does not necessarily imply a turn toward a real erotic other. Nor does it necessarily imply a break with the family romance (to use Freud's term); note that Ashbery traces his new passage *among* the correctness (a loaded word) of the familial maze. What we do feel is an abandonment of one strategy toward the self replaced by another, one that does not acknowledge otherness so much as it demystifies the prestige of the self. Otherness is denied by the insistence upon "familiar" patterns as the ground for erotic salutation of whatever sort, and the sense of the lone self is also rebuked by the recognition that, as Dickinson says, the "perished patterns murmur" in us—the ghostly ancestors constitute the hushed undertone of our deepest longings. Finally, the crucial notion of fictionality is introduced: "The stance to you / Is a fiction, to me a whole." Once again, Ashbery's syntax operates to create an interpretive dilemma. The sentence seems to imply contrast: "the stance to you [on the one hand], to me [on the other]." But I do not think it works this way: instead Ashbery forces the reader, by his device, to decide what the difference is between a fiction and a whole. We desire such a difference and are reluctant to concede that a whole *might be* only a fiction, a stance, but we cannot really justify the desire for such a state except as nostalgia for a lost sense of objective plenitude.

To Ashbery, then, there is no essential paradox in calling a fiction a *whole* (this issue, of course, bears upon the poem's title); it comes down to a question of belief in the fiction, a Stevensian notion. Moreover, the only difference between "you" and "me" involves shades of belief. Both are, indeed, pronouns or substitutions; the second-person substitution grants that the fictional or linguistic self lives among others, is a partial fiction, while the more proximate "me" regards itself and the self it "replaces" as the whole of things. The sense of you and me converging in one compact—a mutual defense treaty—is sung in the poem's fourth stanza: "You exist only in me and on account of me / And my features reflect this proved compactness."

The fiction of wholeness, taking wholeness *as* a fiction, is accompanied throughout "Fragment" by a quest for the center both as origin and as present focal point. "Fragment" opens, as we have seen, with a double statement about origin or starting point: what comes before must be repeated and ruptured at the same time. We end in order to begin again; we *continue* to begin. The sense we gather of the increased tension in Ashbery's verse as it moves from "The Skakers" to "Fragment" very likely results from the severity of his concern with origins, not merely beginnings, with the center and not those wheeling circles upon which "The Skaters" focuses: "The figure 8 is a perfect symbol / Of the freedom to be gained in this kind of activity." Now this distinction certainly does not mean that Ashbery ever comes to rest on a point of pivot in "Fragment"; rather, he is preoccupied with establishing a relation to a center, however absent, however shifting and elusive. For the reader of current criticism as well as poetry, one of the most remarkable things about "Fragment" is its plethora of terms for describing both the quest for centered space and the issue of that quest. No present writer, whether poet or philosopher, can offer us such a rich prism of sensuous tropes for the invisible core. Indeed, Ashbery's startling alternation of abstract and concrete modes of diction reminds one of Dickinson's sixth sense for apprehending unexpected sights on the verge of the formless, the invisible.

The poem's fifth stanza offers an "opening" emblem of the center— "that stable emptiness"—and deliberately pairs it with a dry and reductive vision of erotic union: "that coming together of masses." The one, we are told, "coincides" with the other, and this is hardly surprising; to valorize the self for its stability (its "warm antiquity," to use a phrase of Stevens's) to view any union with another as a mere random collision of physical particles. This flat and somewhat sterile opposition is deliberately put forth by Ashbery as a statement of the given, the ordinary predicament of retentive and self-absorbed inwardness. This is Ashbery's condition, though he presents it here, near the beginning of the poem, in a minor key; more triumphant assertions will follow, when stable emptiness gives way to motion and more fertile cavities. A few stanzas later, for example, the emptiness speaks, the stable center becomes a roaring wind tunnel:

> The hollow thus produced
> A kind of cave of the winds; distribution center
> Of subordinate notions to which the stag
> Returns to die: the suppressed lovers.

Cliché, as usual with Ashbery, only partially deflates; to call this Aeolian cavern a "distribution center" somehow glamorizes the stock term. The feel of the line remains powerful, and we can momentarily forget, as Wordsworth does at a similar juncture in *The Prelude* when earth winds also speak to him, that the rush of sound issues from a hollow. "Hollow," indeed, is close enough to "hallow" for us to think of this cavern as a sacred void or grotto. A touch of myth also creeps in with that most emblematic of creatures, the stag, here invoked as a thirsting for primal waters. The unpredictability of Ashbery's style allows him this use of the stag because it has been preceded by the hopelessly worn phrase "subordinate notions"—a term that, having found itself stranded in a poem, looks forward to some saving figure of speech. Both the source and the quester for that source are fictional creations, illusory but necessary. The hollow must seem to produce the desired sound: it must be the very echo of that desire.

Ashbery soon gives the eye its place, too, at the vacant center. The poem's ninth stanza represents the momentarily centered consciousness standing in "the center of some diamond," coordinating sharp images as they move toward him in a kind of crystal dance. The rhythm is slow and stately; the world moves in upon the poet's eye. The stanza should be read as a refinement of the eye that earlier saw only the coming together of crude masses. Here sight is so sharp that only particulars or particles are at first visible, until even they are broken down into their constituent colors. The idea is to sharpen focus so intensely that the customary world is no longer visible. Sight is supreme, and sight annihilates fact:

> Slowly as from the center of some diamond
> You begin to take in the world as it moves
> In toward you, part of its own burden of thought, rather
> Idle musing, afternoons listing toward some sullen
> Unexpected end. Seen from inside all is
> Abruptness. As though to get out your eye
> Sharpens and sharpens these particulars; no
> Longer visible, they breathe in multicolored
> Parentheses, the way love in short periods
> Puts everything out of focus, coming and going.

The Roethke of "Four for Sir John Davies" would have appreciated the symmetry of this writing. But the real place to go—if go one must—is to the Stevens of "Asides on the Oboe." This stanza of Ashbery's only grows in stature when the Stevens poem is read alongside it. Stevens's crystal man, his diamond globe, is obviously relevant here, but I also think the poem's epigraph is crucial for Ashbery. "Fragment" everywhere endorses this ethos and this rigor:

> The prologues are over. It is a question, now,
> Of final belief. So, say that final belief
> Must be in a fiction. It is time to choose.

There is a deceptively limpid quality to Ashbery's style that readers have mistaken for indecisiveness. Certainly the poet himself at times conspires with some of his readers to create the impression of overly relaxed meditation. "Fragment" may be the most misleading of Ashbery's poems in this regard. Actually, the seeming ease of Ashbery's verse comes from the astonishing rapidity of his thought. He can at times move with a flickering intensity that works to lighten the weight of his lines; Ashbery may prove opaque, but dense he is not. He elongates a thought as molten steel is stretched. The effect can be to attenuate the thread of reference but not really to weaken it. Ashbery knows the heat of his own mind, and so it is natural to find him, in a remarkable stanza of pure lyric energy, declaring that "your only world is an inside one"—and the source of illumination for this inwardness is a blazing candle of artifice:

> Thus your only world is an inside one
> Ironically fashioned out of external phenomena
> Having no rhyme or reason, and yet neither
> An existence independent of foreboding and sly grief.
> Nothing anybody says can make a difference; inversely
> You are a victim of their lack of consequence
> Buffeted by invisible winds, or yet a flame yourself
> Without meaning, yet drawing satisfaction

> From the crevices of that wind, living
> In that flame's idealized shape and duration.

The erotic flame burns by itself, nourishing itself in the absence of meaning. Yet there is a ghost of an Orphic fertility rite in this flaming crevice. If "Fragment" is in some vestigial sense a love poem addressed to a real person, or a poem of consolation over the impossibility of such a relationship, then a stanza such as this offers searing compensation. "Satisfaction" is self-induced. Given that conclusion, the stanza ends on a note of triumph as it discovers "idealized shape and duration." Yet a certain residual ambivalence creeps into a line such as: "inversely / You are a victim of their lack of consequence." Why a victim? How shrewd the phrasing is here: one grieves, Ashbery insists, over others' lack of consequence, one is victimized by it, even while one grows in power as they decline. (It is worth noting that "they" is a sign of remoteness for Ashbery, an indication of reduced filiation.) "Nothing anybody says can make a difference"; yes, but this seems a rueful declaration.

Yet the consequences of contact—indeed, penetration—with the other are more than rueful: they inspire a sense of loss and waste. Perhaps the poem's most startling image serves to verify Yeats's adage: "the tragedy of sexual intercourse lies in the perpetual virginity of the soul." The moment of intercourse should be a passage to the center, but, as if we did not already know the score, Ashbery reminds us and his "lover" that "The volcanic entrance to an antechamber / Was not what either of us meant." Elsewhere in the poem physical contact is rendered as a species of violence— the last stanza, for example, speaks of two people who "collide in this dusk"—and beyond or after collision lies the violence of achieved impact. The cruel and perpetual surprise of erotic union, even physiologically considered, is that any sexual orifice can be only an antechamber. We reach it only to feel somehow more exiled than before: "outside within the periphery." Even in the act of intercourse we find ourselves voyeurs; we are sure that beyond this dividing wall lies the secret. This emblematic episode reverberates throughout the poem and has something to do with the pervasive tone of sober realization in "Fragment," found even at its most visionary moments. Brooding on this picture of tantalizing proximity to the source, one thinks ahead to the poem's penultimate stanza, where the self is caught in its essential isolation:

> . . . back to one side of life, not especially
> Immune to it, in the secret of what goes on:
> The words sung in the next room are unavoidable
> But their passionate intelligence will be studied in you.

It is fully characteristic of Ashbery to extend a "gloss" on an important passage to more than three hundred lines. This is only another way of noting the breathtakingly rich tapestry of "Fragment": every swirl of metaphor leads the reader to a related arabesque elsewhere in the poem. This play of tropes may strike us at first as erratic, governed only by chance; but as we stay with the poem "chance" gravitates toward "dance," to use a revealing internal rhyme found late in the poem and one that stays in the mind as a perfect description of the asymmetrical symmetry of "Fragment."

The "volcano" stanza startles us with its dead-endedness. How *are* we to recover from the fate of being "outside / Within the periphery"? This is really only another way of asking after the true center, or at least a truer sense of centeredness than is available in the erotic relationship. For Ashbery, as for other American poets, the way to this sense lies in a marriage, however stormy, of flesh with air. This union more often takes the form of an *agon* between two sources of power, two living allegories of natural process. When self and other meet, the "meeting escapes through the dark / Like a well." But when the seer confronts nature he can feel "the oozing sap of touchable mortality." This line occurs in a sequence just before the passage into the antechamber of failed eros, a sequence in which Ashbery takes on the wholly American and wholly Romantic enterprise of matching the self first against the sun and then against the emblematic blood orange, fruit of natural process. At the close of stanza twelve Ashbery situates himself at the threshold moment and prepares for the event, or the advent, of the sun's rising. Ashbery calls it the "active memorial," a phrase that refers both to the sun and to the poet's chant of welcome. The break between stanzas eleven and twelve elides not only the sunrise but the whole passage of day, passing through this vacancy to another conventional spot of time—sunset. At this point the poet's powers fail him and "convention gapes."

> This time
> You get over the threshold of so much unmeaning, so much
> Being, prepared for its event, the active memorial.
>
> And more swiftly continually in evening, limpid
> Storm winds, commas are dropped, the convention gapes,
> Prostrated before a monument, disappearing into the dark.
> It would not be good to examine these ages
> Except for sun flecks, little on the golden sand
> And coming to reappraisal of the distance.
> The welcoming stuns the heart, iron bells
> Crash through the transparent metal of the sky

> Each day slowing the method of thought a little
> Until oozing sap of touchable mortality, time lost and won.

Through the passage of day, the sun has hardened into a monument; but tomorrow will bring an attempted recovery, not in an effort to battle the sun directly—that is Whitman's way—but in a more "reasonable" measuring of sun flecks on the sand. At this point Ashbery will not heave himself at the sublime. He is open, however, to being shattered anew by the magnitude of sunrise. And yet Ashbery does not quite turn away from the challenge, either, although he appears to ground his sublime aspiration in "a touchable mortality," redirecting his gaze from the sun to the golden fruit of the sun: the blood orange.

> Like the blood orange we have a single
> Vocabulary all heart and all skin and can see
> Through the dust of incisions the central perimeter
> Our imagination's orbit.

In this tiny globe, like a good metaphysical poet, Ashbery sees the great globe and his own spherical nature. The discovery leads him to a sense of his imagination's orbit as being one with the sun's path. The crucial phrase in this magnificent stanza describes that route as "the central perimeter / Our imagination's orbit." What a play on the concept of centrality! The stanza shows us an inside lodged within the periphery, as the periphery; it speaks of centrality wandered away from the center yet not errant, but moving in a fixed path. Each word in this gnomic phrase redefines and creates space for the others: central opens the way for perimeter, perimeter is redeemed by central. This is the point upon which Ashbery wishes to take up his stance: the central man on the edge, never lulled into believing that the center will hold nor ever quite willing to view all things as falling apart.

The process of centering and decentering the self is Ashbery's major passion in "Fragment"; line after line works toward making the axis of vision coincident with the axis of things, only to discover that art requires a necessary disjunction or asymmetry. This quest to fix the place of the poetic self in regard to the external world is triggered by the movement toward the poem's ghostly, erotic other, followed by the harsh recognition that the self is necessarily alone. This detachment toward the erotic object is one aspect of the poem's mystery: Ashbery speaks at a distance from the beloved usually encountered only in formal elegy. In fact, "Fragment" often takes on the eerie tonality of epitaph: the title may be read, on one level at least, as an elegiac epitaph to a lost and impossible attempt to center the self in another.

There is a related peril, however, in regarding any one achieved stance, any one moment, as central: this is the danger of self-limitation or resistance to motion and change. Keats, always open to the temptations of permanence but aware of how they "tease us out of thought," stated the dilemma acutely in his famous letter to Shelley: "My imagination is a monastery, and I am its monk." In the Psyche ode, Keats was careful to leave a window in the mind *open*—"To let the warm Love in!" And we remember those magic casements opening on perilous seas. (Is there a connection here to the title of a poem from *Houseboat Days:* "Wet Casements"?) Stevens goes even further toward resisting this temptation to achieve the center. The epigraph to "Notes toward a Supreme Fiction" regards "the central of our being" as a place in which we rest "for a moment." More graphically yet, in a direct allusion to the Keatsian emblem, Stevens's hermit of a poet's metaphors (his first idea) "comes and goes and comes and goes all day."

The to-and-fro movement of this hieratic persona is something Ashbery affirms everywhere in his poetry. To feel centered is, of course, to feel powerful, to be all one thing. To remain in this feeling is to become a monument to oneself, and this is spiritual death. One must open out new passages of being even while recognizing that the passage begins from the center and moves outward to another center, there to begin again. This kind of movement brings freedom as well as power. The freedom of new passages is a fine trope for the whole concept of the *quest,* and so it is no surprise to find Ashbery, at one point in "Fragment," bestowing the regalia of the quester upon himself as he prepares to invade that other "room," the world:

> To persist in the revision of very old
> Studies, as though mounted on a charger,
> With the door to the next room partly open
> To the borrowed density, what keeps happening to
> So much dead surprise, a weight of spring.

"A weight of spring" may also be read as a "spring weight": when the density of self becomes too pronounced we turn to the borrowed density "out there" as a release.

By putting himself on a charger in this fashion, Ashbery risks the countercharge that he is being merely quixotic. But he keeps the figure in mind and returns to it some nine stanzas later:

> Out of this intolerant swarm of freedom as it
> Is called in your press, the future, an open
> Structure, is rising even now, to be invaded by the present

As the past stands to one side, dark and theoretical
Yet most important of all, for his midnight interpretation
Is suddenly clasped to you with the force of a hand
But a clear moonlight night in which distant
Masses are traced with parental concern.
After silent, colored storms the reply quickly
Wakens, has already begun its life, its past, just whole and
        sunny.

The uncanny alternation of abstract and concrete tropes continues: where we would expect to find a castle, instead we glimpse "an open structure." If anyone objects that I am pushing the chivalric metaphor too far by seeing this invasion as a grand charge, the next line—"As the past stands to one side, dark and theoretical"—should clinch the comparison. Who is this onlooker if not the Lady of Romance? The dark lady turns out to be no lady at all, but a parent, an "ancestor," as the next stanza informs us. Ashbery has never parodied more subtly and never been more serious in his adherence to the parodied stance. His wit is bewildering here; the quest romance survives, although the quester is not quite a solitary. His companion, no longer an erotic ideal, has become something of a magus, a friendly wizard. The turn from the beloved toward the true subject of the poem could not be clearer. Ashbery quests for a kind of visionary wisdom, or *gnosis*, rather than erotic comfort. In fact, this moment of contact with the ancestor is the closest Ashbery comes to another person in the poem.

    Who might this Merlin persona be? We could simply call him an anterior poet figure, a great poet who now appears in the guise of a prophet. This line of poet-prophets starts with Vergil, so it is entirely appropriate to find a poem in *The Double Dream* entitled "Sortes Vergilianae." I would venture a closer guess, however, as to the identity of this ancestor. "Silent, colored storms": these must be the auroras, and whose key signature are they, if not Stevens's? The rendering of Stevens as magus is a shrewd commentary on the stance that poet does indeed take in "The Auroras of Autumn," and an acknowledgment on Ashbery's part that the two share a common sense of apocalyptic threat.

    But just as Stevens moved to unmake the malice of the auroras by "a flippant communication under the moon," so Ashbery, having paid homage to his true theme, even more than his ancestor, now responds with a flippancy of his own:

Thus reasoned the ancestor, and everything
Happened as he had foretold, but in a funny kind of way.
There was no telling whether the thought had unrolled

> Down to the heap of pebbles and golden sand now
> Only one step ahead, and itself both a trial and
> The possibility of turning aside forever.

Alongside the rhetoric of homage there is the language of dismissal: "The possibility of turning aside forever." The dialectic between the two accounts for poetic strength. What makes this strength especially hard to come by is that "the fathers," as a later stanza puts it, also recognized the need to strike out against the background of a relatively fixed order:

> The fathers asked that it be made permanent,
> A vessel cleaving the dungeon of the waves.
> All the details had been worked out
> And the decks were clear for sensations
> Of joy and defeat, not so closely worked in
> As to demolish the possibility of the game's ever
> Becoming dangerous again, or of an eventual meeting.

The ancestors' sanctification of perpetual questing gets in the way of the new poet, even if the decks remain clear. Better to banish all such pictures of the heroic—auroras, ships—and turn to the difficult freedom of the present image:

> I can tell you all
> About freedom that has turned into a painting;
> The other is more difficult, though prompt—in fact
> A little too prompt: therein lies the difficulty.

No one moment in "Fragment" can be definitive; here the banished pictures return. The reader will find Ashbery toying throughout with the idea of the poem as picture (he is, after all, a professional art critic). At one point, Ashbery seems to regard his framed stanzas as "pictures / Of loving and small things." The bit of Spenserian "season pageantry" that follows this phrase tries for an intentional allegorical stiffness, as if to mock the poem's vigorous spontaneity. So the seasons pass, filled with details that accrue to "an infinity of tiny ways." Having done with the pretence of controlled picture-making, Ashbery turns against this kind of storytelling in the interests of larger brush strokes. The turn is characteristic of Ashbery's procedure in "Fragment" and elsewhere: offer one mode of working toward the subject, then shatter that way with a truer act of imagination:

> The other pictures told in an infinity of tiny ways
>
> Stories of the past: separate incidents
> Recounted in touching detail, or vast histories

> Murmured confusingly, as though the speaker
> Were choked by sighs and tears, and had forgotten
> The reason why he was telling the story.
> It was these finally that made the strongest
> Impression, they shook you like wind
> Roaring through branches with no leaves left on them.
> The vagueness was bigger than life and its apotheosis
> Of shining incidents, colored or dark, vivid or serious.

This credo prefers apocalypse over apotheosis, the image of imaginative power (here ironically troped as "vagueness") over the "shining incidents" of pictorial mimesis. Such rich "vagueness" does not betray the present to a static image, nor does it freeze (frieze) the past. Even the old studies must be "revised," as we have seen; the past as well as the future is an open structure in constant need of revisionary invasion by the present. Words for this kind of revision fill "Fragment," suggesting that the whole can never be satisfactorily captured, even when the whole is "past": "version" and "interpretation," in particular, stand out from the text in a number of important passages. The poem's fourth stanza confronts the issue directly, conceding that the poem is a version (in the root sense of "translation") of what is the "only real one"—namely, the external event posited not so much as a stable existence in itself, but rather as the uncapturable referent to which interpretation and revision always point, the *idea* of a referent. For if the real event is truly outside, then all relation ceases:

> Not forgetting either the chance that you
> Might want to revise this version of what is
> The only real one, it might be that
> No real relation exists between my wish for you
> To return and the movements of your arms and legs.

What is important to note here is Ashbery's free acknowledgement that his poem is one version, one possible text among others. At its strongest it can make us forget other texts, just as its author's centered consciousness can make us oblivious of other centers; but there still remains the specter of a sequence of endless translations:

> And as one figure
> Supplants another, and dies, so the postulate of each
> Tires the shuffling floor with slogans, present
> Complements mindful of our absorbing interest.

We return to the concept of the central perimeter, which may be rephrased here as the notion of a central text continually revising itself and displacing its own center, seeing itself and its world anew: "Then the accounts must be reexamined, / Shifting ropes of figures." This "figure" says it all: in "Fragment" we are dealing with columns of *figures*—tropes—to be added up or interpreted. It makes no difference how the figures are placed: the sum will be the same. (Again, I would argue that only the opening and closing stanzas of the poem cannot be shifted at will.) All that is required of the interpreter is agility enough to climb up or down these "shifty" ropes suspended between no discernible termini.

Or *does* "Fragment" aim at a resolution? The final lines of the poem predict only "flat evenings / In the months ahead," but a few stanzas before this Ashbery ventures on what seems like a more optimistic prophecy:

> People were delighted getting up in the morning
> With the density that for once seemed the promise
> Of everything forgotten.

This "lighthearted" density might be a resolution we could achieve: a present peace in the absence of memory. But even before this vision fully takes hold, Ashbery imagines the counterpart within us of such healthiness—the invalid inside us who cannot forget that history means death:

> . . . and the well-being
> Grew, at the expense of whoever lay dying
> In a small room watched only by the progression
> Of hours in the tight new agreement.

What then would be a good agreement between the various hours? To answer this, I must go outside the bounds of "Fragment" to one of the shorter lyrics in *The Double Dream*, "Years of Indiscretion." All versions of the self as presented in this rich volume of poetry can, I believe, subscribe to the poetic ethic of this poem's closing chant:

> Fables that time invents
> To explain its passing. They entertain
> The very young and the very old, and not
> One's standing up in them to shoulder
> Task and vision, vision in the form of a task
> So that the present seems like yesterday
> And yesterday the place where we left off a little while ago.

HELEN VENDLER

Understanding Ashbery

It seems time to write about John Ashbery's subject matter. His "As We Know" will, of course, elicit more remarks on his style—a style so influential that its imitators are legion. It is Ashbery's style that has obsessed reviewers, as they alternately wrestle with its elusive impermeability and praise its power of linguistic synthesis. There have been able descriptions of its fluid syntax, its insinuating momentum, its generality of reference, its incorporation of vocabulary from all the arts and all the sciences. But it is popularly believed, with some reason, that the style itself is impenetrable, that it is impossible to say what an Ashbery poem is "about." An alternative view says that every Ashbery poem is about poetry—literally self-reflective, like his "Self-Portrait in a Convex Mirror." Though this may in part be true, it sounds thin in the telling, and it is of some help to remember that in the code language of criticism when a poem is said to be about poetry the word "poetry" is often used to mean: how people construct an intelligibility out of the randomness they experience; how people choose what they love; how people integrate loss and gain; how they distort experience by wish and dream; how they perceive and consolidate flashes of harmony; how they (to end a list otherwise endless) achieve what Keats called a "Soul or Intelligence destined to possess the sense of Identity."

It is worth quoting once more Keats's description of this world not as a vale of tears but as a vale of what he called "soul-making." We are born, according to his parable, with an intelligence not yet made human; we are destined to the chastening of life, which, together with painful labor on our part, tutors our chilly intelligence into a feeling and thinking

---

From *The New Yorker* (March 16, 1981). Copyright © 1981 by *The New Yorker*.

soul. "I will put it in the most homely form possible," wrote Keats to his
brother George in Kentucky:

> I will call the *world* a School instituted for the purpose of teaching little
> children to read—I will call the *human heart* the *horn Book* used in that
> School—and I will call the *Child able to read, the Soul* made from that
> *school and its hornbook.* Do you not see how necessary a World of Pains
> and troubles is to school an Intelligence and make it a soul?

In a less passionate tone, Keats added in another letter that the mind in
uncongenial company is forced upon its own resources, and is left free "to
make its speculations on the differences of human character and to class
them with the calmness of a Botanist."

In these passages, Keats writes very generally—in the first with the
generality of parable, in the second with the generality of taxonomy.
Ashbery, too, is a generalizing poet, allegorizing and speculating and
classifying as he goes, leaving behind, except for occasional traces, the
formative "world of circumstances," which, as Keats says, by the trials it
imposes proves the heart, alters the nature, and forms a soul. Ashbery
turns his gaze from the circumstances to the provings and alterations and
schoolings that issue in identity—to the processes themselves. He has
been taking up these mysteries with increasing density in each of his
successive volumes.

I was only one of many readers put off, years ago, by the mixture of
willful flashiness and sentimentality in "The Tennis Court Oath" (1962).
And I was impatient for some time after that because of Ashbery's echoes
of Stevens, in forms done better, I thought, and earlier, by Stevens
himself. Ashbery's mimetic ear, which picks up clichés and advertising
slogans as easily as "noble accents and lucid inescapable rhythms" (as
Stevens called them), is a mixed blessing in the new book (which has
undigested Eliot from the "Quartets" in it), as in the earlier ones. But
though some superficial poems still appear in these new pages, poems of
soul-making and speculative classification—evident in "Rivers and Mountains" (1966) and taking expository form in the prose of "Three Poems"
(1972)—have been in the ascendant since "Self-Portrait in a Convex
Mirror" (1975) and "Houseboat Days" (1977). In "Self-Portrait," Ashbery
gives his own version of the Keatsian soul-making:

> It is the lumps and trials
> That tell us whether we shall be known
> And whether our fate can be exemplary, like a star.

"Bright star, would I were steadfast as thou art," Keats wrote, echoing
Shakespeare and Wordsworth. The Ashbery touch comes in the word

"lumps," as in "to take your lumps"—the word anchoring the lofty sentiment to our ironic existence in the world.

Increasingly, Ashbery's poems are about "fear of growing old/ Alone, and of finding no one at the evening end/Of the path except another myself," as the poem "Fear of Death" (from "Self-Portrait") rather too baldly puts it. The distinct remove of his subject matter from immediate "experience" also concerns Ashbery:

> What is writing?
> Well, in my case, it's getting down on paper
> Not thoughts, exactly, but ideas, maybe:
> Ideas about thoughts. Thoughts is too grand a word.

Something—which we could call ruminativeness, speculation, a humming commentary—is going on unnoticed in us always, and is the seedbed of creation: Keats called it a state of "dim dreams," full of "stirring shades, and baffled beams." We do not quite want to call all these things "thoughts." They nonetheless go on. Do we have ideas about them? Well, yes, as Keats did when he thought of them as shadowy stirrings, perplexed shafts of light. Our "ideas" about these "thoughts" that are not thoughts are, as Keats said, the stuff of poetry before it is put into a neater mental order. Intuition, premonition, suspicion, and surmise are the characteristic forms of Ashbery's expression. Otherwise, he would not be true to the stage of spiritual activity in which he is interested. In Ashbery we find, above all, what Wordsworth called

> . . . those obstinate questionings
> Of sense and outward things,
> Fallings from us, vanishings,
> Blank misgivings of a Creature
> Moving about in worlds not realized. . . .

These misgivings and questionings are often put quite cheerfully by Ashbery, in a departure from the solemnity with which truth and beauty are usually discussed. The chaos we feel when one of the truths we hold to be self-evident forsakes us is generally the source of lugubrious verse; for Ashbery, for whom a change of mood is the chief principle of form, "the truth rushes in to fill the gaps left by/Its sudden demise so that a fairly accurate record of its activity is possible." In short, a new truth sprouts where the old one used to grow, and the recording of successive truths is what is on Ashbery's mind.

A certain coyness attacks poets, understandably enough, when they are asked about their subject matter. It seems too self-incriminating to reply, "Oh, love, death, loneliness, childhood damage, broken friend-

ships, fate, time, death, ecstasy, sex, decay, landscape, war, poverty."
Back in 1965, the Interview Press, in Tucson, published "John Ashbery
and Kenneth Koch (A Conversation)," in which the following exhange
occurs:

> ASHBERY—I would not put a statement in a poem. I feel that poetry must
> reflect on already existing statements.
> KOCH—Why?
> ASHBERY—Poetry does not have subject matter, because it is the subject.
> We are the subject matter of poetry, not vice versa.
> KOCH—Could you distinguish your statement from the ordinary idea,
> which it resembles in every particular, that poems are about people?
> ASHBERY—Yes. Poems are about people and things.

To this playful warding off of banality (all the while including it),
Ashbery truthfully adds, "When statements occur in poetry they are
merely a part of the combined refractions of everything else." One can't,
in short, extract the discursive parts from a poem and think they are the
poem, any more than one can substitute the discursive remark "Beauty is
truth, truth beauty" for the ode of which it is a part. However, the
relation that was agitating Keats in the ode was surely the relation
between truth and beauty, between the representational and the aesthetic,
and there is no harm in saying so. Similarly, for Ashbery, it is no
disservice to his eloquent fabric of "filiations, shuttlings . . . look,
gesture,/Hearsay" ("Self-Portrait") to speak of what the shuttlings are
shuttling around, what the gestures are gesturing to.

An eminent scholar told me recently, more in sorrow than in anger,
that he had read and reread the poem "Houseboat Days" and still he could
not understand it. This can happen, even as people read Ashbery with
good will, because Ashbery has borrowed from Stevens a trick of working
up obliquely to his subject, so that the subject itself makes a rather late
appearance in the poem. The poem begins with a thought or image that
provides a stimulus, and the poet works his way into the poem by an
exploratory process resembling, Ashbery has said, philosophical inquiry.
The beginning, Ashbery modestly adds, may eventually not have very
much to do with the outcome, but by then it has become enmeshed in the
poem and cannot be detached from it. If a reader proceeds past the rather
odd and off-putting beginning of "Houseboat Days," he will come to a
meditation, first of all, on how little either the mind or the senses finally
give us. In youth, we are appetitive, mentally and physically, and are
convinced we are learning and feeling everything; as we age, we find how
much of what we have learned is corrupted by use, and how fast the surge
of sensual discovery ebbs:

> . . . The mind
> Is so hospitable, taking in everything
> Like boarders, and you don't see until
> It's all over how little there was to learn
> Once the stench of knowledge has dissipated, and the trouvailles
> Of every one of the senses fallen back.

After the next meditation (on the insusceptibility of our inmost convictions to reason and argument) comes a meditation on the ubiquitous
presence, no matter what your convictions make you praise or blame in
life, of intractable pain:

> . . . Do you see where it leads? To pain. . . .
> . . . it . . . happens, like an explosion in the brain.
> Only it's a catastrophe on another planet to which
> One has been invited, and as surely cannot refuse:
> Pain in the cistern, in the gutters. . . .

Oddly enough, our first response to emotional pain all around us, down in
the cisterns, up in the gutters, is to deny we are feeling it; it is, Ashbery
muses, "as though a universe of pain/Had been created just so as to deny
its own existence." In the manifesto that follows, Ashbery sets forth a
Paterian ethics of perception, introspection, memory, art, and flexibility.
He argues, given the nature of life, against polemic and contentiousness.

> But I don't set much stock in things
> Beyond the weather and the certainties of living and dying:
> The rest is optional. To praise this, blame that,
> Leads one subtly away from the beginning, where
> We must stay, in motion. To flash light
> Into the house within, its many chambers.
> Its memories and associations, upon its inscribed
> And pictured walls, argues enough that life is various.
> Life is beautiful. He who reads that
> As in the window of some distant, speeding train
> Knows what he wants, and what will befall.

What we hear in these lines, with their ethos of sweetness and Hellenic
light borrowed from Arnold, is a syntax borrowed from Yeats: "He who
can read the signs nor sink unmanned" and "May know not what he
knows, but knows not grief." But Yeats would not continue, as Ashbery
does, by readmitting in the next line a Keatsian melancholy: "Pinpricks of
rain fall again." Hope, he says, seems in middle age a futile emotion:
"hope is something else, something concrete/You can't have." Hope exists
still, but suppressed, confined to the subterranean life of dream, repressed
until the force of desire becomes unmanageable—a tidal wave:

> . . . It becomes a vast dream
> Of having that can topple governments, level towns and cities
> With the pressure of sleep building up behind it.
> The surge creates its own edge
> And you must proceed this way: mornings of assent,
> Indifferent noons leading to the ripple of the question
> Of late afternoon projected into evening.

And what results from the balked torrential surge and earthquake of desire? They find their way much diminished, says the poet, into these poems, these addresses, these needle-tracings of disturbance:

> Arabesques and runnels are the result
> Over the public address system, on the seismograph at Berkeley.

And what do they cost, these houseboat days, our days in this fragile ark, adrift on the Byronic tide? They cost precisely (by a "little simple arithmetic") everything, and they point to the end of the vacation, that "last week in August" which the poem envisages, with not much time left at all, as the rain gathers, and we notice this instant "for the first and last time," as one would notice a place on the dustcover of a book one is closing, "fading like the spine/Of an adventure novel behind glass, behind the teacups." In this light, the mournful beginning of the poem— about a break in a previously healthy surface, about thinking, over the hotel china, at breakfast, about the end of one's stay—is also about the common heresy of thinking oneself immortal and finding the wing of death rushing above, about the tendency of the mind to linger (to "botanize," to borrow Keats's metaphor) on these questions of time and death, and about the equal tendency of life (a dazed daisy, or life "dazed with the fume of poppies," to quote the unrevised ode "To Autumn") to blossom again in its inhospitable environment:

> "The skin is broken. The hotel breakfast china
> Poking ahead to the last week in August, not really
> Very much at all, found the land where you began . . ."
> The hills smouldered up blue that day, again
> You walk five feet along the shore, and you duck
> As a common heresy sweeps over.
> We can botanize
> About this for centuries, and the little dazey
> Blooms again in the cities. . . .

Life for Ashbery, as everyone has noticed, is motion. We are on boats, on rivers, on trains. Each instant is seen "for the first and last time;" each moment is precious and vanishing, and consequently every poem is unique, recording a unique interval of consciousness. This is a consoling aesthetic, since by its standards every utterance is privileged as a nonce affair; it is also mournful, since it considers art as fleeting as life. In an interview he gave to the *New York Quarterly* (reprinted in "The Craft of Poetry;" Doubleday, 1974), Ashbery spoke unequivocally on various topics—his subject matter, his supposed "obscurity," his method of writing, his forms, his influences. There are occasional self-contradictions in the piece, as might be expected in conversation on matters so complex. But, for the record, some of Ashbery's helpful remarks bear repeating:

> All my stuff is romantic poetry, rather than metaphysical or surrealist. . . .As far as painting itself goes . . . I don't feel that the visual part of art is important to me, although I certainly love painting, but I'm much more audio-directed. . . . French poetry on the whole hasn't influenced me in any very deep way. . . . I'm attempting to reproduce in poetry . . . the actions of a mind at work or at rest. . . . ["The Skaters"] is a meditation on my childhood which was rather solitary. I grew up on a farm in a region of very hard winters and I think the boredom of my own childhood was what I was remembering when I wrote that poem— the stamp albums, going outside to try and be amused in the snow. . . . Also an imaginary voyage prompted by the sight of a label or a postage stamp was again a memory of childhood. . . . In the last few years I have been attempting to keep meaningfulness up to the pace of randomness . . . but I really think that meaningfulness can't get along without randomness and that they somehow have to be brought together. . . . The passage of time is becoming more and more *the* subject of my poetry as I get older. . . . ["Fragment"], like maybe all of my poems, [is] a love poem. . . .

The entire interview is a revealing one, and links Ashbery conclusively to the Western lyric tradition. In short, he comes from Wordsworth, Keats, Tennyson, Stevens, Eliot; his poems are about love, or time, or age.

And yet it is no service to Ashbery, on the whole, to group him with Stevens and Eliot; when he echoes them most compliantly, he is least himself. In any case, though he descends from them, he is not very much like them: he is garrulous, like Whitman, not angular, like Eliot; he is not rhetorical, like Stevens, but, rather, tends to be conversational, for all the world like Keats in his mercurial letters. The familiar letter, sometimes the familiar essay are his models now that he has forsaken the formal experiments of his earlier books. We open "As We Know" already included, by its title, in a complicity of recognition and inquiry. The book clarifies itself over time, and is itself the clearest of all Ashbery's books; his special allusiveness, a private language perfected over the past twenty years, appears in it, of course, but there are long stretches of accessible table talk, so to speak. These appear chiefly in "Litany," a long poem written in double columns, in what I find a somewhat trying imitation of the bicameral mind. It is full of perfectly intelligible and heartfelt ruminations on soul-making in art, life, and criticism. On the whole, it wonders why—placed, as we are, on this isthmus of our middle state—we go on living and doing the things we do: inventing, imitating, and transforming life.

> . . . Earthly inadequacy
> Is indescribable, and heavenly satisfaction
> Needs no description, but between
> Them, hovering like Satan on airless
> Wing is the matter at hand:
> The essence of it is that all love
> Is imitative, creative, and that we can't hear it.

Ashbery, like Coleridge, who found all life an interruption of what was going on in his mind, lives in the "chronic reverie" of the natural contemplative. As often as not, his contemplation is chagrined, reproachful of the world that promised us so much and gave us so little. At times, he even doubts whether we are doing any soul-making at all:

> . . . And slowly
> The results are brought in, and are found disappointing
> As broken blue birds'-eggs in a nest among rushes
> And we fall away like fish from the Grand Banks
> Into the inky, tepid depths beyond. It is said
> That this is our development, but no one believes
> It is, but no one has any authority to proceed further.
> And we keep chewing on darkness like a rind
> For what comfort it can give in the crevices
> Between us. . . .

These are the dark passages that Keats foresaw and feared, sketched by Ashbery in his characteristically speckled humor.

Ashbery has said that his long poems are like diaries, written for an hour or so a day over long periods, and "Litany"—a "comic dirge routine," like so many of his poems—has to be listened to as well over a long stretch of time. Such a form of composition, he says in a poem at the end of "Houseboat Days," has to do with "The way music passes, emblematic/Of life and how you cannot isolate a note of it/And say it is good or bad." Nor can a line, or a passage, or an inception or conclusion from Ashbery be isolated as good or bad: "the linear style/is discarded/though this is/not realized for centuries." It is our wish to isolate the line as touchstone which makes us at first find Ashbery baffling; once we stop looking for self-contained units we begin to feel better about our responses, and soon find a drift here, a meander there that feels, if not like our old beloved stanzas or aphorisms, at least like a pause in the rapids. What we find in him (to quote again from "Houseboat Days") is "branching diversions around an axis": the axis of loss, or forgetfulness, or remorse, or optimism, or human drama—since we are all, as Ashbery wittily says, "characters in the opera *The Flood*, by the great anonymous composer."

"Houseboat Days" is the volume containing Ashbery's most explicit short accounts of his own intent. His model there is a tapestry done in the form of a Möbius strip; this metaphor, with its (literal) new twist on an ancient figure for the web of art, coexists with the metaphor of the litany, the chain of words, the sequence of lessons in the heart's hornbook:

> We may as well begin the litany here:
> How all that forgotten past seasons us, prepares
> Us for each other, now that the mathematics
> Of winter is starting to point it out.

As things are reduced, once leafless, to the harsh geometry lesson of winter, we learn the diagrammatic forms of life, and chant its repetitive and lengthening chant. Such is the mournful view. On the other hand, Ashbery is irrepressibly sanguine. Something will always turn up to change the mood, as it does in a sonata. Never was there a "castaway of middle life" (Ashbery was born in 1927) more confident of his daily bread from the ravens:

> . . . Impetuously
> We travel on, life seems full of promise,
> . . . Surely
> Life is meant to be this way, solemn
> And joyful as an autumn wood. . . .

Of course, this cannot last, and the wood is "rent by the hunters'/Horns and their dogs." But a renewal does keep happening: the sun brings, as is its wont, a zephyr, a cowslip.

Not only is Ashbery perennially hopeful, he is perennially generous, especially toward the whole enterprise of art—its origins in experience, the collecting of data that might help it along, its actual, stumbling efforts, its stiffening into print or onto canvas, its preservation by the academies. In "Litany," he is quite willing, for example, for the academy and the critics to exist. After all, his fresco or his "small liturgical opera," this litany, will be preserved by the academy, described by critics, long after the author dies, and even while time threatens to devour everything:

> Certainly the academy has performed
> A useful function. Where else could
> Tiny flecks of plaster float almost
> Forever in innocuous sundown almost
> Fashionable as the dark probes again.
> An open beak is shadowed against the
> Small liturgical opera this time.
> It is nobody's fault. And the academy
> Has saved it all for remembering.

As for critics, they are there, like the poets, to keep reminding people of what is in fact happening to them:

> . . . People
> Are either too stunned or too engrossed
> In their own petty pursuits to bother with
> What is happening all around them, even
> When that turns out to be extremely interesting. . . .
> . . . who
> Can evaluate it, formulate
> The appropriate apothegm, show us
> In a few well-chosen words of wisdom
> Exactly what is taking place all about us?
> Not critics, certainly, though that is precisely
> What they are supposed to be doing.

The despair of language here is a sign of Ashbery's yearning for a vision less than preformulated, more than foreseeable: for something done by great poets ("and a few/Great critics as well," he adds generously); that is, to

> . . . describe the exact feel
> And slant of a field in such a way as to
> Make you wish you were in it, or better yet
> To make you realize that you actually are in it
> For better or for worse, with no
> Conceivable way of getting out. . . .

I quote these lines even though they are not among Ashbery's best—they haven't his eel-like darting—because they show his earnestness about the whole enterprise of art, as he asks for a new criticism, deriving from the actual current practice of poetry, for only in this way do we make our poetry intelligible to ourselves:

> It is to count our own ribs, as though Narcissus
> Were born blind, and still daily
> Haunts the mantled pool, and does not know why.

It is as though poetry were incompetent to see its own image until reflected in the discursive analysis of criticism. And it may be so.

The best moments in Ashbery are those of "antithesis chirping/to antithesis" in an alternation of "elegy and toccata," all told in a style of "ductility, its swift/Garrulity, jumping from line to line,/From page to page." The endless beginnings and endings in Ashbery, the changes of scenery, the shifting of characters ally him to our most volatile poets—the Shakespeare of the sonnets, the Herbert of "The Temple," the Keats of the letters, the Shelley of "Epipsychidion." He is different from all but Keats in being often very funny; in "Litany," for example, he gives himself mock commands and injunctions:

> . . . And so
> I say unto you: beware the right margin
> Which is unjustified; the left
> Is justified and can take care of itself
> But what is in between expands and flaps. . . .

And in a parody of Blake he goes "bopping down the valleys wild;" the poetry of pastoral, parodied, becomes both touching and ridiculous:

> The lovers saunter away.
> It is a mild day in May.
> With music and birdsong alway
> And the hope of love in the way. . . .

Then, in a trice, the pastoral grows grim:

> . . . Death likes to stay
> Near so as to be able to slay
> The lovers who humbly come to pray
> Him to pardon them yet his stay
> Of execution includes none and they lay
> Hope aside and soon disappear.

And so the small liturgical opera of "Litany" goes on through three parts, in a Protean masque of genres. Different readers will prefer different arias and, through the device of the double columns, different counterpoints. My current favorite is an ode to love:

> . . . It is, then,
> Gigantic, yet life-size. And
> Once it has lived, one has lived with it. The astringent,
> Clear timbre is, having belonged to one,
> One's own, forever, and this
> Despite the green ghetto that intrudes
> Its blighted charm on each of the moments

> We called on love for, to lead us
> To farther tables and new, surprised,
> Suffocated chants just beyond the range
> Of simple perception.

This ode continues for nearly forty lines; the part I have quoted is paired, in the other column, with a reflection on solitude, perhaps preceding death:

> . . . The river is wanting
> On. Now no one comes
> To disturb the murk, and the profoundest
> Tributaries are silent with the smell
> Of being alone. How it
> Dances alone, in winter shine
> Or autumn filth.

As always in Ashbery, there is a new beginning, an upswelling. Even the end of "Litany" shows us caught in the reel of life, as the naïf speaker earnestly addresses us for help:

> Some months ago, I got an offer
> From Columbia Tape Club, Terre
> Haute, Ind., where I could buy one
> Tape and get another free. I accept-
> Ed the deal, paid for one tape and
> Chose a free one. But since I've been
> Repeatedly billed for my free tape.
> I've written them several times but
> Can't straighten it out—would you
> Try?

We all think life's first reel is free; we always find ourselves billed for it over and over; we can never "straighten it out." Never has Freud been so lightly explicated.

The rest of "As We Know"—forty-seven short lyrics—is not any more easily summarized than "Litany." There are poems (I begin this list from the beginning) about growing up, about fidelity, about identity, about death, about (I have skipped two) the permanence of art, about construction, deconstruction, and perpetual creative joy in the face of death:

> . . . We must first trick the idea
> Into being, then dismantle it,
> Scattering the pieces on the wind,
> So that the old joy, modest as cake, as wine and friendship
> Will stay with us at the last, backed by the night
> Whose ruse gave it our final meaning.

One could go on, listing the subjects of all forty-seven poems. They are all "about" something. Some are carried off better than others; some seem destined to last, to be memorable and remembered—none more so than the calmly fateful "Haunted Landscape."

"Haunted Landscape" tells us that we all enter at birth a landscape previously inhabited by the dead. We all play Adam and Eve in the land; we then suffer uprootings and upheaval. We are all—as Ashbery says, quoting Yeats—"led . . . / By the nose" through life; we see life and ourselves dwindle into poverty, and it is only our naïveté (some would say stupidity) that lets us construct castles in air, which of course collapse. Life is both a miracle and a non-event. At the end, we die, and become part of the ground cover and the ground; we become ghosts, as we are told by an unknown herald that it is time to go. The transformation takes place without our knowing how, and our history becomes once again the history of earth's dust. This is the "plot" of "Haunted Landscape;" there is no plot more endemic to lyric. I quote the middle lines, about the eternal reappearance and sexual conjunction and final undoing of the archetypal human couple:

> She had preferred to sidle through the cane and he
> To hoe the land in the hope that some day they would grow happy
> Contemplating the result: so much fruitfulness. A legend.
> He came now in the certainty of her braided greeting. . . .
>
> They were thinking, too, that this was the right way to begin
> A farm that would later have to be uprooted to make way
> For the new plains and mountains that would follow after
> To be extinguished in turn as the ocean takes over
>
> Where the glacier leaves off and in the thundering of surf
> And rock, something, some note or other, gets lost. . . .

It is from Stevens that Ashbery learns the dispassionate recording of horror, as here the farm is uprooted, the plains are extinguished, and the irretrievable note (of hope, of happiness, of love) is lost, if not under the glacier then in the crash of surf and rock. And what can we look back on? Only the ruined pastoral, our quenched dreams, our diminished life:

> And we have this to look back on, not much, but a sign
> Of the petty ordering of our days as it was created and led us
>
> By the nose through itself, and now it has happened
> And we have it to look at, and have to look at it
> For the good it now possesses which has shrunk from the
> Outline surrounding it to a little heap or handful near the center.

"Others call this old age or stupidity," comments Ashbery. We cannot bear to utter those words of ourselves.

In the meantime, the only heroism, even when life becomes shaming and humiliating, is to attain the eye that misses nothing:

> The wide angle that seeks to contain
> Everything, as a sea, is an eye.
> What is beheld is whatever lives,
> Is wildly unappetizing and inappropriate,
> And sits, and fits us.

With every construction of pleasure, there arises, says Ashbery, a precisely equivalent and simultaneous construct of criticism, and vice versa: "They are constructing pleasure simultaneously/in an adjacent chamber/That occupies the same cube of space as the critic's study." The perplexed relations between these two—pleasure and criticism, beauty and truth— are shown in constant flux in these poems, the question perpetually reëxamined:

> The contest ends at midnight tonight
> But you can submit again, and again.

Ashbery is an American poet, always putting into his poems our parades and contests and shaded streets. He sometimes sounds like Charles Ives in his irrepressible Americana, full of "dried tears/Loitering at the sun's school shade." There is nonetheless something monkish in these poems, which, in spite of their social joy and their hours of devoted illumination in the scriptorium, see a blank and blighted end. The poem with the portmanteau title "Landscapeople" sums up our dilemma—the intersection of humanity and nature. It tells us, in brief, all that Ashbery has to say at this moment about our lives, a summary both scarred and sunlit:

> Long desired, the journey is begun. The suppliants
> Climb aboard the damaged carrousel:
> Some have been hacked to death, one has learned
> Some new thing, and all are touched
> With the same blight. . . .

It is the blight man was born for, we remind ourselves. We travel in circles on the carrousel, going nowhere:

> And the new ways are as simple as the old ones.
> Only more firmly anchored to the spectacle
> Of the madness of the seasons as it unfolds
> With iron-clad rigidity, filling the sky with light.

The sacred seasons, Keats wrote, must not be disturbed. But they bring the chilly auroras of autumn, as Stevens said, filling the sky with "the color of ice and fire and solitude." At the close of "Landscapeople," Ashbery thinks of Wordsworth's "Immortality" ode, and of his own art as a Rilkean Book of Hours:

> We began in an anonymous sensuality
> And lived most of it out before the difference
> Of time got in the way, filling up the margins of the days
> With pictures of fruit, light, colors, music, and vines,
> Until it ceases to be a problem.

I have been extracting chiefly the more accessible parts of Ashbery, but it is possible to explain his "hard" parts, too, given time, patience, and an acquaintance with his manner. It is possible also to characterize that manner—by turns so free-floating, allusive, arch, desultory, mild, genial, unassertive, accommodating, wistful, confiding, oscillatory, tactful, self-deprecatory, humorous, colloquial, despairing, witty, polite, nostalgic, elusive, entertaining. It is within our grasp to schematize his practice, categorize his tics—opaque references, slithering pronouns, eliding tenses, vague excitements, timid protests, comic reversals, knowing clichés. We can recognize his attitudes—the mania for collection, the outlandish suggestions, the fragrant memories, the camaraderie in anguish. If we ask why the manner, why the tics, why the attitudes, and we do ask it—at least, I have sometimes asked it and heard it asked—the answer, for a poet as serious as Ashbery, cannot be simply the one of play, though the element of playfulness (of not being, God forbid, boring or, worse, bored) always enters in, and enters in powerfully. The answer lies in yet another of Ashbery's affinities with Keats. Keats said that the poet had no identity of his own but, rather, took on the identities of other things—people, animals, atmospheres—which pressed in upon him. "I guess I don't have a very strong sense of my own identity," said Ashbery in the New York Quarterly interview. "I find it very easy to move from one person in the sense of a pronoun to another and this again helps to produce a kind of polyphony in my poetry which I again feel is a means toward greater naturalism." "A crowd of voices," as Stevens called it, is spoken for by the single poet; as we feel ourselves farther and farther from uniqueness and more and more part of a human collective, living, as Lowell said, a generic life, the pressure of reality exerts a pressure on style—a pressure to speak in the voice of the many, with no portion of their language (whether the language of cliché, the language of the media, the language of obscenity, or the language of technology) ruled out. Our denoucement is a collective fate; we are "already drenched in the perfume of fatality." What the poet can do is remind us of "the gigantic/Bits and pieces of knowledge we have retained," of that which "made the chimes ring." If anything, in Ashbery's view, makes a beautiful order of the bits and pieces and the chimes ringing, it is poetry:

> If you listen you can hear them ringing still:
> A mood, a Stimmung, adding up to a sense of what they really were.
> All along, through the chain of lengthening days.

JOHN BAYLEY

The Poetry of John Ashbery

The poet's mind used to make up stories; now it investigates the reasons why it is no longer able to do so. Consciousness picks its way in words through a meagre indeterminate area which it seems to try to render in exact terms. Most contemporary American poetry wants only to offer what Helen Vendler has called 'an interior state clarified in language'. 'Clarified' is an ambiguous word here, meaning the poetry's effort to achieve the effect of being clear on the page. In John Ashbery's case the wordage trembles with a perpetual delicacy that suggests meaning without doing anything so banal as to seem to attempt it. Poetic syntax is constructed to express with a certain intensity a notion of the meaningful that does not convey meaning.

Or does not do so by the normal linguistic route. Inventive poetry, that makes up stories, does so by emphasizing the usual ability of language to embody them, makes that ability into a positive power. 'Jabberwocky' emphasizes it by inventing its own words as it goes along, to demonstrate how completely and finally they then make up the tale. It parodies the charged language of poetry—particularly romantic poetry—in which the force of denotation itself produces connotation.

> St Agnes' Eve—Ah, bitter chill it was!
> The owl, for all his feathers, was a-cold . . .
>
> . . . And they are gone: aye, ages long ago
> These lovers fled away into the storm . . .

The poetry of the Romantics shows consciousness in two kinds, the kind that uses words to tell stories to and about itself, and the kind that knows

---

words cannot express its intuitional being, even though that being can only become aware of itself by using them. Wordsworth, like Keats, can tell stories, stories about himself, but his poetry is also beginning to investigate the power of language in poetry to deny explicit meaning, to be precise about nothing more than itself, 'and something ever more about to be'.

The language of the *Prelude* or of Shelley's 'Mont Blanc', seeks a mode for the inexpressible. Its clarity is a way of abdicating from the inexpressable mode of being that it also sustains. The clarity may be illusory, but the Romantic dawn and the Age of Reason unite to give it a great and naive confidence, so that the reader feels it is trembling on the verge of some great revelation, some breakthrough about the state of the universe and man's nature. As this kind of poetry develops and survives throughout the nineteenth century and into our own day, it learns how to use the effect without any expectation of getting beyond the effect. Most, though by no means all, of Wallace Stevens's poetry works on this principle. In Wordsworth the language of much of the *Prelude* is very different from that of a narrative poem like 'Resolution and Independence'.

Criticism of poetry in American universities, dominated as it is by the writings on romantic effect of Bloom, Hartman, de Man and others, seems to have brought to an abrupt end the fashion for narrative poetry. Berryman and Lowell were the great contemporary narrators, compulsive tellers of stories about the self, and their style was sharply and wholly comprehensive, perfectly expressing what Berryman's mentor R.P. Blackmur called 'the matter in hand', as well as 'adding to the stock of available reality'. Such poetry invented the self as Keats invented his lovers in their winter castle, or Hopkins the wreck of the *Deutschland*, or Milton the loss of Paradise: it was indeed a comparable feat of inventive artifice. By contrast, Ashbery's poetry, warmly admired by Bloom, perfectly illustrates Bloom's own thesis that 'the meaning of a poem is another poem'.

No question of adding to the stock of 'available reality'. The poem succeeds if it creates the image of another poem, and so on *ad infinitum*, like the advertisement picture that contains a picture of itself. Clearly, the poem in my eye and mind is not the poem that Keats or Lowell or Ted Hughes wrote, however absolute and real an artefact it may seem to be: but this is like saying that I am not really seeing a coloured surface but only a refraction of atoms that gives the appearance of colour, etc. The truth of art is the truth of appearance, and its invention is like that of the eye inventing the object it sees. That, at least, is the art of inventive and narrational poetry. The ghost or shadow poetry of Stevens and Ashbery and others can equally claim the title of art, but it is based upon a different premise: that we can never see the object or the poem as it really is, never quite know what we see or see what we know. Such art is born from a uniquely American mixture of influences. The metaphysical climate of Coleridge's, of Wordsworth's and Shelley's poetry is transmuted by Thoreau and Emerson. On the other hand, the scientific climate of physics and semantics destabilizes the confidences of art: the American poet knows that nothing exists in its own self and that Heisenberg's electrons cannot be objectively observed because the art of observation changes their nature. Such mental attitudes produce their own techniques, which rapidly become as conventionalized as any others in the history of poetry.

Ashbery has great skill in these conventions and something that can only be called charm, which has increased with each volume he has produced. The monochrome sixteen-line poems of *Shadow Train* have a great deal of charm, and an elegance of diction which can be heard by the inner ear reciting itself at poetry meetings on campuses, an elegance that mimes the act of evanescence, swooping on the sixteenth line to a vanishing point which echoes the dying fall in the alexandrines at the end of some of the stanzas of *The Faerie Queene.*

> In the time it takes for nothing to happen
> The places, the chairs, the tables, the branches,
> were yours then.

> I mean
> He can pass with me in the meaning and we still
> not see ourselves.

> young people and their sweet names falling,
> almost too many of these.

Some of these sonnet-like poems have a deftly suggested 'inside' to them, as in a Mannerist picture. Ashbery's long poem "Self-Portrait in a Convex Mirror' dealt in great apparent detail with the Parmigianino self-portrait in Vienna, described with admiration by Vasari.

> Francesco one day set himself
> To take his own portrait, looking at himself for that purpose
> In a convex mirror, such as is used by barbers . . .
> He accordingly caused a ball of wood to be made
> By a turner, and having divided it in half and
> Brought it to the size of the mirror, he set himself
> With great art to copy all that he saw in the glass.

The implications of this, for space and time, absorbed Ashbery; and he spent hundreds of delicate lines apparently talking about them.

> The words are only speculation
> (From the Latin *speculum*, mirror):
> They seek and cannot find the meaning of the music.
> We see only postures of the dream,
> Riders of the motion that swings the face
> Into view under evening skies, with no
> False disarray as proof of authenticity.

The tone is of a pastel Stevens, a mildly camp Eliot, yet it has a sureness and confidence of its own, however much we seem to have heard before what it seems to say. The artist's eyes in the mirror proclaim

> That everything is surface. The surface is what's there.
> And nothing can exist except what's there.

The poetry gently nibbles at an old paradox. Art is appearance, but while inventive, story-telling art ignores this and gets on with its invention and story, Mannerist art pauses, circles and remains, enchanted by the beauty of the paradox itself, 'the pure/Affirmation that doesn't affirm anything'. This kind of art is intent on the detritus of living that takes place beyond the enchanted glass, as if Keats, having launched the owl huddled in its cold feathers, and the hare limping through the frozen grass, had gone on to talk about the ordinary evening he was having in Chichester, Sussex. The paradox gives way to another. The strange thing about 'The Eve of St Agnes' is that the more we become absorbed in its tale, its invented truth, the more conscious we are of Keats leading his ordinary life in and around the poem. A very vivid inventive art, in fact, has it both ways: leading us into the story, and also into the being of the story-teller. By dwelling on the precariousness of its existence in the midst of life a Mannerist art such as Ashbery's causes both to fade into nothing on every instant and at every word, like the grin of the Cheshire cat.

But that is the point of the business. The art of fading in this way is a perfectly genuine one, like Sylvia Plath's attribution to her poetry of the art of dying. It is an art to suggest that 'Tomorrow is easy but today is uncharted', that the people who come into the studio, like the words that come from the poet's mind, influence the portrait and the poetry, filter into it

> until no part
> Remains that is surely you.

Everything, says the poet, merges into 'one neutral band', surrounding him on all sides 'everywhere I look'.

> And I cannot explain the action of levelling,
> Why it should all boil down to one
> Uniform substance, a magma of interiors,
> My guide in these matters is yourself.

Parmigianino, that is. The poet cannot explain, but he can suggest how poetry can now be made, not of course out of the things themselves, but by speaking of

> The small accidents and pleasures
> Of the day as it moved gracelessly on,

and of how

> What should be the vacuum of a dream
> Becomes continually replete as the source of dreams.

In one of the most satisfying moments of the poem the consciousness both of life and of art is seen as in the 'Ode on a Grecian Urn'.

> Like a wave breaking on a rock, giving up
> Its shape in a gesture which expresses that shape.

And the poet concludes:

> Why be unhappy with this arrangement, since
> Dreams prolong us as they are absorbed?
> Something like living occurs, a movement
> Out of the dream into its codification.

Something like living occurs; something like art occurs. Although his range is wider than all this might suggest, Ashbery founds the substance of his verse on the ideas explored in 'Self-Portrait in a Convex Mirror', and this is particularly true of the sequence of poems in *Shadow Train*. But a further dimension has been added: the 'magma of interiors' now proffers the notion of drama, the shadow of a story. We write it ourselves, of course, according to the Bloomian recipe that the meaning of a poem is itself another poem, the recipe that is both entailed on the Deconstructionists and repudiated by them.

Not that Ashbery is in any true sense related to or influenced by these still contemporary intellectual fashions, although their leading exponents admire his work. His other 'ideas', as embodied in his extended prose poems (*Three Poems*, 1972), some of the pieces in *The Double Dream of Spring*, in his elegant little plays and in *A Nest of Ninnies*, the novel he wrote with James Schuyler, have more in common with those of the French aesthetes Bachelard and Blanchot. One of the good things about Ashbery is that he never seems in the forefront of the fashion. *Three Poems*, not one of his more successful works—prose poems are not his forte—has the rather *passé* air which is both deft and comfortable in his best poetry but somehow not right in prose.

> You know that emptiness that was the only way you could express a thing? The awkwardness around what were necessary topics of discussion, amounting to total silence on all the most important issues. This was our way of doing.

Maybe it was, but Ashbery's presentation of experience does not lend itself to manifesto. The important issue for a poet like Larkin is what he has to say, and if he has nothing to say he is silent. Ashbery, on the contrary, gets going when he has nothing to say. The absence of a theme is what he both starts with and describes. 'The poetry talks about itself. That is mainly what it does.'

Poets who say such things are usually in fact evangelists who want their poetry to change our lives. Like any other *bien pensant* of the game, Ashbery has given interviews and spoken of the 'pleasure of poetry that forces you back into life'. Such protesting too much means very little, although there is an odd kind of truth involved. Certainly this poetry is not a substitute for life, offering, as the magic of inventive poetry must do, an alternative drama. When Ashbery begins a poem with the line 'A pleasant smell of frying sausages' or (in inverted commas) 'Once I let a guy blow me. I kind of backed away from the experience', we know that an anecdote or drama, with Auden's or Larkin's narrative punch, will not follow. And yet the absence of a drama in some of the poems of *Shadow Train* is also its presence. A good example is the poem called 'Drunken Americans'. Like Wallace Stevens, Ashbery uses rather chunky, bizarre or coy titles, laid-on-the-line invented positives that seem not to connect with the negatives of the poem but to offer a kind of jaunty fiction for its dumb metaphysics. These titles 'see through' the inventions of living day by day, in which this moment is life but so was the last one. The two moments connect: Ashbery says he likes the 'English' spelling 'connexions'. In 'Drunken Americans' the poet sees a reflection in the mirror, a man's image

> . . .fabricating itself
> Out of the old, average light of a college town;

and after a bus trip sees the same 'he' 'arguing behind steamed glass,/With an invisible proprietor'. These glimpses and moments have some importance to the poet that is unknown to the reader: it appears to prompt the reflections of the second two quatrains.

> What if you can't own
>
>> This one either? For it seems that all
>> Moments are like this: thin, unsatisfactory
>> As gruel, worn away more each time you return to them.
>> Until one day you rip the canvas from its frame
>>
>> And take it home with you. You think the god-given
>> Assertiveness in you has triumphed
>> Over the stingy scenario: these objects are real as meat,
>> As tears. We are all soiled with this desire, at the last
>>> moment, the last.

Something obscurely moves in the poem, and perhaps moves us, but what is it exactly? The intensity of vision in an alcoholic moment, which is yet not intense but merely watery and distasteful until the will and the ego assert themselves in an act of artifice which is also an act of destruction? 'Tears' mutely and significantly represents the will to believe that something has happened; the ego lives by meat and tears, and desires its moments to seem as real as they are. What the 'something' is may be suggested in the next poem, entitled 'Something Similar', in which the poet gives a colour photo, 'to be sweet with you / As the times allow'.

It is a very oblique way of suggesting romance. But then this poetry seems not to wish to own anything, not even the words for the moments of which it is made up. The sonnet-like form recalls, perhaps intentionally, the mysterious drama in the Shakespearean sequence. But there is a difference, apart from the obvious one. No one would claim that our lack of knowledge is Shakespeare's actual specification in what he is writing. There is something 'true' in there, even if—particularly if—it is being invented. But Ashbery is a poet who stylizes into apparent existence the non-events of consciousness, sometimes contrasting them in a rather witty way with the perpetual work of art that consciousness has to make up as it goes along. As he wrote in a poem called 'No Way of Knowing',

> It has worked
> And will go on working. All attempts to influence
> The working are parallelism, undulation, writhing
> Sometimes but kept to the domain of metaphor.
> There is no way of knowing whether these are
> Our neighbours or friendly savages trapped in the distance

> By the red tape of a mirage. The fact that
> We drawled 'hallo' just lazily enough this morning
> Doesn't mean that a style was inaugurated.

The feel of the poetry is compulsive enough for us to see life for a moment the Ashbery way, as the young Auden once made us see it his way. Auden's world of spies and significances, solitary women and derelict works, distilled from its excitingness in the thirties the absolute authority of a new fashion. Much more muted, Ashbery's manner has some claim to be the new voice of the late seventies and today, replacing the old-fashioned directness of life-studies and confessions. He depresses the properties of early Auden to give his own version of a new sense of, and employment of, time, of alienation as amiability.

> Someone is coming to get you:
> The mailman or butler enters with a letter on a tray
> Whose message is to change everything, but in the meantime
> One is to worry about one's smell or dandruff or lost glasses—
> If only the curtain-raiser would end, but it is interminable.
> But there is this consolation:
> If it turns out to be not worth doing I haven't done it;
> If the sight appals me, I have seen nothing.

Those lines from 'Grand Galop' skilfully synthesize the minatory style of Auden with Larkin's stylization of the non-life that we are vaguely conscious of mostly leading. Ashbery has since slowed down into more elegant and friendly kinds of pseudo-precision, somehow reminiscent of a campus art-shop, Virginia Woolf's shadow features on a clean tee-shirt, like the Turin shroud.

> Yes, but—there are no 'yes, buts'.
> The body is what all this is about and it dispenses
> In sheeted fragments, all somewhere around
> But difficult to read correctly since there is
> No common vantage point, no point of view
> Like the 'I' in a novel. And in truth
> No one never saw the point of any.

Tell that to Henry James. The sonnet poems of *Shadow Train* have something of the Jamesian absence of specification, of events suggested which, as in *The Turn of the Screw*, are not intended by the author to have taken place either one way or another. But James's absence of solution is not the absence of a story. Ashbery's popularity, like that of Virginia Woolf, which has proved so durable throughout the fashion changes in America, is connected with the air of being too helpless to organize a story.

>   It connects up,
>   Not *to* anything, but kind of like
>   Closing the ranks so as to leave them open.

Helplessness is a pose: the real thing is hard to turn into an art that makes it seem authentic. What is more impressive about Ashbery's poems is their tactile urbanity, the spruce craft of their diction, which, like James's prose, becomes more enjoyable and revealing, in and for itself, each time one makes one's way through it.

Moreover, a typically modern kind of intimacy grows out of the very absence of what one conventionally understands by that quality. It is an odd paradox that Ashbery as an American poet is more 'shy', more distant in his manner, than any English equivalent of comparable talent writing today. This kind of good taste, a poetic version of 'Wasp' characteristics, is a comparatively recent phenomenon in American poetry. Nothing could be more different, for example, from the gamy, compulsively readable anecdotage of late Berryman, in *Love and Fame.* Robert Creeley (much derided by Berryman), Richard Wilbur, Robert Bly and A. R. Ammons share something of this verbal stand-offishness, but Ashbery is better at it than they are and uses it in more diverse and interesting ways.

The question remains whether it is not in some respects a way of escape from the reader, a means of teasing him or amusing him in order to avoid saying anything of real interest. Wasps have good manners, but not necessarily that completely personal perception and utterance—the two fused together—which in the context of modern poetry produces something really interesting. The point is of some significance, for English poets today tend to be braver than Americans in fashioning their view of 'the matter in hand', even though usually without thereby adding to 'the stock of available reality'. I take this at random from a recent review:

>   On Saturday morning a drove of joggers
>   Plods round the park's periphery
>   Like startled cattle fleeing
>   The gad-fly specture of cholesterol.

That is the poet actually speaking to us, in an old-fashioned, mildly witty manner, in a way that Ashbery, for all his colloquial ease ('Yes, but— there are no "yes, buts" '), would never dream of doing. The quotation above makes it clear, rather depressingly so, that the poet lives in just the same world that we do. Though Wordsworth called himself 'a man speaking to men', his experiences and the words he put them in are unique, by definition quite different from ours: no one else has had them or could utter them. And by that criterion Ashbery is a very genuine poet.

Yet there remains a discrepancy between his expression and what is personal to his vision: the first is wholly his own; the second—if he inadvertently lets us catch sight of it—can seem very second-hand. Larkin never writes a poem in which the two do not coincide, and that gives his vision its compelling directness. It is possible to get the impression that Ashbery may take some little shared cliché—the loneliness of urban America, or the contingency of its appearances—and very carefully work this up until the poem stands unique and upright by virtue of its own indistinct distinction. 'Märchenbilder' shows how successful the process can be.

> How shall I put it?
> 'The rain thundered on the uneven red flagstones.
>
> The steadfast tin soldier gazed beyond the drops
> Remembering the hat-shaped paper boat that soon . . .'
> That's not it either.
> Think about the long summer evenings of the past, the queen
>   anne's lace.

The poet's own vision enters and transforms the fairy-tale but is too homeless to reside within its pat invention.

> Es war einmal . . . No, it's too heavy
> To be said.

Saying, for Ashbery, requires the lightest and most evasive of touches. His poems hate to be held down; his style seems to have trouble sometimes with its own simplicity. This is shown by the opening of 'City Afternoon', a poem that ties itself to a famous photograph which shocked American sensibilities in the thirties, a snap of pedestrians waiting for the lights to change, their features significantly empty of the American dream.

> A veil of haze protects this
> Long-ago afternoon forgotten by everybody
> In this photograph, most of them now
> Sucked screaming through old age and death.

But the poem disappears into the photograph. It is instructive to compare it with that masterpiece of invention, Larkin's poem on looking at a young girl's photograph album.

Shadow Train is composed of poems that repeat with an appropriately greater faintness Ashbery's gift of his own version of this negative capability. There is something soothing about poems that do not assert themselves, but vanish in performance into what they appear to be about. Since the days of *The Tennis Court Oath* (1962) and *Rivers and Mountains*, the poems have become steadily clearer and more simple, more effective at distancing themselves from the self-consciousness of the 'poetry scene'. And that means much in terms of their originality and their quality. Like other good modern American poets, Ashbery has been careful to keep Englishness out of his voice: instead of it one can hear the French tone (he spent ten years studying in France), the Italian of Montale, something, too, of the later Mandelstam in translation and of more recent Westernized Russian poets, such as Brodsky. But these international overtones have produced a voice that can be heard reading itself in a purely and distinctively American context.

The point is of some significance in terms of the contrast between Englishness and Americanness in the contemporary poetic voice. The usually positive and robust reality of what the English voice is saying is often let down (as in the four lines I quoted above) by a fatal overpresence. The poem has exposed itself, and is caught there on the page in all its unavoidability of being. Keats, most English of English poets, has this kind of reality at it best, but the permanence can be embarrassing if the poem has failed quite to make it (in the nature of things, not many can) and has to stand for ever on the magazine page or in the collection, all its shortcomings honestly revealed. Still more revealed, on the radio or at a reading, by the exposed and exposing tones of the English poetry voice. That could never happen to Ashbery. He avoids definition as America does, in the 'No Way of Knowing' which is one of his titles. In a poem he once made a joke of it, referring to English writers:

> They're so clever about some things
> Probably smarter generally than we are
> Although there is supposed to be something
> We have that they don't—don't ask me
> What it is.

Ashbery's poetry, the later poetry especially, shows what it is with a singular felicity. What his poetry does is finely told in a sentence from 'A Man of Words':

> Behind the mask
> Is still a continental appreciation
> Of what is fine, rarely appears and when it does is already
> Dying on the breeze that brought it to the threshold
> Of speech.

JOHN HOLLANDER

"Soonest Mended"

It is a poem not overheard, but one which more dangerously responds to the request for a word at a time of disaster—a quarrel, a dish dropped and broken, both perhaps amid the barely heard sounds of distant, rotten warfare. The very title of John Ashbery's "Soonest Mended" is half the proverb ("Least said, soonest mended") that it tries with self-descriptive *triage* to follow. It seems aware that we risk more, imaginatively, by speaking when we are spoken to than by merely being out of turn. Ashbery's opening flat, public diction, a pitch of the quotidian to which he frequently tunes on setting out, is in this poem immediately rescued—in the absence of Pegasus, in the loss even of the hippogriff of romance who replaced him—by the flapping wings of outlandish allusion. And thereby he takes seriously his three improbable opening clichés and is off on his poem in lieu of an apology:

> Barely tolerated, living on the margin
> In our technological society, we were always having to be rescued
> On the brink of destruction, like heroines in *Orlando Furioso*
> Before it was time to start all over again.
> There would be thunder in the bushes, a rustling of coils,
> And Angelica, in the Ingres painting, was considering
> The colorful but small monster near her toe, as though
>   wondering whether forgetting
> Might not in the end be the only solution.

Allusion—here, to Ariosto—and secondary allusion (to a problematic illustration of Ariosto, itself poised on the margins of silliness) have a

From *The Yale Review* (Winter 1981). Copyright © 1981 by *The Yale Review*.

strange power that keep for the user as much as they give. One of Ingres's studies for the Ruggiero and Angelica painting (at the Fogg Museum) is labeled "Perseus and Andromeda," the foreshadowing types of Ariosto's pair. But for the modern poet, the later figures are the fallen ones; and the losses are incurred in moving from myth to romance to gooey illustration to the contemporary moment of remembering all this in a time of need. This much the poet keeps for himself; what he gives us are the limits to the possibility of rescue. But forgetting, even in the presence of the toe of a muse imprisoned in academic painting's *fini*, is not only not the only solution: it is impossible. Even those of us who require wisdom seek after a sign. What next for Ashbery?

> And then there always came a time when
> Happy Hooligan in his rusted green automobile
> Came plowing down the course, just to make sure everything was O.K.,
> Only by that time we were in another chapter and confused
> About how to receve this latest piece of information.
> *Was* it information?

The hero astride the flying hippogriff or popping out of the rusted green automobile: unlike the "pagan in a varnished car" which Wallace Stevens had denied could descend into our lives as a capable fiction, the Imagination's rescuers dart in and out of the chapters of our daily story without the fanfare even of the certainty of their arrivals. This is the residue in major American poetry of the Wordsworthian view that redemptive vision will be there, when it is to be there at all, in the light of our ordinariness. The answer to Ashbery's question is that it *was* information, but could be authenticated only by having been able to elicit our doubt.

> *Was* it information? Weren't we rather acting this out
> For someone else's benefit, thoughts in a mind
> With room enough and to spare for our little problems (so
> they began to seem).
> Our daily quandary about food and the rent and bills to be paid?

That daily quandary is the high noon of our usual attention, the state that W. H. Auden, whose language is indeed suggested in that last line, invoked as "the time· being." It is not that succession of days from which we are, or desire, to be rescued; at the beginning of his great later poem, "Grand Galop," Ashbery makes clear that it is both *through* such a realm, as through an allegorical surrounding region, and by means of it, that the force of what we know can become the possible joy of what we do. At the beginning of a great walk through urban dreck which yields him as many seeds of light as ever glinted out at Henry Vaughan strolling through the

West Country, Ashbery's vision of desiccated spring can lead him to the horrendous sequence of days in which poetic language need only name in order to act: "The weigela," he says,

> . . . does its dusty thing
> In the fire-hammered air. And garbage cans are heaved against
> The railing as the tulips yawn and crack open and fall apart.
> And today is Monday. Today's lunch is: Spanish omelet,
>   lettuce and tomato salad,
> Jello, milk and cookies. Tomorrow's: sloppy joe on bun,
> Scalloped corn, stewed tomatoes, rice pudding and milk . . .

(not an ecstatic Whitmanian catalogue, but more like a recital by W. C. Fields, trying to incapacitate further an already nauseated bank examiner).

It is through, not from, the time of the dreadful lunches that our spirits are to pass, perhaps out into sunlight.—Or, at any rate, in "Soonest Mended,"

> To reduce all this to a small variant,
> To step free at last, miniscule on the gigantic plateau—
> This was our ambition: to be small and clear and free.

In an almost cinematic movement, the poem zooms away from this innuendo of sublimity; and the next strophe of the poem (although unmarked as such typographically) acknowledges its turn away from vision with an allusive touch of older tunes in its diction. Although with a Stevensian exclamation of "Pardie!" as unavailable to him now as a Horatian "Eheu!", the poet must minimize his wail, and move immediately to a confrontation with the difficulty of making poetic arrangements in a late time:

> Alas, the summer's energy wanes quickly,
> A moment and it is gone. And no longer
> May we make the necessary arrangements, simple as they are.

We want to ask, "But how simple *are* they?" What Ashbery elsewhere calls "Using what Wyatt and Surrey left around,/Took up and put down again/Like so much gorgeous raw material," is, after all, simple like the arrangements of the daily quandary from which poetry so differs and yet for which it stands. What is never simple is doing what we have to do at the time, at this time, whenever it is. How can fictions even less than supreme be of any importance now? How can poetry mirror what Shelley calls "the gigantic shadows which futurity casts upon the present" when the covering shade of the past makes such mirrored shadows almost unreadable? Ashbery's answer starts out with a terrifying acknowledgment of the ancestry of all our rhetorical and visionary reticence, and then moves into the central passage of the first half of the poem:

> Our star was brighter perhaps when it had water in it.
> Now there is no question even of that, but only
> Of holding on to the hard earth so as not to get thrown off,
> With an occasional dream, a vision: a robin flies across
> The upper corner of the window, you brush your hair away
> And cannot quite see, or a wound will flash
> Against the sweet faces of the others, something like:
> This is what you wanted to hear, so why
> Did you think of listening to something else? We are all talkers
> It is true, but underneath the talk lies
> The moving and not wanting to be moved, the loose
> Meaning, untidy and simple like a threshing floor.

This "meaning," its own chaff and fruit unwinnowed yet, is not only the meaning of our talk, our poems, our representations to each other of our lives, neat and complex as such deep structures have been held to be. It is more significantly the messy meaning of the word "meaning," the meaning of life. It is as if the poem had come upon its own central concern at the thirty-sixth of its seventy-one lines: Ashbery's resolved major theme of Getting On With It.

In "Soonest Mended" the theme manifests itself in its discovery that significances, moralizations, intentions—all the untidinesses of meaning—reach out from talking to what is talked about. Specifically, in the middle of the poem, the postmeridional time in the history of poetry, in the very chronicle of imaginings, resolves itself into the time of middle age. This is a poem of being forty-two or forty-three; what one had set out upon, whether or not in response to some vocation, twenty-five years or so earlier, will have been arrived at only in a surprising way. It is not only that the time of heroic rescues is over and that one finds oneself, in middle age, in America, awakening to the condition in which all the available heroisms are part of the predicament rather than the means of its dissolution. One discovers that acts of consciousness can be great acts as well:

> These then were some hazards of the course,
> Yet though we knew the course *was* hazards and nothing else
> It was still a shock when, almost a quarter of a century later,
> The clarity of the rules dawned on you for the first time.
> *They* were the players, and we who had struggled at the game
> Were merely spectators, though subject to its vicissitudes
> And moving with it out of the tearful stadium, borne on
>   shoulders, at last.

What kind of action is it, then, to try to grasp the meaning of what had been overflowing with possible significances? All our modern kind of poetic knowledge, all of the ways in which, from the major romantics on, we could possibly be instructed by our moments of vision as to how to live in between them, preclude the possibility of direct answers to such questions. The landscape or scene which is moralized by the very asking of the question, rather than, in the older poetry, an ultimately anagogic formula, returns in some hardened or reduced form as if in answer to the questioning. In Ashbery's poem, "the end that is past truth,/The being of our sentences, in the climate that fostered them" brings together our lives, what we have said of them, what we have—in both senses of the word—made of them. It is not only that men say things because they know they have been sentenced to death: what we say makes up our life sentences. What we could call "the poem of our lives" is at once the poem *about* our lives and the poem that *is* the individual life itself. What then, Ashbery goes on to ask, of the early poem when we awaken to our own request for a prose paraphrase? There is something scary about either refusing the request or trying to meet it; in any event, the early life affronts abstraction:

> These were moments, years,
> Solid with reality, faces, namable events, kisses, heroic acts,
> But like the friendly beginning of a geometrical progression
> Not too reassuring, as though meaning could be cast aside some day
> When it had been outgrown. Better, you said, to stay cowering
> Like this in the early lessons, since the promise of learning
> Is a delusion, and I agreed, adding that
> Tomorrow would alter the sense of what had already been learned . . .

"and," Ashbery continues, "probably thinking not to grow up/Is the brightest kind of maturity for us, right now at any rate."

The difference between "thinking not to grow up" and pretending not to have done so is, in a way, the difference between a trivial, reductive reading of Ashbery's lines and the full—and, I hope that I have been suggesting, fully moral—one. Politically speaking, American visions of maturity—particularly during the nineteen-sixties and -seventies—should drive the good man screaming to the cradle. The businessman, the governor, and the soldier, they who represented the potent maturity of being all "balls" and, alternatively, the uncooperating stud who represented the potent maturity of being all cock—these maintained a cloven fiction of manliness, of being grown-up in America, that has always existed, but which the tasks and injunctions of our earlier history put to active use. Poetically speaking, this is the problem of how to get better, how to go on in any art without merely replicating what one can do well, without producing forgeries of one's earlier genuine work. In our losses, in our sense of time promised and time past slipping away from us, we American artists cannot say with Wordsworth in his *Elegiac Stanzas* "I have submitted to a new control"; instead, we move toward a subsequent messiness which we hope will redeem us from our successes.

For Ashbery in this poem, the dilemma about what to do with our beginnings resolves in the very act of contemplating ourselves as we are now. The astonishment at the realization of having arrived makes for a pause, but not a lack of motion. Life and art come together again in the lesson to be learned: our poems must get better, and we must all keep going. "And you see," he continues,

> . . . both of us were right, though nothing
> Has somehow come to nothing; the avatars
> Of our conforming to the rules and living
> Around the home have made—well, in a sense, "good citizens" of us,
> Brushing the teeth and all that, and learning to accept
> The charity of the hard moments as they are doled out . . .

Ashbery's continuous clarity makes us overlook the way his poetic surface is occasionally so beautifully wrought—I am thinking here of the precise and powerful definite article in "living / Around the home" (just "home" would give a sense of "hanging around," while "the home" makes it a purposive center of life). Similarly, "brushing the teeth" seems a powerful and delicate alteration of the more Audenesque "our teeth," the combined "our" of prayer, the editorial, and the nursery. If we think of the "hard moments"—difficult, windowless, durable in the memory—as being those of Ashbery's hard poem, we can understand how, in that poem, they are the moments of life itself. The difficulties of, and in, our fictions recapitulate those of the rest of our lives. Ashbery's final, firm, almost measured lines conclude his poem with a substitute for the traditional openings-out of landscape, or closings-in of shadows, which the visionary lyric in English derived from Virgil's eclogues and made its own. The conclusion they draw, in an expository sense, is a substitute for heroic resolution, or reductive hope, or a tired, tragic commitment to keeping the inner beasts of disorder chained up as well as one can. The poem has acknowledged its response to the truth about lives to be "a kind of fence-sitting/Raised to the level of an esthetic ideal"; how can it draw itself to a close? Ashbery's measured appositives to "not being sure" hide their startling revisions of the ordinary language—even the cliché—of resolution almost until they have themselves drifted by:

> For this is action, this is not being sure, this careless
> Preparing, sowing seeds crooked in the furrow,

Making ready to forget, and always coming back
To the mooring of starting out, that day so long ago.

One of these revisions accounts for the deep resonance of "making ready to forget"—not making ready to forget life, and to be forgotten, in death, making ready to die; but in fact, making ready to live and to be living. The other brings about the apparent oxymoron of "the mooring of starting out." Not only is there an alteration of the expected "the morning of starting out." There is also rather a matter of condensation than contradiction; at a more purely Stevensian rhetorical moment in his work, Ashbery might have glossed his image more by playing about with the consequences of the metaphor. "It is not that starting out on artistic and, indeed, generally human courses of wisdom is a matter of cutting loose from moorings—no complex consciousness could without the crudest of ironies utter 'I'm adrift, I'm adrift' in avowal of its uncertainty. It is only that the starting out itself, the vocation, the initiation of serious life, is all that we can be, or authentically *be said in a real poem to be*, moored to. The trope of moorings and the sea voyage of life can only apply when troped itself." Something like this, in dialectic but certainly not in language, might have provided a passage of an earlier style of American poetic meditation. The very difficulty of this kind of poetry is the difficulty of having it be true of our lives, of having its art unfold in wisdom.

This is a very different kind of poetic difficulty from that of modernism, some of whose obliquities and ellipses of the expository have already become conventional idiom, but whose other mode of allusive elusiveness, of mandarin closure, functioned as a kind of *trobar clus*, as the troubadours called it, a rhetoric which would lock away the expression of perhaps common feelings from the understanding of the vile and the base. There is some deep justification for this hermetic impulse when one is writing of love: announcing a desire for a particular person—or, perhaps even more emotionally dangerous, announcing the condition of one's inner states to the degree of saying "I love you"—both depend upon the same words that *anybody* will use. And yet, Eros being most blind of all to its own lack of specialness, the poetic impulse to say "I don't mean what they, the others, mean by this: I mean *you* and *me*" is one of the most venerable. To extend this to all poetic expression was a different matter. Contemporary poetic difficulty in America (and we are flooded now as always with bad, easy poems, as easy to read as not to read, and probably easy to write—as Karl Kraus said of aphorisms, poems are easy to write when you don't know how), contemporary poetic difficulty in America, at its most important, results from our own critique of our sense of uniqueness, our distrust of the forms of affirmation which belie its continuing necessity. Ashbery has said that all of his poems are love poems, but this is not because the name of a beloved is coded in a pseudonym, or that desires and the sad knowledge we have about desires are clothed in trope or clouded in scheme. He is concerned, as I think all our important poets are now, with what our imagination makes of our ordinariness, with what the possible rescues are actually like. He starts with a rusty old saw which rebukes all poets, all talkers, with the advice to "shut up and then everything may be O.K." He chops it in half, and then says most. Ashbery's poems are full of the unspecial: stretches of banal phrases that stumble against peaks of visionary image, faceted clichés in the ordinarily cheap settings of inverted commas. But to confuse this use of the givens of our lives (as some of his sillier admirers have done) with what has been called "pop art" is a little like confusing Emerson with Mary Baker Eddy. The banalities are hard; the difficulty of the poems as poems is the difficulty of making sense out of our lives. "Reality," noted the young Wallace Stevens, "is so Chicagoan, so plain, so unmeditative" and yet it alone must bear the weight of all our unfancying meditation. In this sense, the truest poetry is New Yorkean, complex, reflective.

But this does not mean that its mode must necessarily be urban: "the need of being versed in country things" is as much a need of being versed, of being mythologically prepared to read any region of experience, as of the mind's hunger for rural truths. In an astonishing little one-line poem, Emerson once implied that poetry associates the extra-urban scene with the broadcasting of knowledge which in the city is kept pent: "A man tells a secret for the same reason that he loves the country." Emerson's image is the exultant yell of openness here, but it must not be mistaken for an echo of the country's own voice, which broadcasts nothing in the way of truth. Like the urban scene, it presents emblems to be read, and it presents the general enigma of emblem—of making sense out of what we know we are amidst. Whether for Whitman's post-initiate consulting the oracle of the sea after hearing the great Ode of the mockingbird's loss, or for the guarded Frost, not even inquiring of his long scythe (in "Mowing") whether it knew the relevant text in Deutero-Isaiah, the voice of nature could only come in a whisper. Straining to hear that whisper has been a major American poetic act always, just as squinting at our scenes for the shadows cast upon them by our lives has been one of the major visions of "that wilder image" (as Bryant called it) of our painting. In one sense, the poet should not want to have nature's voice, for no matter how mighty in decibels the roaring wind, it is a philosopher with laryngitis; the truth of audibly moving water can only be hearsay.

And yet the poet's longing for nature's way of making things, and of making things happen (beyond breed to brave Time when he takes you hence), reflects so many of our general longings for authenticity in the manufacture of our lives.

HAROLD BLOOM

Measuring the Canon:
"Wet Casements" and "Tapestry"

I begin with a critic's apologia for some autobiographical remarks, but they do come under the heading of what these days is called "reception." Anyway, the apologia may be redundant, since Oscar Wilde was always right, and here is his *persona* Gilbert speaking in the grand dialogue *The Critic as Artist*:

> That is what the highest criticism really is, the record of one's own soul. It is more fascinating than history, as it is concerned simply with oneself. It is more delightful than philosophy, as its subject is concrete not abstract, real and not vague. It is the only civilized form of autobiography, as it deals not with the events, but with the thoughts of one's life; not with life's physical accidents of deed or circumstance, but with the spiritual moods and imaginative passions of the mind. . . .

The only civilized form of autobiography—I know no more adequate characterization of the highest criticism. And so I start with autobiography. I heard Ashbery's poem *Wet Casements* read aloud by its poet at Yale, before I had seen the text. Only the pathos of the traditional phrase "immortal wound" seems to me adequate to my response, both immediate and continuing. For me, it had joined the canon, directly I had heard it, and it transcended the poet's customary, beautifully evasive, rather flat delivery. What persuaded me, cognitively and emotionally, was the poem's immediate authority in taking up and transuming the major American trope of "solitude," in the peculiar sense that Emerson invented, by way of misprision out of Montaigne. Montaigne, in his essay *Of Solitude*, warned

From *Agon.* Copyright © 1982 by Oxford University Press.

that "this occupation with books is as laborious as any other, and as much an enemy to health." But American solitude seems to be associated always with bookish ideals, even if not directly with books, from Emerson and Thoreau to the present moment. Emerson, in his essay *The Transcendentalist*, prophesied that his disciples would choose solitude:

> They are lonely; the spirit of their writing and conversation is lonely; they repel influences; they shun general society; they incline to shut themselves in their chamber in the house. . . .

It seems a more accurate prophecy of Emily Dickinson than of Walt Whitman, but that is because Whitman's *persona*, his mask, was so profoundly deceptive. Though Whitman proclaims companionship, his poetry opens to glory only in solitude, whether that be in the phantasmagoria of *The Sleepers*, in the struggles with his waxing and waning poetic self in the *Sea Drift* pieces, or more intensely in the uniquely solitary elegy for Lincoln, *When Lilacs Last in the Dooryard Bloom'd.*

The poetry of our century has its major spokesmen for solitude in Wallace Stevens and Robert Frost, both of whom flourished best when most perfectly alone. Stevens particularly is closest to a sense of triumph when he proclaims his isolation:

> In solitude the trumpets of solitude
> Are not of another solitude resounding;
> A little string speaks for a crowd of voices.

The darker side of solitude, the estrangement from life brought about by so literary an ideal, is more a burden of contemporary American poetry. Prophecy here belongs to Hart Crane, who drowned himself in 1932, three months before what would have been his thirty-third birthday. His elegy for himself, the immensely poignant *The Broken Tower*, possibly takes from Walter Pater's unfinished prose romance, *Gaston de Latour*, a beautiful phrase, "the visionary company," and converts it into an image of loss, of hopeless quest:

> And so it was I entered the broken world
> To trace the visionary company of love. . . .

Such a tracing would have taken the poet beyond solitude, but Crane's life and work ended more in the spirit of his late poem *Purgatorio*, which pictures the poet in exile and apart, cut off from country and from friends.

The contemporary poet John Ashbery is the culmination of this very American solitude. His recent poem *Wet Casements* records the loss of a beloved name, or perhaps just the name of someone once loved, and then expresses the creative anger of a consciousness condemned to a solitude of lost information, or a world of books. "Anger" becomes Ashbery's substitute word or trope for what Montaigne and Emerson called "solitude":

> I shall use my anger to build a bridge like that
> Of Avignon, on which people may dance for the feeling
> Of dancing on a bridge. I shall at last see my complete face
> Reflected not in the water but in the worn stone floor of my bridge.

Is this not the most American of solitudes, where even the self's own reflection is to be observed, not in nature, but in the self's own solitary creation? The solitude that Montaigne both praised and warned against, but which Emerson wholly exalted, attains a climax in Ashbery's final lines:

> I shall keep to myself.
> I shall not repeat others' comments about me.

Indeed, no American feels free when she or he is not alone, and it may be the eloquent sorrow of America that it must continue, in its best poems, to equate freedom with solitude.

Freedom, or rather the stances or positions of freedom, might be called the determining element, above all others, in canon-formation, the complex process through which a few poets survive, and most vanish. I want, in this chapter, to perform three separate but related critical acts, all of them quests for stances of freedom. Taking as my texts two poems by Ashbery, *Wet Casements* from *Houseboat Days*, and *Tapestry* from *As We Know*, I want to offer interpretations that will aid others in reading more fully and recognizing as canonical two marvelous short meditations. More briefly, I then will go on to an analysis of contemporary canon-formation, and will conclude with a defense of my own antithetical mode of criticism, as against all merely rhetorical analyses. To conduct a defense of that kind, however briefly, necessarily will involve a proclamation of credo as to the use of criticism and the use of poetry, at this time.

Like many other readers of Ashbery I first encountered the text of *Tapestry* in its magazine appearance, and like some of those readers I again responded immediately, as I had on first hearing *Wet Casements*. I do not believe that a canonical response is a mystery, but I defer an account of that response until I have offered a rather close reading of the poem. Though I have observed already that *Tapestry*, unlike *Wet Casements*, yields to rhetorical criticism, whether of the New or current Deconstructionist variety, I will read *Tapestry* rather strictly on the High Romantic crisis-poem model of six revisionary ratios, that is to say, by a kind of criticism overtly canonical and antithetical, a poor thing doubtless but my own.

In the broadest sense of High Romantic tradition, *Tapestry* is a poem in the mode of Keats's *Grecian Urn*, since its *topos* is at once the state of being of an art-work, and the stance or relation of both artist and viewer to the work. In a very narrow sense, there is a fascinating analogue to *Tapestry* in Elizabeth Bishop's wonderful poem, *Brazil, January 1, 1502*, which we can be sure that Ashbery both knows and admires. Bishop's epigraph, which is also her central trope, is from Kenneth Clark's *Landscape into Art:* ". . . embroidered nature . . . tapestried landscape." It is worth recalling, as we read both Bishop's poem and Ashbery's, that "tapestry" in its Greek original sense was a word for a carpet, and that what the two poets exploit is the carpet-like density of tapestry, its heavy fabric woven across the warp by varicolored designs. Bishop contrasts the tapestry-like Brazilian nature that greets her eyes in January with the same nature that greeted the Portuguese four hundred fifty years before. "The Christians, hard as nails, tiny as nails, and glinting," as she grimly calls them, are seen as lost in the illusions of a tapestry-like nature, as they pursue "a brand-new pleasure":

> they ripped away into the hanging fabric,
> each out to catch an Indian for himself—
> those maddening little women who kept calling,
> calling to each other (or had the birds waked up?)
> and retreating, always retreating, behind it.

This negative Eros, and nature/art continuum/conflation, alike are alien to Ashbery's poem. What he shares however is a deeper level of troubled meaning in Bishop's text, which is an apprehension that the dilemmas of poem and of poet are precisely those of tapestry; as Bishop phrases it: "solid but airy; fresh as if just finished/and taken off the frame," which I would gloss as: a representation yet also a limitation, with a black hole of rhetoric, or *aporia*, wedged in between. Ashbery is bleaker even than Bishop, or their common precursor in the later Stevens, and his opening swerve is an irony for that *aporia*, that impossible-to-solve mental dilemma:

> It is difficult to separate the tapestry
> From the room or loom which takes precedence over it.
> For it must always be frontal and yet to one side.

Reductively I translate this (with reservations and reverence) as: "It is impossible to separate the poem, Ashbery's *Tapestry*, from either the anterior tradition or the process of writing, each of which has priority, and illusion of presence, over it, because the poem is compelled always to 'be frontal,' confronting the force of the literary past, 'and yet to one side,' evading that force." The tapestry, and Ashbery's poem, share an absence that exists in an uneasy dialectical alternation with the presence of the room of tradition, and the loom of composition.

The next stanza moves from the artistic dilemma to the reader's or viewer's reception of poem or tapestry, conveyed by a synecdoche as old as Plato's Allegory of the Cave in *The Republic:*

> It insists on this picture of "history"
> In the making, because there is no way out of the punishment
> It proposes: sight blinded by sunlight.
> The seeing taken in with what is seen
> In an explosion of sudden awareness of its formal splendor.

"Sight blinded by sunlight" is Plato's trope, but for Plato it was a phase in a dialectic; for Ashbery it is a turning-against-the-self, a wound beyond rhetoric. Ashbery's genius makes this his reader's wound also; a poetic insistence, a moral proposal that contains the mystery and the authority of the canonical process, which after all is one of *measurement,* particularly in the sense of quantification. Ashbery's trope proper here, his wounded synecdoche, is the "history" he places between quotation marks. Though an intense reader of Whitman and of Stevens, Ashbery asserts he knows little of Emerson directly; but his "history" is precisely Emerson's, probably as filtered through Whitman. "History," like the tapestry and poem, is a textual weave always confronting the force of anteriority and yet evading that force "to one side." Emerson, repudiating Germanic and British "history" in favor of American "biography" or "self-reliance," remarked in an 1840 Journal entry: "self-reliance is precisely that secret,—to make your supposed deficiency redundancy." But "history" in Ashbery's making is his poem's Platonic prospect of the punishment of sight by sunlight, a kind of Oedipal blinding. This is Emerson's trope reversed into its opposite. Contrast to Ashbery the majestic final sentence of Emerson's manifesto, *Nature:*

> The kingdom of man over nature, which cometh not with observation,—a dominion such as now is beyond his dream of God,—he shall enter without more wonder than the blind man feels who is gradually restored to perfect sight.

This is Emerson's triumphant Orphic poet speaking, while Ashbery's *persona,* at least since his great book *The Double Dream of Spring,* is what I remember describing once as a failed Orphic, perhaps even deliberately failed. Such a failure is the intentionality of the two remarkable lines that end *Tapestry:*

> The seeing taken in with what is seen
> In an explosion of sudden awareness of its formal splendor.

Emerson said of American poetic seeing that it was, in essence, more-than-Platonic. Indeed, I would cite this Emersonian blending of the mind's power and of seeing as being more a Gnostic than a Neoplatonic formulation:

> As, in the sun, objects paint their images on the retina of the eye, so they, sharing the aspiration of the whole universe, tend to paint a far more delicate copy of their essence in his mind. . . .
> . . . This insight, which expresses itself by what is called Imagination, is a very high sort of seeing, which does not come by study, but by the intellect being where and what it sees; by sharing the path or circuit of things through forms and so making them translucid to others.

As I have remarked, in other contexts, this is the indisputable American Sublime, by which I intend no irony but rather a noble synecdoche. That synecdoche Ashbery turns from, against himself, in favor of the mutilating synecdoche that executes two turns, both deconstructive, away from the Emersonian cunning. One is to refuse the valorization of seeing over what is seen; the other is to substitute for translucence "an explosion of sudden awareness" of the formal splendor of the seen. Against the passage of things through forms, we are given the more static splendor of the form, the tapestry's actual design. But this is hardly that wearisome Modernism, Poundian and Eliotic in its origins, that pretends to de-idealize a Romantic agon. Instead, it leads to what Romantic convention would accustom us to expect, a *kenosis* of the poet's godhead, an ebbing-away and emptying out of poetic energies:

> The eyesight, seen as inner,
> Registers over the impact of itself
> Receiving phenomena, and in so doing
> Draws an outline, or a blueprint,
> Of what was just there: dead on the line.

This is a *kenosis* of sight, like Whitman's in the *Sea-Drift* poems, or like Stevens in his Whitmanian *Stars at Tallapoosa:*

> The lines are straight and swift between the stars.
> The night is not the cradle that they cry,
> The criers, undulating the deep-oceaned phrase.
> The lines are much too dark and much too sharp.

> Let these be your delight, secretive hunter,
> Wading the sea-lines, moist and ever-mingling,
> Mounting the earth-lines, long and lax, lethargic.
> These lines are swift and fall without diverging.

For Whitman, to be "dead on the line" was the experience of being "seiz'd by the spirit that trails in the lines underfoot," of pondering his own identity with the windrows and the sea-drift. For Ashbery his eyesight, confronting the tapestry, performs the psychic defense of isolation, burning away context until the self-reflexiveness of seeing yields an outline of what was *just* there, in both senses of just, barely and temporally belated, *dead on the line.* In that immensely suggestive Ashberian trope, how are we to read that adverbial "dead"? Presumably not as meaning lifeless nor inanimate nor unresponsive nor out of existence, though these are the primary significations. Lacking excitement, weary, lusterless are possibilities, but more likely "dead on the line" means completely, precisely, abruptly on the line, the line of vision and tapestry, and the poetic line itself. But more probable even is the sports meaning of being out of play, as well as the technical meaning of being cut off from energy, from electric current. Let us translate "dead on the line" as being the burning-out-and-away of context, and most particularly of poetic context.

I recur here to one of my own critical notions, that of "crossing" or the disjunctive gathering of topological meanings between one kind of figuration and another. Outward reality, isolated to outline or blueprint, and rendered dead on the line, as tapestry or poem, is replaced by a tercet that substitutes a repressive "blanket" in a trope at once Keatsian and Stevensian:

> If it has the form of a blanket, that is because
> We are eager, all the same, to be wound in it:
> This must be the good of not experiencing it.

This revises a famous tercet of Stevens's *Final Soliloquy of the Interior Paramour:*

> Within a single thing, a single shawl
> Wrapped tightly round us, since we are poor, a warmth,
> A light, a power; the miraculous influence.

Both poets without design remind us of the Emersonian trope of "poverty" for imaginative need, but the High Romantic: "A light, a power; the miraculous influence" plays against the toneless: "This must be the good of not experiencing it," hyperbole against litotes. In the Sublime crossing to a greater inwardness, Stevens's pathos is strong, invoking the language of desire, possession and power, but Ashbery's language is again what we might call the real absence, the achieved dearth of the tapestry's substitution for experience. As Keats turns to another scene upon the Urn, so Ashbery moves his gaze to some other life, also depicted on the now blanket-like tapestry:

> But in some other life, which the blanket depicts anyway,
> The citizens hold sweet commerce with one another
> And pinch the fruit unpestered, as they will.

The humor charmingly conceals Ashbery's sublimating metaphor, which is his outside removal from this free world inside, or depicted anyway on the blanket-tapestry. The "as they will" at the tercet's close prepares for two Stevensian "intricate evasions of as" that govern the startling final stanza:

> As words go crying after themselves, leaving the dream
> Upended in a puddle somewhere
> As though "dead" were just another adjective.

This "dead" presumably is not identical with "dead on the line," since there "dead" is adverbial. I read this second "dead" as a trope upon the earlier trope "dead on the line," that is to say, as a transumption of Ashbery himself and of his Whitmanian-Stevensian tradition. "Words go crying after themselves" because words are leaves are people (readers, poets), and so "the dream/Upended in a puddle somewhere" is the Shelleyan dream of words or dead thoughts quickening a new birth, as though indeed "dead" were one more adjective among many.

I want to distinguish now, for later development, between strong poems that are implicitly canonical, like *Tapestry*, and those whose designs upon the canon are explicit, like *Wet Casements*. The implicitly canonical *Tapestry* yields to merely rhetorical criticism, while *Wet Casements* requires a more antithetical mode of interpretation. Nevertheless, I have ventured an antithetical reading of *Tapestry*, pretty well relying upon my apotropaic litany of revisionary ratios, and now I will extend contrariness by a reading of *Wet Casements* neither formal nor antithetical, but freestyle, eclectic, perhaps wholly personal.

Ashbery shies away from epigraphs, yet *Wet Casements* turns to Kafka's *Wedding Preparations in the Country* in order to get started. The epigraph though is more about not getting started:

When Eduard Raban, coming along the passage, walked into the open doorway, he saw that it was raining. It was not raining much.

Three paragraphs on from this opening, Raban stares at a lady who perhaps has looked at him:

> She did so indifferently, and she was perhaps, in any case, only looking at the falling rain in front of him or at the small nameplates of firms that were fixed to the door over his head. Raban thought she looked amazed. "Well," he thought, "if I could tell her the whole story, she would cease to be astonished. One works so feverishly at the office that afterwards one is too tired even to enjoy one's holidays properly. But even all that work does not give one a claim to be treated lovingly by everyone; on the contrary, one is alone, a total stranger and only an object of curiosity. And so long as you say 'one' instead of 'I' there's nothing in it and one can easily tell the story; but as soon as you admit to yourself that it is you yourself, you feel as though transfixed and are horrified."

That dark reflection is the *ethos*, the universe of limitation, of the poem *Wet Casements*, whose opening irony swerves from Kafka's yet only to more self-alienation:

> The conception is interesting: to see, as though reflected
> In streaming windowpanes, the look of others through
> Their own eyes.

"Interesting" is one of Ashbery's driest ironies, and is a trope for something like "desperate," while the "look of others through/Their own eyes" is an evasion, wholly characteristic of Ashbery's self-expression through his own reflexive seeing. Yet the conception *is* interesting, particularly since it is both concept and engendering. How much can one catch of the look of others or of the self, through their eyes or one's own, when the look is reflected in wet casements, in streaming windowpanes? The question is desperate enough, and the slightly archaic "casements" of the title means not just any windows opening outwards, but the casements of Keats's odes, open to the vision of romance. Keats concluded his *Ode to Psyche* with the vision of "A bright torch, and a casement ope at night, / To let the warm love in!" In *Ode to a Nightingale*, there is the still grander trope of the bird's song: "that oft-times hath / Charmed magic casements, opening on the foam / Of perilous seas in fairy lands forlorn." *Wet Casements* is a strange, late, meditative version of the Keatsian ode, obviously not in mere form, but in rhetorical stance. Perhaps we might describe it as Keats assimilated to the Age of Kafka, and still it remains Keats. Lest I seem more extreme even than usual, I turn to the merely useful point that must be made in starting to read Ashbery's poem. It could not be entitled *Wet Windows*, because these have to be windows that open outwards, just as Kafka's Raban walked into the open doorway to see that it was raining. There must be still, even in Kafka and in Ashbery, what there always was in Keats, the hope, however forlorn, of open vision, and of a passage to other selves.

Yet *Wet Casements* is a beautifully forlorn poem, a hymn to lost Eros, not an *Ode to Psyche* triumphantly opening to Eros even as a poem attempts closure. The conception is indeed interesting, to see the self-seen look of others reflected in a window closed against the rain, but that could and should be opened outwards in a season of calm weather. "A digest," Ashbery writes, meaning a daemonic division or distribution of self-images, ending with the overlay of his own "ghostly transparent face." We are back in one of Ashbery's familiar modes, from at least *Three Poems* on, a division of self and soul of a Whitmanian rather than Yeatsian kind, where "you" is Ashbery's soul or re-imagined character, in the process of becoming, and "I" is Ashbery's writing self or reduced personality. But the "you" is also the erotic possibility of otherness, now lost, or of a muse-figure never quite found. This is the "you" described in the long passage that is a single sentence and that takes up exactly half of the poem's length:

> You in falbalas
> Of some distant but not too distant era, the cosmetics,
> The shoes perfectly pointed, drifting (how long you
> Have been drifting; how long I have too for that matter)
> Like a bottle-imp toward a surface which can never be approached,
> Never pierced through into the timeless energy of a present
> Which would have its own opinions on these matters,
> Are an epistemological snapshot of the processes
> That first mentioned your name at some crowded cocktail
> Party long ago, and someone (not the person addressed)
> Overheard it and carried that name around in his wallet
> For years as the wallet crumbled and bills slid in
> And out of it.

Call it a Whitmanian "drifting," an episode in Ashbery's continuous, endless Song of Himself. "Drifting" is the crucial word in the passage, akin to Whitman's "sea-drift" elegiac intensities. What precisely can "drifting" mean here? "You"—soul of Ashbery, lost erotic partner, the other or muse component in lyric poetry—are attired in the ruffles, frills, cosmetics, ornamental shoes of a studied nostalgia, one of those eras Stevens said the imagination was always at an end of, a vanished elegance. Like an Arabian Nights bottle-imp you are drifting perpetually towards a fictively paradoxical surface, always absent. If it were present, if you could approach it ever, then you would be pierced through, you would have pierced through, into a true present, indeed into the ontological timelessness of an energy of consciousness that would pass judgment upon all drifting, have its own opinion, presumably negative, of drifting. Again, why "drifting"? The best clue is that the drifter is "an epistemological snapshot of the processes" of time itself, which has a wallet at its back, a crumbling wallet, with bills and alms for oblivion sliding in and out of it. The unreachable surface of a present would have timeless energy, but "drifting" means to yield with a wise passivity to temporal entropy, and so to be reduced to "an epistemological snapshot" of time's revenges.

Yet that is only part of a dialectic; the other part is naming, having been named, remembering, having been remembered. Your overheard name, carried round for years in time's wallet, may be only another alm for oblivion, and yet its survival inspires in you the poet's creative rage for immortality, or what Vico called "divination": "I want that information very much today,/Can't have it, and this makes me angry." The striking word is "information," reminding Ashbery's readers of the crucial use of that word in *Wet Casements*'s meditative rival, *Soonest Mended* in *The Double Dream of Spring*:

> Only by that time we were in another chapter and confused
> About how to receive this latest piece of information.
> *Was* it information? Weren't we rather acting this out
> For someone else's benefit, thoughts in a mind
> With room enough and to spare for our little problems. . . .

"Information" in both poems means a more reliable knowledge communicated by and from otherness, than is allowed by one's status as an epistemological snapshot of a drifter through temporal processes. But the casements do not open out to otherness and to love, and where information is lacking, only the proper use of the rage to order words remains:

> I shall use my anger to build a bridge like that
> Of Avignon, on which people may dance for the feeling
> Of dancing on a bridge.

The round-song of the bridge of Avignon charmingly goes on repeating that the bridge is there, and that people dance upon it. As a trope for the poem *Wet Casements*, this tells us both the limitation and the restituting strength of Ashbery's ambitions. But the song of the self, as in Whitman, movingly and suddenly ascends to a triumph:

> I shall at last see my complete face
> Reflected not in the water but in the worn stone floor of my bridge.

The dancers are Ashbery's readers, who as Stevens once said of *his* elite, will do for the poet what he cannot do for himself: receive his poetry. Elegantly, Ashbery reverses his initial trope, where the reflection in streaming windowpanes did not allow seeing the complete face either of others or of the self. The worn stone floor of the bridge of words has replaced the wet casements, a substitution that prompts the strongest of all Ashberian poetic closures:

> I shall keep to myself.
> I shall not repeat others' comments about me.

If the sentiment is unlike Whitman's, its sermon-like directness still would have commended it to Whitman, or to Thoreau, or even to the Founder, Emerson. For this is the Emersonian Sublime, a belated declaration of self-reliance, or a repression of every fathering force, even the American ones. I note Ashbery's uncharacteristic but very welcome bluntness, and turn to consider how and why I would assign a canonical strength both to this poem and to *Tapestry*. Yet this means I must turn first to the vexed problematic of the canonical process itself.

There is no innocence, and only a small degree of chance, in the canonical process. As a Western procedure, it has combined three main elements: the Jewish tradition of forming Scripture, with its Christian misprision and subsequent refinements, is ideologically the most important. The Alexandrian Hellenistic tradition of literary scholarship is the most instrumental for us, since it inaugurated the canonization of what we would now call secular texts. But the Greek poets themselves, at least from Hesiod on, invented poetic self-canonization, or self-election. I am going to suggest the antithetical formula that a contemporary American poem, to have any hope of permanence, necessarily builds the canonical ambition, process and agon directly into its own text, as Hesiod, Pindar, Milton, Pope, Wordsworth and Whitman did also, as indeed all the poetic survivors have done.

Homer and his unknown precursors were primarily storytellers, and to tell a story is very different from the act of measuring the canon. That act is a genealogy, and perhaps necessarily a cataloging. We sometimes call Whitman the American Homer, but it might be more accurate to call him the American Hesiod. Nietzsche followed Burckhardt in seeing the agonistic spirit as being central to Greek culture, and here is Nietzsche upon *Homer's Contest:*

> Every talent must unfold itself in fighting. . . . Whereas modern man fears nothing in an artist more than the emotion of any personal fight, the Greek knows the artist *only as engaged in a personal fight.* Precisely

where modern man senses the weakness of a work of art, the Hellene seeks the source of its greatest strength. . . . What a problem opens up before us when we inquire into the relationship of the contest to the conception of the work of art!

This agonistic spirit, as expounded by Nietzsche, finds expression in the genealogies and catalogues of Hesiod, who in sorting out and so canonizing the gods, becomes the first Greek theologian. But though epic and drama were conducted as contests, it was in the Greek lyric that the agon became truly internalized, to the extent that the canonical process itself became the structure—rather than the gesture—of the poet's stance. Here is the final stanza of Pindar's *First Olympian Ode* (as rendered by Richmond Lattimore):

> For me
> the Muse in her might is forging yet the strongest arrow.
> One man is excellent one way, one in another; the highest
> fulfills itself in kings. Oh, look no further.
> Let it be yours to walk this time on the height.
> Let it be mine to stand beside you
> in victory, for my skill at the forefront of the Hellenes.

Hieron of Syracuse and his fellow contestants in the race for horse and rider are clearly not so much in Pindar's mind as are Simonides and Bacchylides. Milton, opening *Lycidas* with that awesome and shattering "Yet once more," sweeps past Virgil and Spenser and inaugurates a new internalization of the agon, not to be matched until Wordsworth's *Intimations* ode confidently chants: "Another race has been and other palms are won." This is the tradition of the explicitly canonical, subverted by Keats in his implicitly canonical odes. Yet how am I employing the traditional term "canonical" here? Metaphorically, I must admit, that is to say by what I would call "a strong misreading," and here I must present a highly compressed account of a theory of canonization.

A strong poem, which alone can become canonical for more than a single generation, can be defined as a text that must engender strong misreadings, both as other poems and as literary criticism. Texts that have single, reductive, simplistic meanings are themselves already necessarily weak misreadings of anterior texts. When a strong misreading has demonstrated its fecundity by producing other strong misreadings across several generations, then we can and must accept its canonical status.

Yet by "strong misreading" I mean "strong troping," and the strength of trope can be recognized by skilled readers in a way that anticipates the temporal progression of generations. A strong trope renders all merely trivial readings of it irrelevant. Confronted by Ashbery's "dead on the line" or his "I want that information very much today,/Can't have it, and this makes me angry," the weak reader is defeated by the energy of the Sublime. "Dead," "line," "information" and "angry" are available only to the agonistic striver in the reader, not to the reductionist who inhabits always the same reader. Longinus on the Sublime and Shelley defending poetry both make the crucial point that strong, canonical, Sublime poetry exists in order to compel the reader to abandon easier literary pleasures for more difficult satisfactions, or as Freud would have said it, for works where the incitement premium is higher.

There is a true law of canonization, and it works contrary to Gresham's law of currency. We may phrase it: *in a strong reader's struggle to master a poet's trope, strong poetry will impose itself, because that imposition, that usurpation of mental space, is the proof of trope, the testing of power by power.* The nature of that trope in the poetry of the last three hundred years is increasingly transumptive, and with a brief examination of transumption I will offer also an assertion of how criticism can meet the challenge of the canonical process, and then conclude with a coda on the use of poetry.

Transumption is diachronic rhetoric, figuration operating across a time-frame, which is of course a conceptual temporality, or trope of time, not time itself, whatever we take that to be. Theorists from Samuel Johnson to Angus Fletcher and John Hollander have noted that Miltonic simile is uniquely transumptive in nature, that it crowds the imagination by joining Milton to an ancient and complete truth, and by making every poet's figuration that comes between that proper truth and Milton's text into a trope of belated error, however beautiful or valuable. By joining himself to an ever-early candor, Milton thus assured not only his own place in the canon, but taught his poetic successors how to make themselves canonical by way of their transumptive imagery. This remains the canonical use of strong poetry: it goes on electing its successors, and these Scenes of Instruction become identical with the continuity of poetic tradition.

The use of criticism can only be like this use of poetry. Criticism too must display a power at once interpretive and revisionary, and thus, as Hollander says, in some sense make the echo even louder than the original voice. In a time when nearly every other activity of the mind has suffered a de-mystification or a de-idealization, the writing and reading of poetry has retained a curious prestige of idealism. Curious because the nature of poetry, during the last two hundred years or so, may have changed in ways we scarcely begin to apprehend.

Poetry from Homer through Alexander Pope (who died in 1744)

had a subject matter in the characters and actions of men and women clearly distinct from the poet who observed them, and who described and sometimes judged them. But from 1744 or so to the present day the best poetry internalized its subect matter, particularly in the mode of Wordsworth after 1798. Wordsworth had no true subject except his own subjective nature, and very nearly all significant poetry since Wordsworth, even by American poets, has repeated Wordsworth's inward turning.

This no longer seems to be a question of any individual poet's choice, but evidently is a necessity, perhaps a blight, of the broad movement that we see now to be called Romanticism *or* Modernism, since increasingly the latter would appear to have been only an extension of the former. What can be the use of a poetry that has no true subject except the poet's own selfhood? The traditional use of poetry in the Western world has been instruction through delight, where teaching has meant the common truths or common deceptions of a societal tradition, and where esthetic pleasure has meant a fulfillment of expectations founded upon past joys of the same design. But an individual psyche has its own accidents, which it needs to call truths, and its own necessity for self-recognition, which requires the pleasures of originality, even if those pleasures depend upon a kind of lying-against-time, and against the achievements of the past. The use of such a poetry demands to be seen in a de-idealized way, if it is to be seen more truly.

The philosopher of modern poetry is the Neapolitan rhetorician Giambattista Vico, who died in 1744, the same year as the poet Pope. In his *New Science* (1725), Vico strikingly de-idealized the origin and purpose of poetry. Vico believed that the life of our primitive ancestors was itself what he termed "a severe poem." These giants, through the force of a cruel imagination, defended themselves against nature, the gods, and one another by metaphoric language, with which they "divinated," that is, at once they sought to become immortal gods and also to ward off potential and future dangers from their own lives. For them, the function of poetry was not to liberate, but to define, limit, and so defend the self against everything that might destroy it. This Vichian or de-idealizing view of poetry is the truth about all poetry, in my judgment, but particularly modern poetry. The use of poetry, for the reader as for the poet, is at a profound level an instruction in defense. Poetry teaches a reader the necessity of interpretation, and interpretation is, to cite the other great philosopher of modern poetry, Nietzsche, the exercise of the will-to-power over a text.

The strong American poets—Emerson, Whitman, Dickinson, Frost, Stevens, Hart Crane—and the strongest of our contemporaries—Robert

Penn Warren, Elizabeth Bishop, A. R. Ammons, James Merrill, W. S. Merwin, John Hollander, James Wright and John Ashbery—can give their American readers the best of pragmatic aids in the self-reliance of a psychic self-defense. In the struggle of the reader both with and against a strong poem, more than an interpretation of a poem becomes the prize. What instruction is more valuable than that which shows us how to distinguish real from illusory dangers to the self's survival, and how to ward off the real menaces?

ANITA SOKOLSKY

"A Commission That Never Materialized": Narcissism and Lucidity in Ashbery's "Self-Portrait in a Convex Mirror"

There is a certain precocity in Ashbery's poetry which makes its observations seem to come a little too early. Their own sophistication appears to surprise them. They also surprise the reader: notions are exquisitely elaborated that one has not been set up to understand or to understand the importance of. The structure which would make sense of them hasn't yet occurred, and will be outmoded before one can formulate it. In the attempt to interpret, one is prompted to a paraphrase which devolves into echo, blankly repeating what it attempts to elucidate: the spell of the poem's particular formulations.

Perhaps that solicitous echo, as it hovers around a language carefully considering itself, can help explain why the issue of narcissism predominates in criticism of Ashbery's work. Those who are irritated by the echo condemn the poetry's self-absorption and obscurity, equating lucidity and accessibility of meaning with an escape from the self. Those who are moved by it acclaim the insights borne of its reflexiveness. Yet nearly all such assessments take place within a conventional notion of narcissism which assumes that self for self's sake is an inexcusable vice, that self-exploration is justifiable only when it moves inward in order to move, with majestic clarification, out.

Printed for the first time in this volume. Copyright © 1985 by Anita Sokolsky.

Narcissism has not ceased to provoke the mildest men to relish its punishment, a punishment the purer since, as in Ovid's myth, it is inflicted from within: Narcissus requires no other retribution than his insatiable yearning to make him pine away. Thus those who censure narcissism always manage to remain outside its charged circle. Narcissism has the peculiar status of an impulse which inflames the structure of authority which condemns it, yet against which such authority does not even need to raise a finger, secure in the knowledge that narcissism must ultimately destroy itself.

That is what the history of lyric poetry teaches us, and it is precisely in that context that Ashbery's poetry is already being evaluated. The scrutiny to which it is subjected is meant to determine how his work transforms the poetic undertaking by addressing the issues which have informed the history of the lyric. Such criticism examines how Ashbery's poetry is derivative and how it is original, and reveals the ways in which his originality impeccably acknowledges his derivations.

But there is another movement afoot, one which perceives Ashbery as dispelling the values which bolster a canonical history of poetry, such as uniqueness of perception, originality of voice, canonicity itself. Such post-modernist readings jettison an enterprise which reads poetry as a mode of speculation that confirms the centrality of the self in favor of a notion of the subject which is provisional and linguistically engendered. In such terms, Ashbery's work helps to collapse the structures which defend the sanctity of high culture.

The peculiar ingenuity of Ashbery's poetry is that it confounds both a post-modernist and a canonical reading. He seems quite willing to take on the crucial issues of lyric poetry, to address the canon, to explore the limits of poetic speculation. Yet his poetry plays havoc with the nature of originality, the sanctity of art. A poem such as "Self-Portrait in a Convex Mirror" conveys a formality, a sense of immense preparations, combined with an acute sense of the improvisatory nature of experience, which exempts it from being either insurgent or orthodox. And it is from this elusive and peculiarly modest stance, I want to argue, that Ashbery's poetry provides a precise and mobile account of the dynamics of narcissism and of the speculative transactions lyric poetry engages in.

"Self-Portrait" takes for granted that narcissism is the implicit subject-matter of art, generating incessant speculation about its own enterprise and the nature of the poetic subject. The hackneyed scruple which compels Ashbery to remind us that the word "speculation" is "From the Latin *speculum*, mirror," makes that link clear. The speculative enterprise and the narcissistic are one and the same: the attempt to think one's way out of oneself is forever circumscribed by the realization that one has remained all along within a speculative circle which one keeps rethinking. If "Self-Portrait" undertakes to speculate its way out of narcissism, it does so in order to assess whether a reflexive poetry can end reflexivity, whether a poetry based on the dichotomy of self and other can circumvent that split.

Recent psychoanalytic theory has done much to expose why narcissism has been so scorned within a literary tradition which is obsessed with the self, and offers suggestive terms within which to assess Ashbery's poetry. In his *Life and Death in Psychoanalysis*, Jean Laplanche persuasively dismantles Freud's distinction between the perversion of narcissistic fixation on an internalized ego-ideal and the normal externalization of desire in an object-ideal (a distinction Freud himself may be interpreted as considering dubious). By showing the degree to which our investment in rejecting narcissism works to maintain the illusory possibility that one could escape the constraints of the self, Laplanche reveals the inherent narcissism of both ego and object ideals.

In an essay on Ovid's Narcissus myth ("Narcissus in the Text," *The Georgia Review* 30, no. 5, Summer 1976), John Brenkman offers an analogous assessment of the dynamics of literary narcissism, arguing that literature has derogated and punished narcissism in order to bolster a system of beliefs based on privileging voice (Echo) as the guarantor of sincerity, self-authority, and a desire to extend beyond the self, over representation (Narcissus), which is self-seeking, duplicitous, and endlessly deferring of satisfaction, since it cannot embrace the reality it images. He goes on to demonstrate that the values associated with voice are determined by and implicated in a system of writing. Brenkman thus divests narcissism of its moral stigma, and argues for its inescapability in literature.

By making narcissistic representation the subject-matter of "Self-Portrait," Ashbery takes up these concerns. He essentially asks, what happens when such representation becomes primary, becomes the privileged subect of writing? Is it possible to reassess the dynamics of poetic narcissism in these terms?

Ovid's account of narcissism is susceptible of further reinterpretation which calls into play the essential issues of Ashbery's reassessment. It is worth looking briefly at the story which precedes that of Narcissus, and focuses on the question of object idealization. A domestic quarrel arises between Juno and Jove about whether men or women get greater pleasure from sex, each arguing that the opposite sex does. They call in Tiresias to adjudicate, for he has been both man and woman, having been transformed into a woman for seven years when he struck at two copulating serpents with a stick. (He turned himself back into a man by a repetition of this gesture.) Tiresias sides with Jove, claiming that women have greater sexual pleasure, and, in a rage, Juno blinds him, while, to make amends, Jove grants him the power of prophecy.

It is peculiar that both Jove and Juno should so vehemently deny that his or her sex has greater sexual pleasure, and even more peculiar that if Tiresias considers women to be the victors he should have chosen to be turned back into a man. What this tale reveals is that one wants to believe the object of desire capable of greater pleasure than oneself, that in fact desire is generated by that belief. For postulating the greater pleasure of the other ensures that one always cherishes a longing for what one can never have. And what one can never have is the greater capacity for desire, and therefore for greater satisfaction, that the other is wistfully conceived to possess. The banality of fulfillment is instead transformed into a sign of one's own pleasing insufficiency in relation to a phantasmatic model of an inconceivably greater capacity for desire.

The need to posit the greater pleasure of the other is narcissistic even though it seems to ratify an other-centered economy, for it guarantees precisely what fuels narcissism—that desire is tantalizingly unfulfillable. Thus, Juno punishes Tiresias because from her point of view he threatens to undo the narcissistic economy by identifying her own sex, and so herself, as the source of greater sexual pleasure. Tiresias' sexual transformations also result from disturbing a narcissistic economy: by cutting apart two copulating serpents, a vision of like mating with like, Tiresias strikes out at an image of heterosexual and presumably non-narcissistic love which, by its phallic configuration, reveals the narcissism, or, in Freud's terms, homosexual desire, at the heart of non-narcissistic love. Thus, the story which leads up to Narcissus' self-love and consequent punishment ratifies the structure of narcissistic desire while seeming to uphold the law of the gods as generously centered on another. And the tale shows the gift of prophecy or poetic insight to be the dubious reward for disrupting the economy of narcissism.

While Tiresias is punished for ruffling that economy, Narcissus receives a rather inconsistent discipline from Ovid for apparently preserving it. Yet the myth explores the problem of narcissism differently from the way it is ordinarily understood. Narcissus is *not* punished, as one would expect, for loving his own image. That in itself would not be so bad, for, as Tiresias warns, Narcissus will live a long life "if he never knows himself." And certainly Echo is punished equally by her love for another; in fact, her love for Narcissus is shown to be as narcissistic as his for his handsome self, though invested with greater pathos. Narcissus' problem does not seem to be so much a moral one as a surface/depth confusion; he mistakes the surface image he falls in love with for depth, and it is this perceptual naiveté which damns him. Thus, narcissism is revealed by the myth to be based on the illusion of profundity, of substantive concealed meaning. The threat posed by narcissism occurs in the recognition of the illusory nature of personal depths: a recognition which fosters an increased and despairing self-love, even while it recoils from the disaffecting awareness that there is nothing there to grasp onto.

Interestingly, Ovid recoils from his own text's making such a recognition even as he incites Narcissus to do so:

> As he tried
> To quench his thirst, inside him, deep within him,
> Another thirst was growing, for he saw
> An image in the pool, and fell in love
> With that unbodied hope, and found a substance
> In what was only shadow.
> (*Metamorphoses*, trans. by Rolfe Humphries.
> Indiana: Indiana University Press, 1955, p. 70)

Thus Ovid inserts a belief in depth psychology—"To quench his thirst, inside him, deep within him"—precisely when he reveals Narcissus to be deceived by the illusion of hidden substance, as though to circumscribe Narcissus' discovery that what the image or representation reveals is the ungraspable, unémbraceable nature of the self. This I take to be the meaning of the lines:

> Why try to catch an always fleeing image,
> Poor credulous youngster? What you seek is nowhere,
> And if you turn away, you will take with you
> The boy you love.
> (pp. 70–71)

Such taunting on Ovid's part reveals the same heartlessness Narcissus showed toward Echo, and vengefully exposes not only that Narcissus is not a pariah in the economy of the myth, but also that what he learns is the vanity of attempting to conceive the self as substantive and profound.

In the degree to which Ovid's myth shuts down and isolates Narcissus' recognition, then, we find the myth subtly reinstituting the possibility of believing in a substantive self and thus reaffirming the commonly understood notion of narcissism as delusory self-love. The law which refuses to touch narcissism and lets it wither away really upholds narcissism by continuing to hold out the possibility of substantive selves who, out of their depths, can love others and transcend themselves.

Thus, Ovid's law must guarantee a belief in depth; it keeps clear of the recognition of its illusory nature because, so long as narcissism operates within a system which privileges depth psychology, the law knows that Narcissus will wither away from recognizing the impossibility of recovering his image. Narcissism demands self-punishment because it still operates within a system of yearning for the other. And the law needs to dissociate itself from the recognition of depth as illusion because it cannot be scrutinized from that point of view; to do so would betray the degree to which the law, like narcissism, relies on a belief in depth and the other.

In choosing to explore the issue of aesthetic narcissism by focusing on Parmagianino's self-portrait, Ashbery starts where Narcissus left off: at the self-dissolving recognition of representation's illusory depths. The poem mirrors a portrait which mirrors a mirror image, in a regress which induces a performance anxiety only replicated in certain high-fashion ladies' rooms. The poetic narcissism which believes in its own concealed meanings and substantive insights is put to the test. As the mirror of a mirror of a mirror, the poem extends around it a Platonic chill which makes us ask what kind of poem it is which refuses the consolation of believing in its own profundity, which concedes nothing to the stern imperative at least to feel nostalgia for the real thing.

At the outset of the poem, Ashbery reads in Parmagianino's self-portrait Ovid's first stage of narcissism, that which believes in the enticing delusion of depth.

> The soul establishes itself.
> But how far can it swim out through the eyes
> And still return safely to its nest? The surface
> Of the mirror being convex, the distance increases
> Significantly; that is, enough to make the point
> That the soul is a captive, treated humanely, kept
> In suspension, unable to advance much farther
> Than your look as it intercepts the picture.
> Pope Clement and his court were "stupefied"
> By it, according to Vasari, and promised a commission
> That never materialized. The soul has to stay where it is,
> Even though restless, hearing raindrops at the pane,
> The sighing of autumn leaves thrashed by the wind,
> Longing to be free, outside, but it must stay
> Posing in this place. It must move
> As little as possible.
>   (*Self-Portrait in a Convex Mirror*, The Viking Press,
>   New York 1972, pp. 68–69)

The portrait's convexity seems to posit humane captivity by depth; it suggests that the portrait offers scope to the painter's soul, expanding the distance to which it can safely swim out. The portrait tempts one to believe in its soulful depths, and the poem ratifies this through a tonally neutral language whose exemplary lucidity seems to invite easy access to those depths. Thus, Ashbery's excursus into Renaissance optics provides a spirit of detached scientific inquiry which pervades the scholarly disinterestedness of the quotations from Vasari.

That limpid context is enhanced by the etymological precision with which Latinate words are invoked in the opening section. Such etymological exactitude creates a sense of the materiality of language, inviting us to suppose that one can reach right through words to pluck up a handful of their roots. The conscientiousness with which we are reminded in the opening section that speculation is "From the Latin *speculum*, mirror" emerges again in the literalness with which words like "intercept" and "advertise" are used. The root of "interception," "To cut off light from," describes the very means by which the mirror image is arrested in its progress. Similarly "advertise" (from the Latin *advertere*, "to turn to," and from the French *avertire*, "to turn away, avert") simultaneously invites attention to and diverts it from the portrait. Thus the word "advertise" itself protects what it advertises; the term enacts a tropism which embodies the very nature of trope. So does the portrait, whose image "swings/Toward and away," tempting us to try to possess its meaning even as it evades possession, with all the practised, serene mockery of Narcissus' image. The poem advertises the identity of trope with literal derivation, of the swerving of meaning with meaning; and it protects that insight in order to betray its inherently tautological nature. Rather than creating a lucid transparency of meaning, the poem reveals the intractability with which its language transforms derivation into tautology, converting the equation "I = I" into an endlessly insufficient and approximate asymptote.

Like Narcissus' pond, Ashbery's language in "Self-Portrait" acts as the limpid medium of narcissism. The poem has all the lucidity which critics accuse Ashbery of lacking; and it works, not as an indictment of narcissism, but as a revelation of the narcissism which lucidity constitutes. For as the Narcissus myth shows, lucidity creates the illusion of depth. By implying the transparency of language to its meaning, it courts the delusive expectation that one could reach right through it to grasp the substance of meaning. Thus, the poem's lucidity extends a mocking invitation to embrace a concealed meaning, and exposes the narcissism of that desire.

For the portrait's illusion of convexity proclaims its depth to be delusive, and thus distorts the apparent naturalism of art-as-mirror. That modest distension of the imagined self presses the limits of narcissistic representation. The hand, "Bigger than the head, thrust at the viewer/And swerving easily away, as though to protect what it advertises," acts as the boundary of the representation; it delimits the painting from the beholder, closing the represented world in on itself. Like the hand in Courbet's "Man with the Leather Belt," which Michael Fried examines in his essay "Representing Representation: On the Central Group in Courbet's 'Studio,' " (*Allegory and Representation*, Baltimore: The Johns Hopkins University Press, 1981), Francesco's hand becomes a metonym for the hand which executed the portrait; its looming obtrusiveness protects what it advertises ("Francesco, your hand is big enough to wreck the sphere") even as it assures closure.

By proclaiming narcissism to be the subject of art, the self-portrait further disrupts the possibility of aesthetically neutral lucidity. The beholder is invited into the process of the artist forever beholding himself, and is then caught out in that narcissistic posture by the amused, tender gaze of the painted image: "But there is in that gaze a combination/Of tenderness, amusement, and regret, so powerful/In its restraint that one cannot look for long." The portrait's convexity imitates the shape of an eye, making it difficult to locate who is beholding and who beholden. We become the image, the painting the perceiver, as we gaze; the self-portrait in a convex mirror traps us in a closed perceptual system in which signifier and signified circulate endlessly.

Thus, the impulse to read meaning into the artist's captive soul is exposed by the self-portrait to be an essentially narcissistic delusion. The poem reads in the portrait an assertion of the soul's illusory nature:

> The secret is too plain. The pity of it smarts,
> Makes hot tears spurt: that the soul is not a soul,
> Has no secret, is small, and it fits
> Its hollow perfectly; its room, our moment of attention.
> (p. 69)

This is the second stage of narcissism: the moment when one realizes the illusion of depth psychology.

Yet each time Ashbery recognizes the portrait's pronouncement that there is only surface he reinserts a yearning for the ineffable, for the unsayable. After recognizing that "the soul is not a soul," he says "That is the tune, but there are no words"; as though the words "the soul is not a soul" need to posit the illusion that the language of disillusion can only approximate an impalpable, greater meaning. Thus, he says "We see only postures of the dream." At one point he says "But your eyes proclaim/That everything is surface. The surface is what's there,/And nothing can exist except what's there." Yet moments later he says "And just as there are no words for the surface, that is,/No words to say what it really is, that it is not/Superficial but a visible core, then there is/No way out of the problem of pathos vs. experience." These lines deliberately reinsert the opposition between the pathos of the unsayable, with its hidden reserve of meaning, and experience's implicit recognition that there is no more to be said than itself. The narcissistic dynamic which posits the greater and unimaginable capacity for gratification in the other emerges in the poem whenever Ashbery reinserts a nostalgic desire for mystery, for the inexpressible nature of experience: the pathos of imagining that words are inadequate to their capacity for meaning. Thus, Francesco's portrait enacts for Ashbery the dynamic between, on the one hand, a recognition of the illusion of hidden meaning, and, on the other, the perpetual need to invest that moment of recognition with a sense of pathos.

This odd complicity between the impulse to tear away and to restore the authoritative status of meaning emerges in the portrait's uncertain legal status. As the site of a dialogue between the impulses to unveil and to ratify narcissism, the portrait occupies a provisional and indeterminate legal territory. "It is what is/Sequestered," says Ashbery. In legal terms sequestration entails removing an object under dispute from the possession of the parties to a controversy and putting it into the keeping of an indifferent third party. Thus, the self-portrait is the contested property in a legal struggle between, presumably, artist and viewer, and is perceived in a suspended, dispossessed state. The viewer connives in that dispossession, for the soul is "unable to advance much farther/Than your look as it intercepts the picture": the beholder's gaze in effect seizes the portrait in transit, contriving to keep it in a state of suspension. Since the portrait is perpetually sequestered, the law, whose power derives from an investment in the notion of the Other, of substantive experience and profundity (the law which Lacan calls "The Name of the Father," and which governs the operations of the Symbolic order) never gets the chance to assert its power over the portrait. Thus, it is fitting that "Pope Clement and his court were 'stupefied'/By it, according to Vasari, and promised a commission/That never materialized." The portrait *could* never materialize, in the terms of the poem. For the law, as represented by Pope Clement and his court, could not support and encourage the portrait's bold declaration that the whole structure on which authority is based—depth, stability of the self—might be a narcissistic illusion. Yet the commission could not materialize from Parmagianino's point of view either, for by undertaking to paint a mirror portrait, he too has accepted a commission that can never materialize, since an image by its nature cannot be made material. Thus, both Pope Clement and Parmagianino are similarly circumscribed, and the poem begins to intimate that narcissism itself connives with authority.

The rest of the "Self-Portrait" becomes a search to negotiate the possibility of a poetry which, operating within the recognition garnered from the portrait of the inescapable narcissism of its representational framework, could speculate its way out of that frame. Yet the first step in that process reveals how powerful those constraints are. The limited exaltation achieved in acknowledging the precarious homeostasis of the portrait's disillusionment with and continued incitement to narcissism is pricked in the section immediately following. "The balloon pops, the attention turns dully away. Clouds/In the puddle stir up into sawtoothed fragments." When the balloon of his attentiveness to the portrait bursts, Ashbery begins to explore the possibility that one need not rest in the englobed state which the portrait authorizes. The puddle, the dribble left of Narcissus' pure sequestered pond, reflects the fracturing of the narcissistic bond when the poet breaks the portrait's circuit of attention. Yet in attempting to break free of the portrait's influence, he finds himself caught in a narcissistic compact with it; the poet's entrapment in his own dimension merely reflects the portrait's self-enclosure.

> Whose curved hand controls,
> Francesco, the turning seasons and the thoughts
> That peel off and fly away at breathless speeds
> Like the last stubborn leaves ripped
> From wet branches? I see in this only the chaos
> Of your round mirror which organizes everything
> Around the polestar of your eyes which are empty,
> Know nothing, dream but reveal nothing.
>
> (p. 71)

The self subsists in as obdurate an encasement as the self-portrait represents.

> The skin of the bubble chamber's as tough as
> Reptile eggs; everything gets programmed there in due course . . .
> What should be the vacuum of a dream
> Becomes continually replete as the source of dreams
> Is being tapped so that this one dream
> May wax, flourish like a cabbage rose,
> Defying sumptuary laws, leaving us
> To awake and try to begin living in what
> Has now become a slum.
>
> (pp. 72–73)

Our effort to condense and solicit meaning from the portrait to feed the dream of a coherent self saps us until we waken from it to realize that all the dream cannot encompass has been sucked dry in the attempt. In the moment of disenchantment with the portrait's perceptual imperialism, the poet realizes the extent to which he has succumbed to its totalizing myth.

In the attempt to disengage himself from the portrait's vision, Ashbery tries to carve out his own artistic primacy. As he retreats into privacy, he feels the influence of "A peculiar slant/Of memory that intrudes on the dreaming model/In the silence of the studio as he considers/Lifting the pencil to the self-portrait." The phrase, "A peculiar slant of memory" echoes Emily Dickinson's "There is a certain slant of light," which evokes "Internal difference where the meanings are." Unlike the careful citation from Vasari at the outset, which makes it clear who is the source and who the original, and which carefully distinguishes Ashbery's voice from another's, this slant of allusion obliquely induces internal difference into the poet's own language. The magnet of the self collects the apparently haphazard miscellany out of which one emerges apparently *as* one, yet the voice which proceeds out of the jumble cannot claim any etymological purity for its ideas. The quaver of Dickinson in Ashbery's voice momentarily hits that excruciating note which cracks glass, and the narcissistic reliance on a locatable origin founders slightly. But according to the laws of an imperative to subtlety just clumsy enough to make themselves known, the very obtrusiveness of the reference to Dickinson keeps the mirror, at least temporarily, intact.

Unmoored from its comforting historical anachronicity by the poet's recognition that its meaning has invaded his territory, the portrait embarks on a kind of wafting guerrilla action, unnerving the poet by its unfixable power over him.

> As I start to forget it
> It presents its stereotype again
> But it is an unfamiliar stereotype, the face
> Riding at anchor, issued from hazards, soon
> To accost others, "rather angel than man" (Vasari).
> Perhaps an angel looks like everything
> We have forgotten, I mean forgotten
> Things that don't seem familiar when
> We meet them again, lost beyond telling,
> Which were ours once. This would be the point
> Of invading the privacy of this man . . .
>
> (pp. 73–74)

Perception has now become encroachment; and such mutual violation by portrait and viewer occurs with the casual intensity of a partial eclipse. In that strange light an old knowledge is released; the portrait reappears like the return of the repressed. The painting's incursions on private boundaries might release an awareness of that which we have repressed so as to constitute ourselves through that. Yet the danger of such invasion is that our image is usurped by the artist.

> You could be fooled for a moment
> Before you realize the reflection
> Isn't yours. You feel then like one of those
> Hoffman characters who have been deprived
> Of a reflection, except that the whole of me
> Is seen to be supplanted by the strict
> Otherness of the painter in his
> Other room
>
> (p. 74)

At the moment of expectant narcissistic self-discovery, when the stems of *heimlich* and *unheimlich* are entwined and thrust at the diligent self-researcher like a therapeutic bouquet, one finds oneself supplanted; it turns out to be the Other who is at home in oneself, who has been subtly inserted there from the start. This thoroughly Lacanian formulation, which for Lacan holds from the inception of the mirror-stage, which is to say from the inception of desire, unnerves the poet because it puts paid to the possibility of escaping a closed narcissistic economy or of securing the sanctity of one's own subjectivity. When one solicits oneself, the Other will always reappear in the mirror with unbudgeable and enigmatic assertiveness, to the endless detriment of the project of self-discovery.

The poem immediately manifests its disquietude with this formulation that the self is constituted only through the strictly Other in a new restlessness. "The city injects its own urgency"—and it is the urgency of a world whose energies challenge, oppress, and tantalize us with a new perception which evades the portrait's assertion that all we have is the interplay of self and Other. The city becomes the poem's provisional alternative to the narcissistic deadlock the portrait represents; its sprawling confusions insert a new energy into the growing airlessness of representational narcissism. Ashbery's congenital urbanity of tone similarly makes him seem capable of detaching himself at any moment from a world of art that threatens to become claustrophobic. Yet the temptation that the self-portrait might yet provide a new accommodation of the old, might yet let one slip back into the metaphor of the self as a little world which encapsulates one's own meaning, is too great to be ignored.

> Your argument, Francesco,
> Had begun to grow stale as no answer

> Or answers were forthcoming. If it dissolves now
> Into dust, that only means its time had come
> Some time ago, but look now, and listen:
> It may be that another life is stocked there
> In recesses no one knew of; that it,
> Not we, are the change; that we are in fact it
> If we could get back to it, relive some of the way
> It looked, turn our faces to the globe as it sets
> And still be coming out all right:
> Nerves normal, breath normal.
>
> (p. 76)

This final wistful attempt to assimilate the portrait's rationale for living within the confines of a cannily narcissistic art, one which accepts the illusion of depth and substantive selves, falters almost immediately; the impulse to resurrect the old argument is crisply denied:

> Mere forgetfulness cannot remove it
> Nor wishing bring it back, so long as it remains
> The white precipitate of its dream
> In the climate of sighs flung across the world,
> A cloth over a birdcage.
>
> (p. 77)

The possibility that the portrait might adapt itself to the city's heterogeneity must fail; for the portrait would have to escape the dichotomy of self and Other only to become its own radical Other. In effect, the renunciation of the portrait as the "unlikely challenger" may be read as Ashbery's rejection of the possibility of resuscitating the values of a canonical poetic, of a radical orthodoxy, for his own work.

The final collapse of the illusion that the portrait might provide a rationale for itself creates the imperative need to escape other structures which are erected to protect the narcissistic enterprise, such as the museum. Yet in his haste to shake off the impulse to sanctify art, to section it off, to encourage narcissistic admiration by the beholder, Ashbery characteristically advertises the duplicity of that impulse. The lines which deny art's sacred time—"That is, all time/Reduces to no special time"—echo those of a consummate museum piece, constructed by a one-time would-be museum demolisher; even despite the irreverent reduction of all time to "no special time," they deliberately reduce the ease or plausibility of escaping the museum.

Amidst such foundering structures, Ashbery posits, with entrepreneurial panache, a world which might manage to capitalize on this recognition. He envisions living in a world of today, a world which has made its terms with narcissism, has subordinated it usefully to its needs.

Today has no margins, the event arrives
Flush with its edges, is of the same substance,
Indistinguishable. "Play" is something else;
It exists, in a society specifically
Organized as a demonstration of itself.
There is no other way, and those assholes
Who would confuse everything with their mirror games
Which seem to multiply stakes and possibilities, or
At least confuse issues by means of an investing
Aura that would corrode the architecture
Of the whole in a haze of suppressed mockery,
Are beside the point. They are out of the game,
Which doesn't exist until they are out of it.

(pp. 79–80)

This new world is essentially narcissistic, "a society specifically organized as a demonstration of itself," yet its disillusioned recognition of that fact permits it to function quite happily. "Play" operates within this system as a specifically organized demonstration that the framework of that society "organized as a demonstration of itself" is *not* narcissistic: it is play which is devoted solely to pleasure, to servicing the self. And society *must* operate thus, must abide by its self-acknowledged illusion that narcissism is merely a trifling mode within a larger structure of authority: "there is no other way, and those assholes/Who would confuse everything with their mirror games . . . Are beside the point" because they want to make the pervasive structure of narcissism clear. They want it to be recognized that there are only mirror games, a recognition which would "corrode the architecture/Of the whole in a haze of suppressed mockery" by revealing the insubstantiality of that framework.

"Those assholes," at whom Ashbery's spurt of irritability betrays his identification, is, I suspect, a technical reference. It invokes Canto XV of the *Inferno*, the canto of the Sodomites and of Brunetto Latini. "Those assholes" have the status of homosexual narcissists who, like Brunetto Latini, create a narcissistic art; his *Tesoretto*, a source for *The Divine Comedy*, describes a city with a blind Cupid at its center, an image of narcissism. Dante, who admires Brunetto intensely, must go beyond his work, as Ashbery presumably must Francesco's. Yet the structure of the *Inferno* is a thoroughly narcissistic one in which punishment mirrors crime, just as Ashbery's self-portrait mirrors the narcissism of Francesco's. Ashbery cannot convincingly dissociate himself from those assholes; the poem's mirror games bespeak his incapacity to accept a world which would need to suppress a sardonic awareness of them as such.

But in the terms of this provisional world "those assholes are out of the game" because "the game" posits a world based on the illusion of depths and surfaces: there can only be "play" if these operate as domesticated forms of subversion within a structure which believes that one can experience otherness. One might come to rest in a belief in "the mute undivided present," content to remain within an unreflective assimilation of the moment,

> which isn't a bad thing
> Or wouldn't be, if the way of telling
> Didn't somehow intrude, twisting the end result
> Into a caricature of itself. This always
> Happens, as in the game where
> A whispered phrase passed around the room
> Ends up as something completely different.
> It is the principle that makes works of art so unlike
> What the artist intended.
>
> (p. 80)

The misrepresentations occur the moment representation begins to call attention to the fact that the architecture of the whole is always a representational and therefore a narcissistic frame. Thus, the possibility of living in a world of today, a world where the narcissistic recognition that images of depth are illusory has its domesticated place, turns out to be untenable.

The poem's dissatisfaction with living in a world which trades with cynical assurance on the complicit denial of its narcissism, the final option for accommodating the painting, contributes to make the poet reject, finally, the portrait.

> Once it seemed so perfect—gloss on the fine
> Freckled skin, lips moistened as though about to part
> Releasing speech, and the familiar look
> Of clothes and furniture that one forgets.
> This could have been our paradise: exotic
> Refuge within an exhausted world, but that wasn't
> In the cards, because it couldn't have been
> The point.
>
> (p. 82)

By renouncing the portrait, which seems now to sport Ashbery's freckles, the poem rejects the aspect of narcissism most difficult to part with: the assurance of the other as more pleasurable and capable of a sensuous delight, which guarantees the unfailing possibility of an aesthetic paradise of perpetuated desire. Ashbery turns the lens on Francesco and with courte-

.ous antagonism distances his perspective until the convex image is flat-
tened and diminished:

> The hand holds no chalk
> And each part of the whole falls off
> And cannot know it knew, except
> Here and there, in cold pockets
> Of remembrance, whispers out of time.
> (p. 83)

The rejection of the portrait's narcissistic invitation leads to a final
flare of disillusioned, useless prophecy. "We have seen the city; it is the
gibbous,/Mirrored eye of an insect." At the moment when the poem casts
out the alternative of sophisticated narcissistic representation by ejecting
the portrait, it destroys the alternative to that alternative. The city,
earlier the portrait's opposite, has now shrunk to a repulsive, self-absorbed
creature whose mirrored eye sees only itself, as at the end of a science
fiction film in which ineffectual humanity is replaced by grotesque, capable creatures. And in this context it is worth noting, with all due frivolity,
that the city, which from the start has been tied to a narcissistic art in the
very name "Parmagianino," makes its pervasive presence felt when the
reader finds that he cannot escape the miniature cosmopolite "burg" of a
poem which houses Sydney Freedberg, Alban Berg, and an Ashberry whose
derivation comes from bury out of burg, the ablative stem of the Old
Teutonic berg, which means to protect or cover. If etymology had a
chance earlier on of protecting what the poem advertises—that the escape
from narcissism only betrays the ineluctable narcissism of language—it
has lost it by the poem's end.

Ashbery substitutes for the portrait its dismemberment, and with
it the apparent dismemberment of narcissism. The ending dismantles the
image and thus what it reflects. The poem has gone beyond both a
narcissism based on a delusion about the other, and one based on the
self-destroying recognition of the illusion of otherness; the notion of a
substantive self gives way to the play of the self in language. Ashbery
seems to end the "Self-Portrait," then, by shattering the mirror.

But I want to turn once again to Ovid to explore this ending a bit
further. The story which immediately follows that of Narcissus is the tale
of Pentheus and Bacchus. The young Pentheus refuses to believe in
Bacchus' godhead, and, to disprove his power, goes up to his mountain
temple. There he sees the holy orgies of the god's worshippers, who, led
by the maddened Agave, Pentheus' mother, rend him into pieces. Such
ecstatic dismemberment is the consequence of disbelieving in the mystery

of the hedonistically self-celebratory god, and of seeing the unseeable. Narcissus too sees what he should not when he recognizes himself in the water, and that narcissistic recognition destroys him. The disintegration of the self is in the service of the preservation of the unseeable, which is a more exalted form of narcissism. Thus, the story of Narcissus occurs in the interstices between the quarrel of Juno and Jove, which might be said to initiate narcissism by ratifying a belief in the primacy of the other's pleasure, and the story of Pentheus, the decrier of mystery who is dismembered for refusing to worship the avowedly narcissistic god Bacchus.

If one returns to the dismemberment of the portrait at the end of "Self-Portrait" one finds a similar reinsertion of the ineffable, of mystery, just at the point where the poem seems to have refused it. The wearily apocalyptic tone, the intense revulsion of the lines,

> We have seen the city: it is the gibbous
> Mirrored eye of an insect. All things happen
> On its balcony and are resumed within,
> But the action is the cold, syrupy flow
> Of a pageant;

the "cold pockets of remembrance, whispers out of time"—all these invest the ending with a sense of Otherness, of ineffable meaning. The poem subtly reinserts narcissism just at the point where it seems to have been eluded.

Ashbery thus confronts the dangers of disturbing the economy of narcissism. For the disgust or disaffection which emerges in his tone at the end of the poem is the consequence of attempting to reject the mystique of language, with its promise of a greater reserve of meaning, which tantalizes the poet's desire. When that mystique is reinserted at the end, it is by making that gloomy recognition itself a source of negative gratification. Thus, by imperiously striking out a division between his poem and the portrait at the end, Ashbery repeats Tiresias' gesture of disrupting a narcissistic economy by dividing the two entwined forces. And Ashbery's punishment, a loss of poetic desire, is like that of Tiresias' blinding: he exposes the structure of narcissism only to recognize the vacancy his work inhabits without it.

In an essay on "The Structure of Allegorical Desire," (in *Allegory and Representation*) Joel Fineman argues that "profoundly self-conscious texts eventually realize their responsibility for the loss upon which their literalness depends, and when this happens, this responsibility is thematized as sin" (p. 49). The poem's loss of the energy and desire which the portrait's narcissistic economy afforded is precisely *not* thematized as sin in

"Self-Portrait in a Convex Mirror." And it is the very fact that it is not which makes the disaffection induced by the attempt to discard narcissism so disturbing to Ashbery. For conceiving the loss of narcissism as neutral reveals that the investment which generates poetry depends on there being something thrillingly transgressive about writing. What the end of "Self-Portrait" reveals is that there is no scandal of the text—and that discovery emerges only as a consequence of attempting to discard narcissism. Ashbery refuses to accept the consequences of this discovery, preferring to resurrect the limits of narcissism rather than to abolish them. "What's wrong with narcissism?" is precisely the question the poem wants to address; but it ought to be asked not as a challenge, but in confirmation of its sinfulness; for narcissism *needs* to be in the wrong in order to keep literature absorbed with itself.

Thus, the poem is "a commission that never materialized," for it fails to execute the commission it assigns itself: that of escaping a framework of narcissistic reflexiveness both for lyric poetry and for the self. Yet the failure is not so much incumbent as preferred; it is a failure caused, not by the inevitable double bind of language, but by a willed refusal of the consequences of dismantling that double bind. This is the endlessly iterable crux for a so-called "post-modernist" poetry, a poetry that tries to disengage itself from a traditional Romantic poetic project. To announce the perpetual renewal of the end of the speculative project is, as the "Self-Portrait" is wryly aware, nothing to pride oneself on. Ashbery does not accede to the mutual sustenance of a law which maintains itself on the basis of a belief in the originality of the poetic self and a narcissism which services those demands, albeit implicitly, even if he does not destroy that complicity.

Yet it is worth noting that the portrait takes on a certain materiality just as it is being dismissed: it leaves "A frozen gesture of welcome etched/On the air materializing behind it"; "Its existence/Was real, though troubled, and the ache/Of this waking dream can never drown out/The diagram still sketched on the wind,/Chosen, meant for me and materialized/In the disguising radiance of my room" (p. 82). There is a sense in which the commission escapes the boundaries of its chosen failure to materialize; and it is in the intractability of its appearance, of its insistence on its meaning at the point of dissolution, that both the portrait and the poem assume materiality. Or perhaps that is the way the poem chooses to appear. For the almost mechanical spurt of investment that occurs at endings, which seems to indicate an upsurge of all that one passionately regrets to divest oneself of, makes it difficult to ascertain whether such investment has not the status of a purely formal illusion.

Chronology

1927   Born July 28 in Rochester, New York, to Chester Ashbery and Helen Lawrence Ashbery. Is brought up on a farm in Sodus, near Rochester.

1949   Becomes editor of *Harvard Advocate* during senior year at Harvard, and publishes work of Frank O'Hara, with whom he forms a lifelong friendship.

1951   Receives M.A. in English from Columbia University.

1951–55   Works as copywriter for Oxford University Press and for McGraw-Hill Book Company.

1953   *Turandot and Other Poems*

1955–56   In Paris, on Fulbright Fellowship.

1956–57   In Rennes, teaching American Studies.

1956   *Some Trees*, with "Introduction" by W. H. Auden.

1957–58   Graduate study at New York University; contributor, with Frank O'Hara, to *Art News*.

1958–66   Returns to Paris; works as art critic of *Paris Herald Tribune*.

1962   *The Tennis Court Oath*.

1966   Death of Frank O'Hara on July 24. Returns to United States in Autumn. *Rivers and Mountains*.

1966–72   Executive Editor of *Art News*.

1969   *A Nest of Ninnies*, a novel written with James Schuyler.

1970   *The Double Dream of Spring*.

1972   *Three Poems*.

1974   Teaches at Brooklyn College, where he is now Distinguished Professor of English.

1975   *Self-Portrait in a Convex Mirror; The Vermont Notebook. Self-Portrait* wins Pulitzer Prize, National Book Award, and National Book Critics Circle Award.

1977   *Houseboat Days*.

1978   *Three Plays*.

1979   *As We Know*.

1981   *Shadow Train*.

1984   *A Wave*.

Contributors

HAROLD BLOOM, Sterling Professor of the Humanities at Yale University, is the author of *The Anxiety of Influence, Poetry and Repression* and many other volumes of literary criticism. His forthcoming study, *Freud: Transference and Authority*, attempts a full-scale reading of all of Freud's major writings. He is the general editor of *The Chelsea House Library of Literary Criticism*.

RICHARD HOWARD, poet and critic, is now writing the definitive biography of André Gide. His books include a translation of Baudelaire's *Fleurs Du Mal*, as well as *Findings*, a volume of his poetry, and *Preferences*, a critical anthology with commentaries.

ALFRED CORN is, together with Douglas Crase, a leading member of the poetic generation following that of Ashbery and James Merrill. His books include *All Roads at Once* and *A Call in the Midst of the Crowd*.

DAVID KALSTONE, Professor of English at Rutgers University, has written on the poetry of Sir Philip Sidney as well as on such contemporary poets as Elizabeth Bishop and James Merrill.

DOUGLAS CRASE'S first volume of poetry, *The Revisionist*, is the most remarkable instance, so far, of Ashbery's intense influence upon many of the best younger poets.

CHARLES BERGER, who teaches at Yale, is the author of a book on Wallace Stevens, and of many essays upon contemporary literature.

HELEN VENDLER teaches both at Boston University and at Harvard. Her books include *Part of Nature, Part of Us*, and studies of Yeats and Stevens.

JOHN BAYLEY is Warton Professor of English Literature at Oxford University. His books include *The Romantic Survival, The Characters of Love* and *The Uses of Division*.

JOHN HOLLANDER is Professor of English and Poet-in-Residence at Yale. His books include *The Untuning of the Sky, Vision and Resonance* and *Spectral Emanations: New and Selected Poems*.

ANITA SOKOLSKY is an Assistant Professor of English at Williams College. She has published critical essays on Yeats, Stevens, Berryman and Ashbery.

Bibliography

Ashbery, John. *Turandot and Other Poems*. New York: Editions of the Tibor de Nagy Gallery, 1953.

———. *Some Trees*. New Haven: Yale University Press, 1956; reprinted, New York: Ecco Press, 1978.

———. *The Tennis Court Oath*. Middletown: Weslyan University Press, 1962.

———. *Rivers and Mountains*. New York: Holt, Rinehart and Winston, 1966; reprinted, New York: Ecco Press, 1977.

———. *A Nest of Ninnies*. A novel written with James Schuyler. New York: Dutton, 1969.

———. *The Double Dream of Spring*. New York: Dutton, 1970; reprinted, New York: Ecco Press, 1976.

———. *Three Poems*. New York: Viking Press, 1972.

———. *Self-Portrait in a Convex Mirror*. New York: Viking Press, 1975.

———. *The Vermont Notebook*. Los Angeles: Black Sparrow Press, 1975.

———. *Houseboat Days*. New York: Viking Press, 1977.

———. *Three Plays*. Calais, Vt.: Z Press, 1978.

———. *As We Know*. New York: Viking Press, 1979.

Auden, W. H. "Foreword." In *Some Trees* by John Ashbery. New Haven: Yale University Press, 1956.

Bloom, Harold. "John Ashbery: The Charity of the Hard Moments." In *Figures of Capable Imagination*. New York: Seabury Press, 1976.

———. "Measuring the Canon: John Ashbery's 'Wet Casements' and 'Tapestry'." In *Agon*. New York: Oxford University Press, 1982.

Boyers, Robert. "A Quest Without an Object." *Times Literary Supplement* (Sept. 1, 1978): 962–63.

Breslin, Paul. "Warpless and Woofless Subtleties." *Poetry* (Oct. 1980).

Cott, Jonathan. "The New American Poetry." In *The New American Arts*, edited by Richard Kostelanetz. New York: Horizon Press, 1965.

Di Piero, W. S. "John Ashbery: The Romantic as Problem Solver." *American Poetry Review* (July-August 1973).

Donadio, Stephen. "Some Younger Poets in America." In *Modern Occasions*, edited by Philip Rahv. New York: Farrar, Straus and Giroux, 1966.

Ehrenpreis, Irvin. "Boysenberry Sherbet." *The New York Review of Books* (Oct. 16, 1975).

Erwin, John W. "The Reader is the Medium: Ashbery and Ammons Ensphered." *Contemporary Literature* 21 (1980).

Evans, Cynthia. "John Ashbery: 'A Moment Out of the Dream'." *American Poetry Review* 8 (1979).

Howard, Richard. "Sortes Virgilianae." *Poetry* (Oct. 1970): 50–53.

Jackson, Richard. "Writing as Transgression: Ashbery's Archaeology of the Moment: A Review Essay." *Southern Humanities Review* 12 (1978).

Keller, Lynn. " 'Thinkers Without Final Thoughts': John Ashbery's Evolving Debt to Wallace Stevens." *English Literary History* 49 (Spring 1982).

Kermani, David K. *John Ashbery: A Comprehensive Bibliography.* New York and London: Garland Press, 1976.

Koch, Stephen. "The New York School of Poets: The Serious at Play." *The New York Times Book Review* (Feb. 11, 1968).

Kostelanetz, Richard. "How to be a Difficult Poet." *The New York Times Magazine* (May 23, 1976).

Lehman, David. *Beyond Amazement: New Essays on John Ashbery.* Ithaca: Cornell University Press, 1980.

Liebermann, Lawrence. "Unassigned Frequencies: Whispers Out of Time." *American Poetry Review* (March-April 1977).

Middleton, Christopher. "Language Woof-Side Up." *The New York Times Book Review* (June 17, 1984).

Molesworth, Charles. " 'This Leaving-Out Business': The Poetry of John Ashbery." *Salmagundi* (Summer-Fall 1977).

Moramarco, Fred. "John Ashbery and Frank O'Hara: The Painterly Poets." *Journal of Modern Literature* 5 (Sept. 1976).

O'Hara, Frank. "Rare Modern." *Poetry* (Feb. 1957).

Perloff, Marjorie. " 'Transparent Selves': The Poetry of John Ashbery and Frank O'Hara." *Yearbook of English Studies* 8 (1978).

———. *The Poetics of Indeterminacy.* Princeton: Princeton University Press, 1981.

Shapiro, David. "Urgent Masks: An Introduction to John Ashbery's Poetry." *Field: Contemporary Poetry and Poetics* 5 (Fall 1971).

Shattuck, Roger. "Poet in the Wings." *The New York Review of Books* (Mar. 23, 1978).

Shetley, Vernon. "Language on a Very Plain Level." *Poetry* (July 1982).

Simon, John. "More Brass than Enduring." *Hudson Review* (Autumn 1962).

Spurr, David. "John Ashbery's Poetry of Language." *The Centennial Review* 25 (1981).

Acknowledgments

"Introduction" (Section I) by Harold Bloom from *The Anxiety of Influence* by Harold Bloom, copyright © 1973 by Oxford University Press. "Introduction" (Section II) by Harold Bloom from *The Map of Misreading* by Harold Bloom, copyright © 1975 by Oxford University Press. "Introduction" (Section III) by Harold Bloom from *Figures of Capable Imagination* by Harold Bloom, copyright © 1976 by Harold Bloom. "Introduction" (Sections IV and V) by Harold Bloom from *Agon* by Harold Bloom, copyright © 1982 by Oxford University Press. All sections reprinted by permission.

"John Ashbery" by Richard Howard from *Alone with America* by Richard Howard, copyright © 1980 by Richard Howard. Reprinted by permission.

"The Charity of the Hard Moments" by Harold Bloom from *Figures of Capable Imagination* by Harold Bloom, copyright © 1976 by Harold Bloom. Reprinted by permission of the Continuum Publishing Company.

"A Magma of Interiors" by Alfred Corn from *Parnassus* 4 (Fall/Winter 1975), copyright © 1975 by Poetry in Review Foundation. Reprinted by permission.

"*Self-Portrait in a Convex Mirror*" by David Kalstone from *Five Temperaments* by David Kalstone, copyright © 1977 by David Kalstone. Reprinted by permission.

"The Breaking of Form" by Harold Bloom from *Deconstruction and Criticism*, copyright © 1979 by The Continuum Publishing Company. Reprinted by permission.

"The Prophetic Ashbery" by Douglas Crase from *Beyond Amazement*, edited by David Lehman, copyright © 1980 by Cornell University Press. Reprinted by permission.

"Vision in the Form of a Task: *The Double Dream of Spring*" by Charles Berger from *Beyond Amazement*, edited by David Lehman, copyright © 1980 by Cornell University Press. Reprinted by permission.

"Understanding Ashbery" by Helen Vendler from *The New Yorker* (March 16, 1981), copyright © 1981 by Helen Vendler. Reprinted by permission of *The New Yorker*.

"The Poetry of John Ashbery" by John Bayley from *Selected Essays* by John Bayley, copyright © 1984 by Cambridge University Press. Reprinted by permission.

" 'Soonest Mended' " by John Hollander from *The Yale Review* (Winter 1981), copyright © 1981 by *The Yale Review*. Reprinted by permission.

"Measuring the Canon: 'Wet Casements' and 'Tapestry' " by Harold Bloom from *Agon* by Harold Bloom, copyright © 1982 by Oxford University Press. Reprinted by permission.

" 'A Commission That Never Materialized': Narcissism and Lucidity in Ashbery's 'Self-Portrait in a Convex Mirror' " by Anita Sokolsky, copyright © 1985 by Anita Sokolsky. Printed for the first time in this volume.

Index

A

"Absolute Clearance," 105
Adagia (Stevens), 3, 50
"Adonais," 67
Aids to Reflection (Coleridge), 63
"Alastor" (Shelley), 66–67
Alcott, Bronson, 136
"All and Some," 105, 113
"America," 29
Ammons, A. R., 8, 9, 49, 64, 73, 203, 232
Ananke, 8, 10, 64, 78
"And Ut Pictura Poesis is Her Name," 92, 104, 140
Apollinaire, Guillaume, 24, 26, 51, 53, 56
apophasis, 138
apophrades, 1, 2, 4, 115, 124
Arnold, Matthew, 183
Art News, 36, 81
"As One Put Drunk into the Packet Boat," 87, 96, 111, 130–31, 136
As We Know, 179, 185, 190, 219
As You Came from the Holy Land, 4, 6, 42
Asides on the Oboe (Stevens), 117, 118, 170
Auden, W. H., 21, 24, 49, 50, 91, 134, 200, 202, 208, 212
Auroras of Autumn, The (Stevens), 175

B

Bacchus, 248–49
Bacchylides, 229
Bayley, John, 195–205
Beaumont, Francis, 10
Beethoven, Ludwig van, 85
Benjamin, Walter, 121–22
Berg, Alban, 125
Berger, Charles, 145–78
Berryman, John, 196, 203
Bishop, Elizabeth, 220, 232
Blackmut, R. P., 196
Blake, William, 56, 61, 158, 189

"Blessing in Disguise," 146
Bloom, Harold, 42, 44, 49–79, 82, 115–26, 140, 159, 196, 199, 217–32
"Blue Sonata," 44
Bly, Robert, 203
Brazil, January 1, 1502 (Bishop), 220
Brenkman, John, 235
Bridge, The, 58
Brinnin, John, 43
Brodsky, Joseph, 205
Broken Tower, The (Crane), 218
Bronzino, Il, 97
Brook, Peter, 91
Browning, Robert, 60, 61, 77–78, 115
Bryant, William Cullen, 214
Burckhardt, J. C., 228
"By Paths Untrodden" (Whitman), 146
Byron, George, 184

C

Cage, John, 7, 53, 91
Calamus (Whitman), 153
Cantos, 58
"Canzone," 22
"Chaos," 23
Chaucer, Geoffrey, 166
Chekhov, Anton, 91
Chirico, Giorgio di, 36, 37, 107, 142
Churchill, Winston S., 23
Circe, 19, 21
"City Afternoon," 204
Clark, Kenneth, 220
Clepsydra, 33, 34, 56–57, 69, 109–10
clinamen, 116, 118, 119
"Clouds," 10–11, 37, 105, 154, 160, 161–64
Coleridge, Samuel Taylor, 10, 57, 61, 63, 115, 117, 119, 120, 124, 157, 186, 197
"Comedian as the Letter C, The" (Stevens), 56, 66
Commager, Henry Steele, 143

Compromise, or Queen of the Caribou, 31
consciousness, 195, 201
continuity, 163, 165–66
Corn, Alfred, 81–89
Counterfeiters, The (Gide), 18
Courbert, Gustave, 240
"Course of a Particular, The," 65, 66
Cowell, Henry Dixon, 7
Crane, Hart, 8, 11, 52, 57, 60, 64, 72,
    115, 119, 218, 231
Crase, Douglas, 127–43
Cravan, Arthur, 165
"Credences of Summer" (Stevens), 7–8, 49
Creeley, Robert, 203
Cunningham, Merce, 91
Cymbeline, 125

D

daemonization, 58
"Daffy Duck in Hollywood," 135, 140
Dante, Alighieri, 152, 246
Definition of Blue, 37, 93, 94, 95, 102–03,
    133
De Kooning, Elaine, 130
De Kooning, Willem, 53, 130
de Man, Paul, 14, 196
Democritus, 10
Dickey, James, 8
Dickinson, Emily, 9, 60, 120, 151, 167,
    168, 218, 231, 243
diction, 143, 207
Dionysus, 8, 10, 11, 64, 162, 164
divination, 10
Divine Comedy, The (Dante), 246
Double Dream of Spring, The, 6, 7, 10,
    35–38, 52, 59, 60, 61, 67, 69,
    81, 93, 95, 105–08, 114, 142,
    145–78, 199, 221, 227
"Drunken Americans," 200

E

"Ecclesiast, The," 156
"Eclogue," 22
Eddy, Mary Baker, 214
Elegiac Stanzas (Wordsworth), 212
Eliot, T. S., 1, 8, 31, 166, 167, 180, 185,
    198
ellipsis, 60
Emerson, Ralph Waldo, 7, 9–12, 14, 15,
    49, 50, 51, 57, 58, 61, 64, 75,
    77, 78, 79, 115, 117, 122, 127,
    128, 131, 136, 140, 150, 197,
    214, 217–18, 219, 221–23, 228,
    231
Epicurus, 10
"Epipsychidion" (Shelley), 189
Eros, 8, 10, 38, 64, 66, 68, 166, 213, 226
"Errors," 23
"Europe," 30, 40, 51, 93
"Eve of St. Agnes, The" (Keats), 198
"Evening in the Country," 53, 59, 63–64,
    66, 73, 105, 134, 153, 154, 155,
    158, 162
Experience (Stevens), 9
Eyck, Jan van, 88

F

Faerie Queene, The, 197
Fantasia on "The Nut-Brown Maid," 115
Far Field, The, 58
"Farewell to Florida" (Stevens), 72
*Farm Implements and Rutabagas in a
    Landscape,* 37, 134, 149, 164
"Faust," 30, 92
"Fear of Death," 181
Feinman, Alvin, 8, 60
Fields, W. C., 209
Final Soliloquy of the Interior Paramour
    (Stevens), 223
Fineman, Joel, 249
Flaubert, Gustave, 62
Fletcher, Angus, 115, 117, 119, 120, 124,
    126, 230
Fletcher, John, 10
"For John Clare," 37, 107
"Forties Flick," 85
"Four for Sir John Davies" (Roethke), 170
Fragment, 1, 2, 3, 37, 53, 56, 59, 64,
    67–73, 74, 75, 76, 92, 107, 108,
    115, 116, 126, 146, 147, 164,
    167–78, 185
Freilieher, Jane, 130
"French Poems," 7, 93, 153
Freud, Anna, 120
Freud, Sigmund, 61, 115, 118, 121–22,
    167, 190, 230, 235, 236
Fried, Michael, 240
Frost, Robert, 8, 32, 146, 214, 218, 231
Frye, Northrop, 32, 60

G

"Garden, The," 133

Gaston de Latour (Pater), 218
Gaudi, 82
"Gazing Grain, The," 140
Gide, André, 18
Ginsberg, Allen, 58
"Grand Abacus," 24–25
"Grand Galop," 84, 110–11, 202, 208
Green, Henry, 18, 19
Gresham, Sir Thomas, 230

H
Hartman, Geoffrey, 196
"Haunted Landscape," 191
Hecht, Roger, 8
Heisenberg, Werner, 197
Herbert, George, 189
Heroes, The, 19, 20, 21, 23
Hesiod, 142, 228, 229
Hollander, John, 8, 43, 124, 207–15, 230, 232
Holy Grail, The (Tennyson), 1
Homer, 228, 230
"Hop o' My Thumb," 111
Hopkins, Gerard M., 196
Horace, 140
Houseboat Days, 13, 14, 43–47, 92, 130, 142, 146, 158, 164, 174, 180, 182, 184, 186, 187, 219
Howard, Richard, 8, 17–47, 57, 82
Hughes, Ted, 196
Humphries, Rolfe, 237
hyperbaton, 139
hyperbole, 139

I
Ibsen, Henrik, 91
"Illustration," 22, 24–27, 31, 104
Impressions of Africa (Roussel), 142
Ingres, Jean, 208
"Instruction Manual, The," 22, 24–27, 30–31, 34
Interview Press, 182
"Into the Dusk-Charged Air," 31, 142
irony, 140
Ives, Charles, 192

J
James, Henry, 75, 202, 203
Johnson, Samuel, 62, 124, 230
Jove, 235–36, 249
Juno, 235–36, 249

K
Kafka, Franz, 224–26
Kalstone, David, 82, 91–114, 149–50, 159
Katz, Alex, 130
Keats, John, 64, 102, 116, 125, 130, 131, 132, 158, 166, 174, 179–80, ·181, 182, 184, 185, 186, 189, 193, 196, 198, 205, 220, 223–26, 229
kenosis, 57, 120–21, 222
Kermani, David, 91
Kinnell, Galway, 8
Kline, Franz, 7, 53
Koch, Kenneth, 6, 8, 49, 130, 142, 182
Kraus, Karl, 213
"Kubla Khan" (Coleridge), 157

L
Landscape into Art (Clark), 220
"Landscapeople," 192–93
Laplanche, Jean, 235
Larkin, Philip, 200, 202, 204
"Last World, A," 7, 52, 53–54
"Latest Freed Man, The" (Stevens), 149
Latini, Brunetto, 246
Lattimore, Richmond, 229
"Leaving the Atocha Station," 52
Leonardo da Vinci, 88
Leslie, Alfred, 31
Life and Death in Psychoanalysis (Laplanche), 235
Lincoln, Abraham, 218
Liszt, Franz, 84
"Litany," 186, 189–90
"Lithuanian Dance Band," 82, 87
Living Theater (New York), 31
Livre est sur la Table, Le, 2, 3
"Long Novel, A," 22
Longinus, 138, 139, 140, 230
Love and Fame (Berryman), 203
Lowell, Robert, 53, 57, 193, 196
"Lozenges, The," 29
lucidity, 233, 239–40
Lycidas (Milton), 229

M
Madonna of the Long Neck (Parmigianino), 141
Mahler, Gustav, 84
"Man of Words, A," 111, 205

Man with the Blue Guitar, The (Stevens), 2–3, 68, 115
"Man with the Leather Belt" (Courbert), 240
Mandelstan, Osip, 205
mannerism, 137–138, 142, 197, 198
"Marchenbilder," 83, 84, 112, 204
Marriage of St. Catherine, The (Parmigianino), 141
Marvel, Andrew, 22, 91, 96, 133, 137–38
Mazzola, Francesco, 136, 138
"Measles," 29
"Melodic Train," 128, 142
Merrill, James, 8, 19, 145, 232
Merrill, Stuart, 84, 85
Merwin, W. S., 8, 10, 64, 232
metalepsis, 115, 124, 126
Metamorphoses (Ovid), 237
Michaux, Henri, 7
Milton, John, 10, 61, 115, 124, 196, 228–30
"Mixed Feelings, 105, 112–13
modernism, 231
Monocle de Mon Oncle, Le (Stevens), 1, 2, 76
Montaigne, Michel E., 217, 219
Montale, Eugenio, 205
Moore, Marianne, 91
Moore, Merrill, 30
"Mythological Poet, The," 50

N
narcissism, 233–50
"Nature" (Emerson), 12, 50, 51, 78, 150, 221
negation, 121
Nest of Ninnes, A, 37, 133, 199
"New Realism, The," 28
New Science (Vico), 231
"New Spirit, The," 39, 73–76
"New York School," 49, 142
Niceron, Jean, 88
Nietzsche, Friedrich W., 9, 52, 53, 228–29, 231
"No Way of Knowing," 105, 114, 201, 205
Notes toward a Supreme Fiction (Stevens), 12, 58, 73, 115, 151, 174

O
"Ode on a Grecian Urn" (Keats), 102, 116, 125, 119, 220, 224

"Ode to a Nightingale" (Keats), 225
"Ode to Psyche" (Keats), 225
"Of Solitude" (Montaigne), 217
O'Hara Frank, 6, 8, 19, 49, 129, 142
"One Thing That Can Save America, The," 113, 134
onomatopoeia, 85
"Ordinary Evening in New Haven, An," 142
Other Tradition, The, 13, 14, 140
Ovid, 124, 234, 235–38, 248
"Owl in the Sarcophagus, The," 11

P
Pack, Robert, 8
"Pantoum," 22
paralipomenon, 141
paranomasia, 138
"Parergon," 53, 59, 65, 66–67, 140, 155, 157, 158, 160, 162
Parmigianino, Francesco, 42, 43, 88, 95–103, 110, 116, 118, 119, 121, 123, 130, 131, 137, 138, 141, 142, 197, 199, 238, 241–42, 244, 246–48
"Pastoral, A," 22
"Pasture, The" (Frost), 146
Pater, Walter, 1, 15, 61, 74, 77, 84, 117, 183, 218
Paterson, 58
Pentheus, 248–49
periphrasis, 138
personification, 124
"Picture of Little J. A. in a Prospect of Flowers, The," 22, 132
Pinsky, Robert, 133
"Plainness in Diversity," 161
Plath, Sylvia, 198
Plato, 221
Poe, Edgar Allan, 85
Poem with Rhythms (Stevens), 118
Poems of Our Climate, The (Stevens), 116, 125
Pollock, Jackson, 7
polyptoton, 138
Pontormo, Jacopo da, 130, 142
Pope, Alexander, 228, 230, 231
"Popular Songs," 22
"Postcard from the Volcano, A," 55
Pound, Ezra, 8, 10, 165
"Prayer for My Daughter, A," 152

Prelude, The (Wordsworth), 169, 196
Preludes To Attitude, 58
prophecy, 141
Proust, Marcel, 44, 134
Psyche (Alcott), 136
Purgatorio (Crane), 218
"Pyrography," 134

R
Ravel, Maurice, 84
"Recent Past, The," 55–56
Recital, The, 12, 39, 73, 74, 78
Reed, Sampson, 75
Republic, The (Plato), 221
Reverdy, Pierre, 7, 51
Rich, Adrienne, 8
Rilke, Rainer Maria, 86, 193
Rimbaud, Arthur, 50
Rimsky-Korsakov, Nicolai, 84
Rivers, Larry, 130
Rivers and Mountains, 52, 55, 60, 146,
    156, 162, 180, 205
Rock, The (Stevens), 54–55
Roethke, Theodore, 170
Romantic style, 1, 49, 195, 231
Rosenberg, Harold, 130
Rosso, Il, 130
Rousseau, Jean Jacques, 62
Roussel, Raymond, 7, 18, 28, 132, 142
"Rural Objects," 105
Ruskin, John, 66, 140

S
St. Augustine, 117
Sandys, George, 124
Sarraute, Nathalie, 81
"Scheherazade," 84, 112
Schuman, Robert, 84
Schumpeter, J. A., 143
Schuyler, James, 37, 49, 130, 134, 142, 200
Season in Hell, A, 83
Self-Portrait in a Convex Mirror, 15, 41–43,
    45, 47, 81–89, 91–114, 115,
    116, 125, 136, 138, 179–82, 197,
    199, 233–50
Self-Reliance (Emerson), 9–10
Shadow Train, 197, 198, 200, 202, 204
Shakespeare, William, 91, 180, 189, 201
Shaw, George Bernard, 91
Shelley, Percy Bysshe, 6, 10, 56, 60, 61,
    62, 66–67, 71, 78, 155, 174,
    189, 196, 197, 209, 230
"Shower, The," 30
Simon, John, 43
Simonides, 229
Skaters, The, 7, 33, 34, 55, 56, 58–59, 69,
    74, 75, 115, 154, 165, 168, 185
"Sleepers, The" (Whitman), 11, 118, 218
Snodgrass, W. D., 8
Sokolsky, Anita, 233–50
solitude, 217–19
Some Trees, 2, 6, 7, 19, 21–27, 30–31, 49,
    52, 53, 61, 67, 92, 93, 104, 162
"Some Words," 156, 164
"Something Similar," 201
Song of Myself (Whitman), 10, 12, 58, 73,
    115
"Sonnet," 22
Soonest Mended, 4, 53, 59, 61–63, 64, 72,
    85, 108–09, 123, 154, 158–62,
    164, 207–15, 227
Sortes Vergilianae, 36, 38, 156, 164, 175
Spenser, Edmund, 115, 123, 124, 176,
    229
"Spring Day," 105, 106, 149–52, 156, 158
Stars at Tallapoosa (Stevens), 222
Stevens, Wallace, 1–3, 5–12, 14–16, 33,
    41, 49–65, 67–70, 72–73,
    76–79, 85, 91, 107, 115–18,
    122–23, 130, 135, 145, 149,
    150, 151, 156, 166, 168, 169, 170,
    174, 175, 180, 182, 185, 191,
    193, 196, 198, 200, 208, 209, 211,
    214, 218, 220–24, 226, 228, 231
Strand, Mark, 8, 64, 67
stream of consciousness, 83, 110
"Street Musicians," 158
style, 137–42, 146, 179, 204
"Summer," 105, 107
Summers, Joseph, 133
"Sunrise in Suburbia," 59, 64, 152–53
surrealism, 140, 142
Swinburne, Algernon, 69
syntax, poetic, 195
Sypher, Wylie, 137
Syringa, 14
"System, The," 39, 73–78

T
Tanguy, Yves, 138
Tapestry, 217–32
"Task, The," 93, 146, 147, 148, 154, 158,
    160

"Temple, The" (Herbert), 189
Tennis Court Oath, The, 6, 28, 30, 31, 40,
    50, 51, 52, 53, 55, 60, 64, 92,
    93, 162, 180, 205
Tennyson, Alfred Lord, 1, 185
"Tenth Symphony," 84
Theale, Milly, 97
"These Lacustrine Cities," 56, 146
Theseus, 19–21, 28
Thoreau, Henry David, 10, 197, 218, 228
"Thoughts of a Young Girl," 30
Three Poems, 6, 7, 12, 38–40, 41, 50, 52,
    56, 57, 59, 60, 61, 64, 73–75,
    77, 81, 86, 93, 103, 104, 109,
    115, 116, 131, 180, 199, 200,
    226
Tiresias, 235–36, 249
"To Autumn," 184
"To His Coy Mistress" (Marvell), 137
"To Redouté," 30
To the Mill, 31
"Tom May's Death" (Marvell), 96
"Tomb of Stuart Merrill, The," 84
Traheme, Thomas, 91
transcendentalism, 8, 9, 12, 57
Transcendentalist, The (Emerson), 218
transumption, 115, 124–25, 230
"Triumph of Life, The" (Shelley), 67
"Triumph of Time, The" (Swinburne), 69
Turn of the Screw, The (James), 202
"Turnadot," 19
"Two Scenes," 22, 49–50
"Two Sonnets," 29

V

Valéry, Paul, 30, 85
"Variations, Calypso and Fugue on a
    Theme of Ella Wheeler Wilcox,"
    37, 164
Vasari, Giorgio, 116, 197, 239, 241, 243
Vaughan, Henry, 208
Vendler, Helen, 55, 57, 179–94, 195
Vergil, 165, 175, 212, 229

Vermont Notebook, The, 130, 140
Vico, Giambattista, 227, 231
Viking Press, 42
"Voyage in the Blue," 87

W

Warren, Robert Penn, 8, 231–32
Waste Land, The (Eliot), 1, 167
Webern, Anton von, 53, 64
Wedding Preparations in the Country
    (Kafka), 224
Weil, Simone, 47
West, Mae, 85
"Wet Casements," 174, 217–32
Wheelright, John, 12
When Lilacs Last in the Dooryard Bloom'd
    (Whitman), 218
"White," 19–20
Whitman, Walt, 5–11, 14–16, 49, 50, 51,
    53, 56–59, 61, 73, 74, 77, 78,
    79, 110, 114, 115, 116, 118, 119,
    134, 146, 148, 153, 158, 173,
    185, 209, 214, 218, 221–24,
    226–28, 231
Wilbur, Richard, 203
Wilcox, Ella Wheeler, 37, 164, 165
Wilde, Oscar, 91, 217
Williams, William Carlos, 8
Wilson, Robert, 91
Wings of the Dove, The, 97
Woolf, Virginia, 202
Wordsworth, William, 5, 10, 53, 57, 61,
    62, 120, 169, 180, 181, 185, 193,
    196, 197, 203, 208, 212, 228, 229,
    231
"Worsening Situation," 105
Wright, James, 8, 64, 232

Y

"Years of Indiscretion," 105, 106, 178
Yeats, William Butler, 61, 74, 152, 162,
    171, 183, 191, 226
"Young Man with Letter," 105–06